THE
McDONALDIZATION
OF THE
CHURCH

I more I read, the more I'm thankful I was raised by you, who honestly live on the cutting edge, without even knowing it.

THE McDONALDIZATION OF THE CHURCH

Spirituality, Creativity, and the Future of the Church

JOHN DRANE

DARTON·LONGMAN + TODD

First published in 2000 by
Darton, Longman and Todd Ltd
1 Spencer Court
140–142 Wandsworth High Street
London SW18 4JJ

ISBN 0–232–52259–6

A catalogue record for this book is available from
the British Library.

Designed by Sandie Boccacci
Set in 9½/12¼pt Palatino by Intype London Ltd
Printed and bound in Great Britain by
Redwood Books, Trowbridge, Wiltshire

CONTENTS

PREFACE

The completion of this book is part of a process that, for me, began in the late 1980s, when I was mission convener of the ecumenical group, the Scottish Churches Council. That period from 1984 to 1990 was one of the most productive and exciting times of my life in relation to Christian ministry, and it was also an experience which moved me on in my own personal spiritual journey in ways that I could hardly have imagined at the time. As I worked with Christian leaders from all the major traditions in the Scottish churches, I soon realized that if our faith was to make a difference to our nation in the twenty-first century, we could not continue to do the same things as our forebears had done before us. It was not that there was anything intrinsically wrong with our inherited patterns of belief and discipleship, just that they belonged to a way of being that – even then – was oriented towards the past, rather than to the present or the future. Previous generations had done a good job of contextualizing the gospel into the culture of their day, but we somehow seemed to have become disconnected from their vision and enthusiasm. Whether by accident or design, my generation has seen a living faith become petrified and moribund to such an extent that some of our churches have, quite literally, become museum pieces, while those which remain are increasingly conscious of the fact that their survival can no longer be taken for granted. What is true in Scotland is increasingly the case among mainline churches throughout the Western world. Even in the USA, whose churches are generally stronger and better attended than would now be the case in Britain or Australasia, the signs of decline are all too evident, and it is more urgent than it has ever been that we find new ways of being church that will enable the Christian message to be heard effectively by today's people.

At about the same time as I began to realize all this, I also became aware of the burgeoning sense of overt spiritual searching that was coming to birth among significant sections of the population in many Western countries, not least through the emergence of what has come to be known as the New Age. I also learned, as I explain in the first chapter, something of the potential of the creative arts to address this search for new ways in which we might relate to one another as well as rediscover the will of God for our lives. It was only when I came across the work of sociologist George Ritzer in the mid-1990s that the final pieces of the jigsaw started to fall into place, and I began to play with the tools that might help to combine awareness of the changing cultural paradigm of our times with some biblical, theological and missiological insights, in the hope that the resulting mixture might identify constructive ways forward for our churches.

In the past, Western culture was largely homogeneous and un-differentiated, but today it is characterized by variety and diversity. Diversity, of course, was the hallmark of God's creative activity as far back as the book of Genesis, and the recognition of our differences as well as our similarities can therefore be viewed positively as an evidence of God at work among us. But it also presents problems for people who have been trained and educated to think that there is always going to be only one way of doing things. Like everyone else of my generation, I was one of them, and the discovery that there are many ways of being human – and, therefore, of being spiritual and Christian – has had a liberating effect on my life. This is why I have deliberately chosen not to offer any one single blueprint for the Church of today and tomorrow, preferring instead to highlight some of the questions, and in the process to provide snapshots of possible ways of engaging these in relation to the biblical traditions which I believe ought always to inform and inspire us. For some, this will no doubt be a frustrating approach, because you would rather be told in clear terms how it is supposed to be. For others, I expect it will open doors of opportunity that you have not noticed before.

Many people have encouraged me in developing the themes of this book. In particular I must mention my wife and best friend, Olive, not just because we have shared our lives together for more than thirty years, but also because in recent years we have increasingly worked alongside one another in Christian ministry. Her faithful discipleship through many challenging circumstances has been a constant inspiration, while the distinctive angle from which she approaches theology has constantly drawn my attention to aspects I would otherwise not have noticed. I have also learned a lot from the perceptions brought by participants in seminars and workshops that we have led together in both Western and non-Western countries all around the world. For me, one of the encouraging signs of life and growth in the

Church has been the discovery that people in places as far removed as Australia and Jamaica, or Scotland and California, are all asking much the same questions about what it means to follow Jesus in today's world.

I must also express my gratitude to my colleagues in the Department of Divinity at the University of Aberdeen, who made it possible for me to take study leave during autumn 1999. Almost all the writing of this book was done during that time, which I spent at Fuller Seminary in Pasadena, California – thanks to the generosity of the faculty of the School of Theology there, who welcomed both Olive and me into their midst and helped make that a profitable and pro-ductive time for us both. One of the most rewarding things I did while there was a weekly seminar for doctoral students on the subject of 'Understanding Cultural Change', and the ideas and insights shared by those who were a part of that added a significant dimen-sion to what I have written. In particular, I need to mention Marilee Harris and Kim Thacker, each of whom gave me original insights into the nature of the post-modern spiritual search and its consequences for the Church that (with their permission) have been incorporated into the last couple of chapters of the book. I am also grateful to Barry Taylor, who was not afraid to ask all the hard questions, even when it was obvious that the answers could be quite threatening.

All these, and others, have regularly asked me exactly what this book is all about. I have sometimes wondered about that myself, and it will certainly be interesting to see where the librarians will place it. In some ways, it is a work of social science, for not only have I taken account of the writings of contemporary sociologists, but I have argued at several points that applying Ritzer's McDonaldization thesis to the Church actually suggests ways in which the thesis itself needs to be changed and extended. Other sections, however, move in a different world altogether, and contain quite detailed exegetical and theological studies of particular passages of the Bible – while yet other features no doubt qualify it as a missiological work. I have not spent much time worrying about such concerns, though, for my over-arching aim has been to inspire and enthuse Christians in their following of Jesus, and in that sense it might even be regarded as a devotional or inspirational book.

Bringing these different discourses together has also been in-tentional on my part, for one of the other lessons I have learned over the years is that, to be authentic to the intention of Jesus, the gospel must always be holistic, bridging the perceived gap between the so-called 'secular' and 'spiritual' aspects of life. That still challenges the way most of our institutions work, and the way that many Christians live out their faith. But perhaps, of all the things that will need to characterize the Church of the future, that is the most important of all.

JOHN DRANE
King's College
University of Aberdeen
Scotland
Easter 2000

1 CULTURAL CHANGE IN PERSONAL PERSPECTIVE

Of all the books I have ever written, this one seems to have caused me more heart-searching than most. In the process of reflecting on its theme, and then trying to express what I have to say in a way that will be both engaging and clear, there have been several moments when I have been forced to step back, and ask myself some fundamental questions about it. For all their diversity, these questions have always come back to a handful of basic issues that can be summarized in a series of questions. What am I trying to do here? What are the significant issues that concern me in relation to the present state and future destiny of the Christian Church in Western culture? How and why have I arrived at this particular understanding of the situation? And what do I hope to achieve by sharing these thoughts with a wider readership?

Of course, I am not coming at these questions from nowhere. This is now the fourth book I have written in as many years, seeking to engage with the challenge facing the Church in the context of the rapid and, to a large extent, unpredictable cultural change that we see all around us.[1] Maybe that is itself part of the reason why I have kept returning to such fundamental questions of purpose and intention. Throughout the 1990s, Christian analysts and church strategists have invested a good deal of time and energy in the effort to understand what has variously been called postmodernism, postmodernity, or (my own preference) post-modernity.[2] But what do we mean, and what difference is all our analysis and speculation actually making to the work and witness of the Church in the world? As I have listened to both academics and church leaders expounding ever more complex definitions of the nature of the cultural change which, quite clearly, is a reality, I have often asked myself whether we really know what we are talking about. Are our efforts at cultural analysis truly describing what is there in any objective sense at all, or are we merely deluding ourselves with the thought that, if we are able to name a thing, we can also be in control of it, and therefore it becomes less of a threat to our familiar systems and lifestyles? The fact that many would dismiss the possibility of objective knowledge of anything at all, claiming that this is in itself yet another sign of the emergence of a new way of understanding reality, only serves to emphasize the importance of the question.[3] Could it be that, in our laudable efforts to understand what is going on, we have ended up being more precise than the evidence allows or requires us to be, and that by carefully crafting our church strategies to match this perception of the needs and concerns of those who as yet are not Christian, we are not only failing to make any discernible difference (wherever we look, the Church is still in serious decline), but we are also, like the emperor in Hans Christian Anderson's famous story, not as well clothed as we imagine ourselves to be?

Facing the Facts

The facts about the Church can hardly be disputed. Throughout the Western world, Christianity has fallen on hard times. No matter how they are reported and interpreted, the statistics of church attendance and membership all paint the same picture, right across all denominations and all theological persuasions.[4] It is impossible to deny or otherwise redefine the obvious fact that all the historic mainline Churches are struggling – more than that, some Protestant groups in particular appear to have no future at all. They are losing ground at an alarming rate, even (especially) among those groups who have traditionally been their most devoted supporters. In Britain and Australasia, it is not uncommon to find even apparently thriving congregations whose members have an average age of well over fifty years. Not only does it seem as if younger generations have lost interest in the Church, but those who are left – of whatever age – are often quite unrepresentative of the wider population, most visibly in the fact that congregations are overwhelmingly female, though that gender balance is not generally reflected among their leaders. The picture is slightly different in the USA, though in this instance the country itself is so large and culturally diverse that generalizations are not necessarily going to be helpful. Not only is there significant variation from one state to another, but also among different ethnic groups. African American or Hispanic Churches face their own problems, but they are not usually the same as those faced by the liberal Protestant tradition or the Roman Catholics. Nevertheless, over the country as a whole the Church is clearly in better shape than it is in Britain and

Europe. Regular commitment to church attendance and involvement among the American population is significantly greater right across the board, and the visitor coming from a context of British or Australian churches will certainly be struck by the obvious fact that, in most congregations of most denominations, both women and men are well represented, as also are all generational groups – while the average age is a good deal lower than would be the case in Britain. There are no doubt many possible explanations for such differences, some of which will not be irrelevant to our understanding of how the Church right across Western culture might now need to reinvent itself if it is to have a healthy future into the twenty-first century. Some are related to differences between the two cultures. For example, Americans as a nation are more likely to join voluntary organizations than are British or other European people.[5] There are also different opportunities available to churches in these two contexts: since the USA has fewer publicly-funded services than Britain, imaginative churches can enter the market-place as effective providers to the whole community of a wide variety of things ranging from child-care and schooling to restaurants, hospitals and sports clubs. The US is also more obviously a consumer society, and that extends to the acquiring of cultural goods – like religion – as well as material possessions. A phenomenon found in American churches that is not so evident in the UK is of people engaging with religion in order to provide their children with a sense of values and a community to belong to.[6] In this context it is natural for parents to shop around in order to identify the best spiritual 'fit' for their family's needs, often in a conscious awareness that what is relevant at one stage of life may not be at another.[7] This only happens on a very limited scale in Britain, and then almost always among people who are already Christians and who are dissatisfied with the church to which they currently belong. In the British context, unchurched people would typically have no sense at all that the Church might enrich their own or their children's lives. This is no doubt related to the paradoxical fact that, at a time of burgeoning spirituality all over the world, Europe (including Britain) appears as what Grace Davies has called 'a ghost at the feast', the one place that seems (on the surface, at least) to buck the international trend.[8] It is a moot point whether the situation would be different if there was more variety among churches for consumers to choose from, for the one thing characterizing British churches is their uniform similarities, often to the point where, without prior knowledge, it can be difficult to identify even denominational distinctives in some congregations, let alone more conscious concerns about meeting the needs of unchurched people. The reality, however, is probably that the competition (if that is the right word) for the average British church comes not from other churches but from non-religious leisure activities. The same competition exists in the USA, and may well intensify in the course of the next few years. If American churches are not to follow their European counterparts, though, it may well be because of yet another difference between the two cultures. For American culture adopts an essentially pragmatic approach – oriented towards getting things done – as distinct from the more reserved and philosophically reflective approach that is typical of European people. Historically, Europeans have tended to feel a need to get the rational, abstract, theoretical framework in place first – out of which practical action can then spring. American culture is more inclined to address the practical questions, and if necessary adjust the theory in the light of experience. There are many reasons for this, largely related to the historical experiences of the two cultures. But in the Church, it can often manifest itself as the difference between conservationists and risk-takers, and arguably we have suffered in Britain from an oversupply of the former and a shortage of the latter.

There is no question that church leaders in the US can take some comfort from all this. But a more nuanced reflection on the trends in both our cultures will also inescapably lead to the conclusion that some of this difference is cosmetic rather than substantial. Right across Western culture, the number of practising Christians expressed as a proportion of the total population is in significant decline. There are of course some Churches that are growing, most notably in the independent sector worldwide (particularly the Pentecostal–Charismatic Churches, which are not necessarily the same as so-called 'fundamentalists'), or in Britain (especially England) among the various New Church networks that are now major players on the Christian scene. It is not always clear where this growth is coming from, though there is a good deal of anecdotal evidence to suggest that much of it relates to the ability of such Churches to attract those who are already Christian but find themselves disillusioned with the mainline Churches. Even in Europe, some people are also coming to faith from completely unchurched backgrounds. All these are positive signs, but when the overall total number of Christians is still declining, it has to be obvious that we have little room for self-congratulation. For the continuing decline means that, in the grand scheme of things, much so-called church growth amounts to little more than moving bodies around from one congregation to another, while for every person who comes to faith there must be quite a few more who are giving up on faith altogether, and leaving the Church for good. This phenomenon is characteristic of churches in America, just as it is in Britain. The difference in the USA is that churches still have enough resources and residual strength to be able to address this more dispassionately than many feel is now possible in Britain, where 'crisis' is a word that I increasingly hear in discussions among church leaders. American church leaders can still address their problems from a position of relative strength and stability, and those who are wise will do so, learning from the experience of British churches, and reinventing themselves as a matter of considered policy before they too are forced into crisis management.

I have mentioned those who leave the Church. Though I described them as giving up on faith, things are not usually that straightforward. Not only do such people rarely abandon faith altogether, they also frequently claim that leaving the Church is actually a way of maintaining their faith. Increasing numbers of people today regard the spiritual search as something that is not necessarily supported or enhanced by involvement in the life of organized religious institutions. In his significant book *Exit Interviews* (subtitled *revealing stories of why people are leaving the church*), William D. Hendricks has identified this as one of the Church's major problems. The statement made by a returned missionary (hardly an uncommitted person) says it all: 'I guess my problem with church is not that I've lost my faith or feel like it's hopeless or that kind of thing. It's more that I'm bored with it. I go to church and I hear sermons and I think, "I just don't want to hear this" . . .'[9] More alarming still is Hendricks' discovery that leaving the Church often seems to be a consequence of people dealing with issues of personal maturity and growth in their lives.[10] I have not carried out the sort of disciplined research reported in his book or others that deal with the same issue, but my own ad hoc observations strongly support such assertions. For much of the last ten years I have been involved in leading seminars and workshops on issues related to spirituality, worship, and mission – among churches of all traditions and denominations, and all around the world – and I have repeatedly heard such sentiments expressed, often by congregational leaders, including clergy. These are the very people, who, one might imagine, would be most likely to be finding their needs for personal spiritual growth satisfied by their involvement with the church. Yet I remember one clergy person commenting to me that church should carry a health warning, much like a packet of cigarettes: 'Taking church too seriously can damage your spiritual health'. While that may sound cynical, it was born out of that person's experience of church, and for that reason alone draws attention to one of our problems, namely that many churches and their leaders have lost a sense of confidence in the ability of the system to address their own deepest needs. If – to use marketing terminology – the product does not seem to work well for the salesperson, that has to be bad news for our endeavours to uncover effective ways of inviting others to join us in following Jesus. Of course, we are not salespersons in that limited sense, and the gospel is not a product to be bought and sold. The struggle to be human, spiritual and Christian is part of the package of discipleship. No one expects instant solutions, least of all those who take seriously the demands of a spiritual approach to life. But we cannot be good evangelists if we ourselves have doubts about the value of our own journey of faith.

This might seem a long-winded way of explaining some of the reasons why I prefer to think of our present circumstance in terms of post-modernity, with a hyphen, rather than speaking of postmodernity or postmodernism as some kind of self-contained philosophical or ideological position. The way I am using it, the hyphen draws attention to the provisionality and continually evolving nature of the changes that are now taking place and affecting all our lives. Far from having some clearly articulated world view or cultural position, today's people – Christians included – actually seem to be faced with nothing but chaos and confusion as we journey toward new ways of being. The values and attitudes of modernity have certainly been rejected (which is why we are post-modern, living after the demise of much that modernity represented). We cannot, however, claim that modernity has been unequivocally replaced by some other world view. As a matter of fact, we still live happily with the products and personal trappings of modernity even though we are disposed to question or reject its underlying value system. Maybe this dialectical process of sorting out what to keep and what to abandon is itself a form of world view, in which (for the present anyway) the journey itself is more important than the destination. If so, we should be looking at what is happening in our churches not only as the end of one era – which it certainly is – but as a potential growth point at which those of faith and vision might bring to birth new ways not only of being church, but of being human.

Though some (especially in Britain) might dismiss it as sentimentality and narcissism, there is no doubt that the search for personal identity and meaning in life is now one of the central concerns of our culture. One of the most striking manifestations of that was the spontaneous outpouring of human emotion following the sudden death of Diana, Princess of Wales, in August 1997. Historians and social commentators will inevitably reach many diverse judgements about the ultimate significance of what took place, but there can be no doubt that it marked a major change in the ways British people express themselves and their search for meaning. Whether (as some think) our growing willingness to display our feelings in public is mere self-indulgence or (as I myself believe) a symptom of a deep – if partly inchoate – spirituality, this is a phenomenon which the Churches cannot afford to ignore.[11] Either way, when viewed in the light of the new ways in which growing numbers of people are now asking spiritual questions, it is almost inevitable that the Church as we know it should be regarded by many as being irrelevant to the spiritual search. When I hear people dismiss the Church as 'unspiritual' I do not necessarily agree with their analysis, though in talking with them I rarely find myself attempting to correct their understandings. I can see clearly enough how such a conclusion can make sense. On the whole, the Church still operates on the world-view assumptions of modernity, and while our inherited tradition has much that can speak to today's world, we have scarcely begun to scratch the surface in discovering what a vibrant community of faith might need to look like if it is to address the needs of post-modern people. It will require a more fundamental overhaul of our own current styles of church than most of us realize, or are ready for.

Methods and Procedures

If some of this seems far too radical already, then we should remind ourselves that it is merely the practical outworking of some significant trends that have emerged not only in theological reflection over the last two or three decades, but also more recently in the writings of some leading sociologists. From the theological point of view, one of the most significant books in this respect is the work by Don Browning, *A Fundamental Practical Theology: Descriptive and Strategic Proposals*,[12] while the work of George Ritzer on what has come to be known as 'the McDonaldization thesis' adopts an essentially similar methodology to provide a sociological subtext for much of what I want to say.[13] This is where I find myself connecting with my original questions about what I am writing, and why, and how. In all my previous books on the subject of Church and contemporary culture I have self-consciously adopted something like Browning's model. He argues that the traditional division of theology into discrete disciplines such as systematic theology, the Bible, historical theology, practical theology, and so on, is a misleading way of understanding the nature of the discipline. Far from being a series of deductions from some previously-established theoretical position, practical theology – which he defines as 'critical reflection on the church's ministry to the world'[14] – is itself the root of all theological work. In the rest of life, 'practical thinking is the center of human thinking and . . . theoretical and technical thinking are abstractions from practical thinking'[15] – something that Browning illustrates not only with reference to his own experience, but also through recent trends in philosophy and the social sciences. In terms of theological discourse, what this amounts to in practice is that the linear model of the Enlightenment, beginning from abstract, rational first principles from which practical conclusions may be deduced, is replaced by a cyclical model in which the starting point is experience, which can then be brought into connection with the accumulated wisdom of the Christian theological tradition, which in turn may facilitate new insights into the nature of the stories – which then raise new questions for the tradition, and so on.

This notion was not new when Browning proposed it, of course. It had already played a significant part in the emergence of Liberation Theology at the hands of people such as Gustavo Gutiérrez, Juan Segundo, and others.[16] But in rereading Browning's book recently, I was struck with the emphasis that he places on the need for the theological commentator to be honest and transparent in locating him or herself in relation to the subjects and objects of study. I have always taken account of that for myself, recognizing that any description of the condition of the Church in today's world (or of anything else, for that matter) is never neutral, but is always going to be determined by the attitudes and understandings that the interpreter brings. Browning, however, encourages us to take it a step further, not only by recognizing for ourselves our own predilections and concerns, but also taking care to spell them out in a way that will enable others to be more aware of what we are trying to do. His own work is a good example of this, as he describes how he himself brought his own experience of Church and theology to bear on three particular congregations that he uses as case studies. In order to enable my own perspective to be more clearly understood (by myself, as well as others), I have concluded that now is the time for me to reflect on my own starting points in more detail than I have previously done. Some readers will no doubt regard this as a form of self-advertisement that they can do without. Those who feel that way can skip the rest of this chapter and move on to the next one. But I am constrained to think that I ought at least to attempt it, in the light of Browning's well-founded insistence that 'Honestly and explicitly positioning the social location of the researcher is . . . an extremely important component of descriptive analysis in the larger practical theological task', a concern that he situates in the necessity for us to determine for ourselves, and explain to others, 'How did your interests and social location influence the questions that guided you?'[17] Moreover, I find myself empathizing with his own starting point, when he comments: 'Most of us stand on the boundary: religious communities attract us; we may even participate in them; but we also wonder if they make sense.'[18] That statement describes exactly where I find myself, and this book is an attempt, in his words, to 'make sense' of the Church in relation to today's changing culture. Working within this frame of reference, I share my own personal baggage not to encourage or indulge in a kind of spiritual voyeurism, but in the hope that it will relate in some way to the sort of questions that others might be wrestling with.

Personal Perspectives

One of the most obvious characteristics in my own thinking is that I am an optimist. If some of the things I have written in later chapters sound somewhat critical or dismissive of the Church, that is largely due to the limitations of the medium of written communication, with its inability to convey tone of voice, gestures, and so on. The fact is that for people (especially men) of my generation, born not long after the end of the Second World War, it was easier to leave the Church than to stay with it. Most of my peers abandoned the Church as teenagers, and the majority of those who stayed beyond those years of their lives then got out before they were thirty. I would easily have followed them had I not been optimistic, both about Jesus and his teaching, and about the prospects for the Church to become an adequate vehicle to reflect a relevant spirituality for today's world. I have repeatedly emphasized in many contexts that the beginning of all effective evangelism will be a recognition that this is God's world, and because of that we can always expect to find God at work in it. Mission for me therefore becomes a matter of recognizing what God is already doing (the *Missio Dei*), and getting alongside that, to affirm those who have already embarked on the search for spiritual meaning and, as appropriate, to challenge them to take the Christian message seriously. In the process, of course, the evangelist can also expect to be challenged and reshaped – a truth that is succinctly expressed in the World Council of Churches' document *Mission and Evangelism – an Ecumenical Affirmation* with its reminder that 'The call to conversion should begin with the repentance of those who do the calling, who issue the invitation.'[19]

I am therefore optimistic not just about the Church, but about the world. As I was in the process of writing this book, I went to see the movie *Stigmata*.[20] It was not the best film I had ever seen, either technically or in terms of its storyline. In fact, the plot was largely implausible, focusing on a young woman who had involuntarily become a channel for the spirit of a dead priest who had been working on a scholarly investigation into the Gnostic *Gospel of Thomas*. The script was full of historical inaccuracies, while the screenplay had much unnecessary repetition of scenes of physical distress as the central character received the traditional stigmata. Nevertheless, I identified several aspects of today's spiritual search reflected in all that: questions about suffering, about psychic powers, about the source of religious authority, about whether the Church could be trusted as a guardian of the truth, and some other themes besides. By the time I left the cinema, I was wondering how all this could be redeemed, and reflecting on the questions it had raised about Christian beliefs and church practice. I was more than surprised when the two companions who went with me – both of them people of wide experience in the promotion of innovative and creative approaches to church life and witness – reacted entirely differently. One of them in particular was really angry at having seen the film, and could see absolutely none of the possibilities that I had identified. Indeed, he was incapable of discussing it at all: for him, this was a manifestation of sin in the most vulgar form imaginable, and the very idea of engaging with it – still less wondering how it might be redeemed – clearly made no sense. I did not especially disagree with his statements about matters of moral principle, but my awareness of the unsatisfactory condition of human life as it was reflected in the film intuitively moved me on to think about possibilities of redemption, whereas his intuitive response was one of condemnation. We both saw the same movie, and as Christians both of us were bringing a similar world view to bear on it – but our responses were so different that we might as well have been from different planets. That is how I sometimes feel about the Church. It frustrates me, as I see the growing spiritual search that is all around us, and reflect on our apparent inability or unwillingness to engage with it. It annoys me, as I see small-minded autocrats (usually, though not invariably, men) refusing to face the reality of the decline and spiritual stagnation that is so obvious a feature of church life in the Western world today. It saddens me as I recall the ways in which even pastoral leaders have on occasion abused me, and I wonder how many others have left the Church not because of loss of faith, but simply because they have had enough of intemperate behaviour and oppressive attitudes. But at the end of it all, I am still left asking how even these things can be redeemed, so that we might yet be the people God intends for us to be.

One of the reasons for my optimistic outlook (though not the only one) is related to my love of the Bible. I do not look upon it as a textbook or blueprint for church life. To change the metaphor, I think I use it more in the way that one might use a compass on a journey – something that will give general direction, but which needs to be supplemented by a detailed route map. This is why reflection on selected Bible passages is central to what I want to say in some of the later chapters of this book – using the compass, in the process of drawing the detailed route map ourselves, to suit our own unique circumstances and opportunities. No doubt this goes back to my own first discovery of the Bible, which was motivated not by any religious purpose, but by pragmatism of a very different sort – the need to be able to argue effectively with a high school teacher of religious education. I realized that in order to do that, I would need to be more familiar with the Bible than at that stage I was, and so I took to reading it in order to equip myself for intelligent debate. As I did so – especially as I read the New Testament Gospels – I found myself transported into a different world, seeing Jesus through different eyes, and appreciating how these stories might indeed become a resource for addressing the mysteries of life as I understood them.[21] This essentially pragmatic approach to the Bible was both continued and reinforced as a student of theology, not least by my personal tutor at that time, Dr William Lillie, who had spent much of his life in India, and was correspondingly less interested in the kind of historical and literary-critical minutiae of biblical study than most other academics of his generation. Though his way of making theology practical was essentially the theory-to-practice model that more recent scholars such as Browning would disapprove of,[22] it still steered me away from the narrowly textual approach to the Christian Scriptures, and when I found myself making a choice for Ph.D. studies between textual exegesis and a much wider conceptual topic, there was really no contest at all. My choice of Gnosticism as a dissertation subject was more fortuitous than I could possibly have realized at the time (this was in the 1970s), for in the immediately following years, it rapidly became one of the hottest topics in the spiritual search that came to be known as the New Age, and without making any effort I found myself receiving many invitations to go and meet with spiritually-oriented groups and help them unlock the secrets of this long-forgotten path and its esoteric texts, many of which were just coming to public attention at that time with the wider publication of the Nag Hammadi texts.[23] No doubt this also helps to explain why I take today's 'alternative' spiritualities so seriously. Unlike many Christians, who have only met the New Age at a distance (not infrequently by reading books written about it by other Christians), this is not for me something remote and therefore easy to caricature, still less to demonize. I know that most of the people now attracted by what would once have been regarded as wacky ideas are exactly the people who, a generation or two ago, would have been pillars of their local churches. That is actually one of the key reasons for the decline of the Church today. The Church in the West has never been able to attract equal numbers of people from right across the social spectrum – but today, we cannot attract the very people who, sociologically and culturally, were the mainstay of the Church even as recently as the middle of the twentieth century. We will need to return to this group and their ongoing spiritual search in a later chapter, where I will designate them the 'spiritual searchers', for our ability – or inability – to reach them will probably hold the key to whatever future there might be for the Church in the West.

One of the other things that I bring to my understanding of the Church is a certain disillusionment with the academy – not so much with the academy per se (I am, after all, also still an academic), as with its self-opinionated conceit that it alone is likely to be able to solve all the world's problems. In recent years, the sheer sense of hubris that has swept through the humanities in particular – including especially the study of religion – has been quite breathtaking. It is now commonplace for today's scholars to sit in judgement not only over one another, but over every previous generation there has ever been. In some disciplines, it would be hard to get an academic job at all without at least paying lip service to the deconstruction of every imaginable world view from all times and places. It has become fashionable and trendy to suppose that one has nothing to say unless one can undermine the insights of the past by reference to the real or imaginary blindness of our forebears, who are regularly dismissed as, at best, conformist hacks or, at worst, sophisticated power brokers who redefined the nature of 'truth' in order to construct and consolidate their own ideological (if not economic) power base. Because of the innate gullibility and herd instinct of academics, this notion has gained far more credibility than it deserves. If there is today an emperor who truly has no clothes, then this pseudo-intellectual pursuit would have a good claim to the title. It has taken an Islamic writer, Ziauddin Sardar, to remind us that 'A meaningful world with meaningful relationships can only be based on meaningful content and meaningful world views' – all of which he finds to be tragically lacking from contemporary Western academia.[24] Such a concept, while commonsense to the majority of the world's people, is anathema to most contemporary scholars of religion, who would label such a statement as being 'confessional', and therefore somehow suspect or wrong. There is an obvious logical fallacy in an argument that would place what is 'confessional' in opposition to what is 'objective', for no one can avoid being 'confessional' in the sense of having a world view. Even atheism is itself a 'confessional' posture. The idea that academic understanding requires one to be empty-headed and have no world view, but simply sit outside it all in judgement, is incoherent as a principle, and unworkable in practice. In reality, this kind of argument is a clumsy effort to silence those who disagree with what has hitherto been the liberal consensus, which is tolerant to itself but not to others – especially not to those who engage in a search for ultimate truth, such as Jews, Muslims, and orthodox mainstream Christians. Moreover, as a world view it is hardly likely to enhance the quality of human life, for who would wish to live in this vacuous 'non-confessional' limbo, in a world where everyone believed nothing? Long before I came across Sardar's book, I was deeply uneasy with a view which seems to say that those of us who are white Westerners know best, and everyone else is or was stupid. His analysis has now also shown that, in the very act of claiming to be liberating the world's peoples from what are caricatured as the darkness and oppression of the past, scholars who think this way are actually the new oppressors, who find it so easy to identify confessional stances with power games because that is precisely what they are engaged in themselves: 'far from being a new theory of liberation, postmodernism, particularly from the perspective of the Other, the non-western cultures, is simply a new wave of domination riding on the crest of colonialism and modernity.'[25]

My dissatisfaction with this aspect of contemporary academic life is probably just the tip of a much larger intellectual iceberg, for what I have described is almost an inevitable consequence of our historic emphasis on rational individualism. It is the end-product of Descartes' insistence that 'I think, therefore I am',[26] interpreted and applied in such a way that each individual has become the arbiter of what is true, defining their own 'truth' in terms of 'what will be to my own advantage and benefit'. In the process, truth itself has been fragmented so as to become a meaningless concept. Of course, we cannot escape the fact that, to a greater or lesser extent, Christians have played their part in all this. Linda Woodhead speaks for many when she complains that

> Academic theology has for too long encouraged a view of theology – and of Christianity itself – as a purely disembodied, intellectual pursuit. So, for example, patristics courses treat the Fathers as disembodied minds, courses in the philosophy of religion present Christianity as a set of contextless propositions, and the rise of modernity is traced by various theologians to intellectual mistakes made by Augustine, or Aquinas, or Duns Scotus, or Descartes rather than to a complex mix of social, political, economic and cultural factors. Similarly, commentaries on (say) Romans are written with little or no reference to the concrete situation of the church in the modern world which such theologies are meant to serve.

She goes on to recommend that what we now require is 'a recognition of the fuller, embodied reality of Christianity.'[27]

Radical Spirituality

What that 'embodied reality' might entail is the final piece of my personal jigsaw that I wish to include here. In many ways, it has been for me the most significant piece of all.

But because 'embodied reality' takes us well beyond our cognitive senses, it is also the most difficult to describe in mere words. At an early stage in my adult life, I encountered the reality of pain in a particularly stark and oppressive form, with the death of my infant daughter. My wife and I both struggled for a long time (in my case, several years) to work through all the repercussions of that. The two of us eventually found healing in quite diverse ways, related no doubt to our predispositions at that particular point in our lives. For me, I was surprised to find new life when I was invited to become the convener of the Mission Committee of the (ecumenical) Scottish Churches Council. I have included a little of that story in a previous book, so will not repeat it here.[28] No doubt that experience goes a long way towards explaining my continued optimism regarding the Church, and my belief that in spite of our weakness we can still play a significant part in the wider purposes of God. But, over the longer term, the one thing that has had an even greater impact on me has been the way my wife emerged from that tragedy. For she found herself moving away from her original professional work in medical science to become – of all things – a clown. And not just any kind of clown, but a clown working (and playing) within the context of Christian ministry and theological education. She has shared some of her own story elsewhere,[29] but the impact of her discovery has by no means been restricted to her own life. It is no exaggeration to say that my entire world view, indeed my life, has been turned upside down as a result of this. I found myself asking much the same question as Don Browning when he first encountered an African-American Pentecostal Church: 'Would I, as a reasonably respected scholar . . . have anything to contribute to the dialogue at all?'[30] I soon realized that the idea that I would be a contributor was not on the agenda. In fact, it was unsettling to see how easily Olive was able to address many of the questions to which I had no clear answer. Whereas I (like all the other male church leaders I knew) could do little more than wonder how we would ever be able to communicate faith to the growing body of spiritually-interested but unchurched people all around us, my wife's clown characters seemed to know exactly how to do it – and just got on with the job. As I travelled with her all around the world during the early 1990s, and saw how warmly people of all ages, races and social classes responded to her message, no matter whether it was in a regular church or in some religiously neutral venue, I found myself forced to compare – and mostly contrast – what she was able to achieve with what I knew of the response to all the carefully-crafted sermons that I had preached over the years. Though I did not have the terminology with which to describe it, it was undeniable that she was touching people's lives at points that were much deeper than the Church usually manages to reach. Moreover, much of it was being accomplished without any words at all, as she regularly adopted the medium of silent mime. From the outset, my instincts told me that she had identified not only a strategically important tool for worship and evangelism, but also a collection of significant insights into the nature of theology itself. It took me a bit longer to appreciate just exactly what that might mean, but my understanding began to broaden when Olive decided the time was right to invite her audiences to join her in having crosses painted on their eyes so that they could, quite literally, in her words 'see the world the way God sees it – through the cross'. The first time she did this was in Sydney, Australia, and a young teenage couple (male and female) came to me to have the cross painted on their hands, 'so that as Christians, we might touch one another in appropriate ways.' As I joined Olive in painting the sign of the cross on literally thousands of people in the twelve-month period following that, I realized that requests of that kind were going to be commonplace – and also that, for whatever reason, regular church was evidently not providing spaces for people to make commitments in ways that would mean most to them in the context of today's lifestyles. But the one thing I did know was that many people seemed to be looking for a way of exploring spirituality that would be community-based, as well as being tactile, sensual, visual, and embodied. More than anything else, it has been this kind of experience (continually repeated wherever Olive gives that same invitation) that has kept bringing me back to some of the central values of the gospel, in the effort to discern exactly what sort of church we now need to be. There could not be a greater contrast between what I have described and the style of what I most typically encounter in today's Church, particularly in the Protestant traditions best known to me – and it was this that sent me back to the Bible to see what resources I might uncover there, both to illuminate and to inform further reflection on possible futures for the Churches, if we are to engage relevantly with the spiritual journey of those people who feel more at home with the exploration of creativity than the discourse of intellectual rationality.

These, then, are my own pre-commitments insofar as I understand and am able to articulate them at this point in time. In line with my previous criticism of the possibility of 'objective', value-free analysis, I want to insist that, far from being a hindrance or a limitation, spelling out my own starting points in this way actually gives some sense of perspective to what I want to say. It at least offers a way of

moving beyond the illusory notion that it is either possible or worthwhile to be a detached observer, and at its best should enable us to
engage in a more properly critical form of theology which, precisely
because it is more transparent, is also both more accessible and, ultimately, more honest. All our cognitive processes and moral and emotional patterns of life are significantly shaped by our inherited stories,
and knowing where we have come from, and how these stories have
impacted our lives, is a fundamental starting point in any serious
reflection. During the course of writing this book, I listened to a
Kenyan speaker in the chapel service at Fuller Seminary, who helpfully contrasted the Cartesian formula, 'I think, therefore I am', with
the wisdom of her own culture, which preferred to say, 'I am, because
we belong'. Of course, we do not thereby leave ourselves imprisoned
or limited by the parameters of our inherited stories: indeed, as
Christians, that should never be allowed to happen because the
bigger story of Jesus should always be challenging us to new hori-
zons and fresh possibilities. But our personal history and social
location are always going to be highly significant. As Browning
reminds us, 'Practical theology always reflects the angle of vision
from which it is done.'[31] Done this way, it also reflects not some exter-
nally-imposed nostrum of what theology is supposed to be, but arises directly from the nature of the Christian revelation, in the incarnation of Jesus Christ. In his poem 'The Incarnate One', the Orcadian
poet Edwin Muir may have been more than a little cynical – and he
was certainly unjustified in singling out Scottish Calvinists as the
only ones to blame for what he regarded as the disembowelling of a
lively and practical belief in the incarnation – but there is a good deal
of truth in his observation that 'The Word made flesh here is made
word again' and we have allowed God to be reduced to

> . . . three angry letters in a book,
> . . . the logical hook
> On which the Mystery is impaled and bent
> Into an ideological argument.

More prosaically – though with no less of a challenge – Don
Browning writes of there being 'estrangement between the reigning
theologies in the mainline denominations and the hearts of their
people. Most of these Churches are declining. There is evidence that
their theologies bring this about.'[32] In order to make any sense of the
Church at all in today's culture, that will perhaps be the one question
to which we will need to return over and over again.

2 RATIONAL SYSTEMS AND HUMAN VALUES

The philosophical and social processes whereby we have reached today's cultural crisis in the West have been well documented elsewhere, and it is not necessary to repeat here in detail what has been more eloquently expressed by others.[1] Though there are still many aspects of our understanding that are in need of further clarification, including some of the basic terminology (the concept of 'the Enlightenment' as well as what we mean by 'postmodernity' are both ambiguous and open to varying understandings), human experience all over the world is telling us that the spread of Western influence during the last five hundred years or so has had a profound impact on the way today's world has developed, and that this has not always been positive. In this chapter, I want to focus not so much on the ideological trends that have led to this, but on the human experience of it. Though there is a legitimate place for philosophical reflection in the service of the Church, an apologetic for Christianity that focuses only on that will, at the end of the day, be inadequate. In keeping with the example of Jesus himself, the Church's primary concern must always be for people, and effective mission cannot be restricted to cognitive discussions, but must enable people to find their souls and empower them to be all that God intends for them, as those who are made 'in God's image' (Genesis 1:27–8). When the Church neglects these human dimensions of the gospel, its own spiritual power is diminished, and its right to say anything at all to the wider culture is seriously compromised.

Setting the Scene
Though the philosophical ideas that fed into it had been developing for some time, it was the onset of the Industrial Revolution that brought about the really significant changes in everyday lifestyles, and ushered us into the modern world.[2] We still scarcely understand the full consequences of that radical shift in working patterns, but

there can be little doubt that this constitutes one of the root causes of the considerable sense of alienation being felt by increasing numbers of people today. Of course, the mass industrialization of our culture, followed up more recently by the arrival of computer technology, has had a good number of positive benefits, which in the grand scheme of things may well outweigh the disadvantages. We are now able to feed many more people than would have been possible in previous generations, because the application of technology to agriculture has led to levels of efficiency that our forebears could not have envisaged. Transportation and mobility have been revolutionized even in recent decades, and it is now possible to travel with ease to places that previously would have been out of the reach of all but the wealthiest or most adventurous. Through the computer revolution, we now have access to more knowledge and information than any other generation before us, and we can carry out mundane and tedious chores quite simply at the touch of a button. Alongside all this, however, other questions about the meaning of life and the worth of people have been raising themselves more and more insistently, particularly in the closing decades of the twentieth century. Even those benefits of technology that I have just enumerated all have a dark side to them. Many would argue that we have been able to increase our agricultural output only by putting at risk the underlying stability and long-term ecological balance of the land itself. Rapid transportation systems are evidently taking their toll on the very atmosphere which we breathe, by creating new levels of pollution. And even the computer is a mixed blessing, for we now have more information than we know how to deal with, and increasing knowledge has not necessarily led to greater happiness and satisfaction, but to growing pressures as we find ourselves with even more things to do than before. The mobility of manufacturing processes, which is an inevitable consequence of the development of industrialized economies, also raises other questions with a human dimension. As production is switched from one country to another in the effort to find ever lower wage costs, we are facing many complex ethical questions, not only in relation to the apparent exploitation of workers in developing countries, who have no choice but to work hard for low pay, but also in relation to the fate of those in the traditional industrial heartlands of Europe and North America, who find themselves in mid-life without employment, and with little prospect of finding any unless they are prepared for a radical reversal of their expectations about life and livelihoods. We are increasingly having to deal with the reality of significant numbers of people who have no work, while those who can still find a place in the system regularly feel that they are overworked. Both groups are becoming increasingly dissatisfied with the kind of society we have created. A world dominated by the pressures of achieving career success, on the one hand, and the insistent demands of consumerism on the other, is becoming less attractive as a sustainable way of life.

To put it somewhat starkly, though not altogether inaccurately, the combined result of all this has been that we have come to value one another mostly in mechanistic terms related to production and output. You only need to go to a party or reception and listen to the way in which people typically introduce themselves to realize the impact that this has had on our sense of self-worth and personal identity. Many people nowadays have no way of defining themselves apart from paid employment (or the lack of it). I have often tried to get to know new people by asking them to, 'Tell me about yourself' – and, in nine cases out of ten, the only thing I ever discover about them is the kind of work they do. Their families, inner life, personal hopes and aspirations – all the aspects of their lives that one might imagine would help to define what we mean by being human – rarely seem to feature. By way of a contrast, I recently met an Indian couple who came to Britain to study. Both of them are intelligent and well-educated people, engaged in significant jobs in their homeland, and who therefore would have had no shortage of such utilitarian facts that they could have shared about themselves – but in answer to the invitation, 'Tell me about yourselves' they spoke first of their own relationship to one another (they were wife and husband), then told me of their respective families, as well as mentioning some of their friends, and telling me what kind of contribution they were hoping to make to the life of their nation. None of this will come as a surprise to most of my readers. For one of the consequences of the way that Western culture has developed in the last two hundred years or so is that daily life is no longer carried out in a relational context – as it has been throughout the world since the beginning of time, and still is to a large extent in non-Western cultures. Though we have come to take it for granted as being 'normal', our way of being is, in the larger perspective, anomalous. We are the only people in the whole of history who have supposed that our mechanistic and individualistic understanding of life is the way to become fulfilled and whole persons. Following the Industrial Revolution, life for men in particular came to be centred around factories and machines. The real purpose of existence was redefined by reference to the products of industrial and commercial processes, something that was in turn facilitated by the Cartesian notion that our bodies and minds are also machines, and undergirded by the kind of cosmology espoused by people such as Isaac Newton, which encouraged us to imagine that the entire cosmos is merely the biggest and most efficient machine of all. Machines have become the truly creative producers of the goods we all want, and for many people, their daily work has quite literally been to serve as cogs in a machine. The eighteenth-century French philosopher Julien de la Mettrie expressed it with more precision than we now feel comfortable with: 'Let us then conclude boldly that man is a machine, and that the entire universe consists only of a single substance subjected to different modifications.'[3]

Management theorists have been aware of the human cost of all this for some time, but it is still proving incredibly difficult to address it in any effective way. Even the apparent solutions, such as the adoption of systems theories of management and workplace organization, themselves easily turn out to be just another (though different) form of mechanistic straitjacket that replaces one form of alienation with another.[4] Meanwhile, increasing numbers of people feel as if their entire lives are being spent dealing with trivia, and wonder if they will ever escape from the spiral of misery and dissatisfaction in which they feel they are enmeshed. At a time when we in the West have more possessions and labour-saving devices than our forebears could ever have imagined, we seem to have lost our souls, and people are dissatisfied with the way our own identities have become false and shallow, apparently without meaning beyond the immediate moment.[5] Even the dawning of a new century – in our case of a new millennium! – has not created the sense of expectancy and hope that has regularly greeted such transitional moments in the past. The twentieth century was heralded with an expectation that it would be a time of prosperity and renewal – an optimism that, of course, was not justified by the subsequent turn of events, which may go some way toward explaining why the mood at the start of the twenty-first century is more one of dull resignation than genuine optimism.

Human misery is nothing new, and our forebears in previous centuries had plenty of experience of it, usually through the impact of external forces on their lives, such as warfare and disease. They were able to seek reassurance and understanding by reference to some larger world view or metanarrative which could enable them to perceive the greater meaning of all things, and of their own lives within that cosmic context. Today, that is more difficult to do. Not only has the grand vision that inspired recent Western culture been discarded, but we are having difficulty in knowing how to set about constructing a new vision. Many commentators assume that the day of the metanarrative is finished, though in a later chapter I will question that position and suggest that, for those prepared to think outside the lines of traditional Western analytical discourse, there is plenty of evidence to show that most of us are actually searching for a new metanarrative. There can however be no doubt that one of the reasons why we are finding the search so difficult is that metanarratives assume some kind of shared experience of life, and today the very notion of community has itself become problematic. In a world where people are regarded as cogs in a machine, they are immediately placed in competition with everyone else, and that in itself creates relationships based not on co-operation but on suspicion. In addition, though, the idea of community was questioned by the philosophical ideology which assured us that autonomous rational individuals held within themselves the key to everything, and therefore the pinnacle of human accomplishment would be for us to exercise our reason in a way that would be completely free and unfettered by personal values or faith principles (world views or metanarratives). As a result, we seem to have adopted as a fundamental underlying principle of life the belief that, in order to be fulfilled and satisfied, we must rely only on ourselves and not on others, and in the process we question the accumulated wisdom of previous generations and doubt the authenticity of the personal support we may be able to get from those who are around us. Communities of interest that may help us to affirm and live out absolute values have been derided because of the way they might be likely to influence (usually interpreted in a negative way) our individual rational discourse and personal free choice. As a consequence, when people now look for sources of meaning in the midst of apparent chaos and discontinuity, they often feel they cannot trust others to stand alongside them in their endeavour. Indeed, we have become positively distrustful of other people, so that we regularly find ourselves desperate for community and meaningful relationships, but quite incapable of accepting either ourselves or anyone else. The fragmentation of neighbourhoods, not to mention the corrosion of family life and constant disintegration of personal relationships, can all be traced back to the way in which we have come to regard ourselves. Far from enabling us to reach our full potential – and regardless of whatever theoretical benefits it was supposed to bestow on us – we are discovering that the rationalist-materialist world view handed down to us from the eighteenth, nineteenth and early twentieth centuries has led to lives that are fractured and broken, and has created personal dysfunction on the grand scale. The reality and the extent of our own dislocation can be seen in the multiplicity of new caring professions that have arisen, in response to personal needs that, in previous generations, would have been met in the natural course of relationships, especially within the family. We now pay therapists for the kind of open ear that we might once have expected to get from our parents or grandparents (who, because they had first-hand acquaintance with our social location, as well as a natural benevolence toward their own people, were also better placed to give truly useful support in times of crisis).

What I describe will be familiar enough to most of us, for these are tensions that we all struggle with on a daily basis. It is what Francis Fukuyama has called *The Great Disruption,*[6] and there is a growing consensus not only with regard to the nature of the problem, but also in relation to its causes. Increasingly influential voices are now insisting that the cultural norms developed in Western society over the last two to three hundred years have played a crucial part in undermining the essential human quest for personal fulfilment and meaningful spirituality. This theme has surfaced repeatedly in Hollywood movies over the last two decades, most recently in *The Truman Show* (1998), *The Matrix* (1999) and the Oscar-winning *American Beauty* (1999), which have highlighted the contrast between the happy, clean, middle-class values that our culture commends and which we all – at some level – strive for, and the underlying reality of people who wear masks all the time, and who have a real struggle to come to grips with what is real and worthwhile in life.[7] This is an example of the moviemakers reflecting back what we already know to be true: the world we have created for ourselves seems not to be real. Moreover, this is not just a perception being promoted by trendy academics, but is increasingly becoming a shared conviction among very ordinary people in all walks of life. Indeed, academics (not to mention church leaders) often seem strangely resistant to recognizing this new social reality – philosophers and theologians in particular.

From the Church's point of view, that is part of the problem. People are now at the point where they are ready to question the values that have shaped our culture, and are more prepared than ever before to step outside the lines by challenging many of our preconceptions about what constitutes 'success', and what might be worth doing and believing. Paradoxically, the systems we have developed and by which we define civilized life have never been stronger, yet in those parts of our lives where we still have some sense of control, our willingness to experiment with alternative ways of doing things seems to be increasing exponentially. Exploring how we as Christians can relate to that will be a major theme of later chapters of this book. But before we come to the specifically church-oriented aspects of the argument, it will do no harm for us to remind ourselves of the diversity of ways in which people are dealing with this dichotomy.

Some have seen the destructive impact of our individualistic culture, and are resolving to use the opportunities they now have (many of them incongruously facilitated by technology) in order to enhance and enrich their own experience and that of the other people who are important in their lives by investing more time in relational matters. For example, increasing numbers of people with apparently secure jobs are leaving them in order to try and establish for themselves a more fulfilled lifestyle, even though there is considerable risk attached to such a move, with no guarantee of the eventual outcome. Many men are concerned about the way in which cultural norms have isolated them from the care of their children – indeed, are realizing that in a world where all adults are in paid employment outside the home, children are most likely to be brought up not even with their own parents' values, but with the values of such child-care providers as they can find, which in many cases will be whatever bland values the State can manage to agree on as representing the lowest common denominator of all its citizens (something that itself is becoming increasingly difficult to accomplish in Western liberal democracies). Whereas a generation ago, concern about such matters would mostly have manifested itself as an unspoken unease, today's parents are more likely to take action to reorganize their lives in order to fulfil what they see as their parental responsibilities, in some cases actually initiating their own personal downsizing by taking lower-paid work which gives them greater flexibility, or negotiating new working styles whose inevitable consequence is that they are disadvantaged in relation to the traditional career path offered by major corporate organizations.[8]

While there are many who would like to change their lifestyle, not everyone is fortunate enough to be able to achieve it, especially not those at the lower end of the income scale, or those who are disadvantaged in other ways. Because of the collapse of traditional relational networks, and the way that material success has become a culturally-approved sign of worthwhile achievement, people right across all social classes are struggling to establish themselves as individuals of true worth, and the extent of the personal alienation that then ensues is leading to pathological behaviour patterns. The only way in which some people can respond to their own sense of inner pain and personal abuse is by inflicting violence on themselves or on other people. Obvious examples of that would be through the misuse of drugs and alcohol, or other addictions – which can seem to be the only available route to transcendence, especially for rootless young people, though such behaviour is increasingly popular among middle-class executives, who do it just for the experience, as if they need to try everything at least once and see how near the edge they can go without damaging themselves. The huge rise in the suicide rate among young people is another manifestation of the same thing: in Britain, suicide is now one of the leading causes of death among young men aged twenty-five and under. In its most extreme form, this disillusionment with society and the self-hatred which it engenders has been behind many, if not all, of the growing number of violent attacks on innocent communities which from time to time have grabbed headlines right across the world. While many aspects of such random, unprovoked mass violence remain a mystery, everything that we know of those tragedies which have been best documented – such as the 1996 shootings at a primary school in Dunblane, Scotland, and the killings at Columbine High School, Colorado in 1999, together with a growing number of unprovoked workplace killings, especially in the USA – suggests that tragedies of this kind have their roots in the deep alienation felt by those who perpetrate them.[9] In less dramatic – though no less painful – circumstances, alienated men are responsible for increasing levels of domestic violence and sexual abuse in all Western countries. While there are many complex reasons behind this also, it stands to reason that one factor has got to be the sense of powerlessness and lack of purpose felt by so many.[10] In a world where we have lost touch with our emotions and where matters of the spirit have been systematically marginalized, many find that the only way left open for them to express grief for their lost prospects and possibilities is either by acting out their anger, or covering it up through drugs, alcohol and other forms of abusive or addictive behaviour.

Fortunately, it is only a minority of people who deal with the discontinuities of contemporary life by indulging in the kind of pathological behaviour that damages other people. But the same trends can be identified elsewhere – for example in the growing popularity of

the ever more extreme sports that we are now inventing to keep ourselves amused.[11] One of the fastest-growing leisure pastimes in North
America is known as BASE, which is an acronym for Building,
Antenna, Span (of a bridge) and Earth (cliffs). The common factor that
unites these apparently diverse things is that they are all high, and
provide platforms from which people can fling themselves at a great
height and increasing velocity, with only minimal control. Devotees
of this 'sport' jump off any high points they can find, with a flimsy
parachute being their only protection from certain death. They do so
mostly without the benefit of secondary parachutes, which in any
case would be useless in an emergency because people are travelling
so fast there is only time for one attempt to arrest their descent. The
dangers are obvious, and real: people do actually kill themselves, and
every BASE enthusiast I have spoken to seems to know somebody
who has, in the grotesque vocabulary of this game, 'gone in', that is
'gone in' to a wall, a dam, a mountainside, or the ground. Those who
'go in' almost never come back out again, and if they do it is to a life
of disability and dependency. But that scarcely seems to deter
devotees. A similar phenomenon can be seen in the numbers of
recreational mountain climbers who take risks that professionals
would never entertain. Even in the Scottish mountains (hardly the
highest or most dangerous in the world), the casualty figures have
been increasing every winter in recent years, partly as a result of
people who go out with little or no equipment, and even less
knowledge, but who presumably are driven by the need to have
transcendent experiences that will somehow lift them from their
predictable everyday lives.

It is ironic that, at a time when everyday life has never been safer,
so many people want to take risks, and get their fulfilment by leaving
safety behind and leaping into whatever void they can find. Jumping
off cliffs, or over canyons, may not be to everyone's taste, but participation in extreme sports is not the only evidence of this search for
transcendence. Other people (sometimes the same people) are resigning from well-paid and secure positions on the off chance that the
Internet will become even bigger than it already is, and they will be
the ones to become the next millionaires of cyber-space. In addition,
there is a rapidly growing band of people who apparently find fulfilment through reckless risk-taking on the stock market, whether by
operating as casual day traders while still maintaining other employment, or by using the Internet to buy and sell their own investments,
precisely because that route allows them to make their own choices,

and take responsibility for them, without having to pay any attention at all to the opinions of professional stockbrokers whose guidance would, in a previous generation, have been considered essential. Amazingly, companies that operate web sites through which it is possible to carry out on-line stock trading are now actually advertising their services with the assurance that individuals who sign up will be free to do absolutely anything they wish (as long as it is legal), without any advice being either sought or offered – and this assurance is clearly a recommendation in the eyes of their potential clients! Others place their trust in the lottery, which is just another form of the same enterprise, with even less likelihood of success. The same desire for excitement is also being reflected in our everyday lifestyles, so that people who will never take to the ski slopes still wear the clothing, and those whose only regular journey is to take their children to school along suburban roads now drive all-terrain vehicles, which at least leaves them feeling that they are ready for any adventure, even if they would neither want nor know how to handle a cross-country chase.

Our grandparents would have made no sense at all out of any of this. In their generation, there was no need to take initiatives in order to encounter danger: it was all around them, and came into their lives uninvited and generally unwelcomed, whether through global warfare, or epidemics and health scares, or more recently the uncertainties of the Cold War. To find a haven of peace and stability would have been regarded as a laudable objective. Now that we have it, we want something else. Of course, in one way human nature has always wanted what it does not have at any given moment in history. But this desire to uncover something more 'authentic' than our regularly prepackaged lifestyle has its deeper roots not in human nature per se, but in the way our culture has developed in the recent past.[12] For that reason alone, it is worth further reflection – and may well turn out to be significant in terms of the Church's ability to engage with people on their spiritual journey. Christians may not like it, but involvement with the church is now only one option among many in which people might engage in their leisure time. In order to bear witness to our faith, we have to be realistic about how people living in this cultural context will be facilitated in hearing the gospel, and what part the church might play in that. Of course, in my broader understanding of the nature of the gospel I do not see following Christ as a leisure activity, but as a radical lifestyle commitment. Nor do I see evangelism simply as an exercise in marketing. But we have to begin where people find themselves, and as I have reflected on what the church typically offers, and compared it with these other pursuits through which people are searching for meaning – not to mention spirituality – I wonder if our ways of being church have not become too much like the kind of rationalized systems that we are all struggling with in other areas of our lives. Or, putting it another way, is church as we know it just too bland, dull and safely predictable for people who crave an experience of radical challenge? And if that is the case, we need to ask ourselves how this might be impacting both our witness to those who are as yet not Christian, and our ability to empower those who are already following Christ. At a time when our culture is so clearly crying out for what in biblical terms could be described as a social *metanoia*, or change of heart, what can the church – which has long been familiar with such terminology – hope to contribute?

McDonaldization

To give some focus to these questions, I want to use a model of social analysis popularized by sociologist George Ritzer, and summarized most comprehensively in his book *The McDonaldization of Society*,[13] with further elaboration in his more recent work *The McDonaldization Thesis*.[14] The term 'McDonaldization' is of course derived from the American hamburger chain which began with humble origins in the mid twentieth century and is now claimed to be the world's largest restaurant franchise. The methodology whereby this has been achieved is not unique to the fast food business, but precisely because of the accessibility of this image, it provides an especially useful way of delineating some significant cultural trends and their impact on our lifestyles. Indeed, Ritzer claims that the paradigm represented by this way of doing things has become 'the way of life of a significant portion of the world', and 'is destined to continue to expand at an accelerating rate in the foreseeable future'. He defines McDonaldization as 'the process by which the principles of the fast-food restaurant are coming to dominate more and more sectors of American society as well as of the rest of the world.'[15] This is, in effect, a specialized form of Weber's understanding of the social process, which postulated that the natural concern to identify the most optimum and efficient ways to achieve given ends would always result in the emergence of what he called 'formal rationality', that is, a collection of rules, regulations, and procedures, and the growth of the bureaucratic systems necessary to ensure the smooth operation of such practices.[16] It is not difficult to see how this kind of rationality now controls our lives at almost every point. Nor is it necessary to be quite as cynical and negative about it as Ritzer seems to be. Some aspects of rationalization are beneficial: they would not have been adopted so widely if that had not been the case. But more often than not, the thoroughgoing way in which rationalization has been pursued seems to carry along with it other aspects that are less than satisfying, precisely because they are mechanical, and therefore dehumanizing. Indeed, in the 1996 revised edition of his book, Ritzer supplemented his original analysis with a new chapter insisting that the Nazi Holocaust – arguably the most dehumanizing of all events of recent history – could best be understood as a manifestation of McDonaldization.[17] Some industrial manufacturers have begun to recognize the shortcomings of over-rationalized systems, and have reorganized their production lines so that workers are not spending hours carrying out apparently trivial operations which have no obvious purpose beyond themselves. But in many more areas of life, rationalized systems are not only tolerated, but growing – not just as a means to an end, but as ends in themselves. Recreation is just one of a number of human activities that have become increasingly rationalized, so that even our own free time has become a 'product' which we purchase from someone else.[18] For example, most British people who go on vacation nowadays choose to buy a package tour, in which all the work has been done for them. That can of course be a time-saving and cost-saving way to travel overseas. For the faint-hearted, it can also offer the reassurance of a basic level of safety and security. But part of the price that has been paid for this is that the experience of international travel has itself been domesticated, and the purpose for which one might imagine it is worth travelling at all – to experience different cultures around the world – is frequently undermined in the process. British visitors go to Mediterranean resorts where everything has been built so that it looks like Britain, where 'British' pubs serve British beer, where people can watch British soccer matches on TV, buy British newspapers, and where no one ever has to speak another language than English because the only people they ever meet are exactly like them. This extraordinary phenomenon is even more exaggerated when people buy all-inclusive holidays in places like the Caribbean, or some West African countries, and end up living in rationalized tourist ghettoes with people who are just the same as themselves, and may even have come from the same cities. In some places, they will find themselves living in holiday accommodation that has been specifically designed to iso-late them from what is perceived as the irrationality of the indigenous culture. I remember visiting Jamaica (not as a tourist), and being amazed to learn that holidaymakers who wanted to 'escape' from their resort in order to meet real people could find it difficult, if not impossible, to do so because their accommodation was likely to be patrolled by armed guards – and even when they got out of the com-pound they were still likely to be escorted and chaperoned by their minders. The same paradox can be illustrated from entirely different areas of contemporary life. In the early 1990s the UK government inaugurated a programme for assessing the 'teaching quality' of its universities. Cumbersome and highly complex procedures were developed for this purpose, and an army of administrators were recruited to make it all work. It was an impressive-looking operation, and many university teachers welcomed it, as they placed a high value on students as a major national and international resource. In the event, even more of them were amazed and disappointed by what took place, for the whole process turned out not to be about teaching (still less about learning), but about the efficiency of bureaucracies and the accuracy of paperwork. Teaching standards were largely monitored by reference to the way in which aims and objectives were spelled out, or the procedures whereby disputes might be handled, or how written projects were catalogued and stored after they had been graded. Even when students were consulted, it was largely in relation to their satisfaction with procedures and practices, with far more attention paid to matters such as their representation on course com-mittees than to fundamental questions such as whether they had actually learned anything, or whether they had become better people as a result of the educational process.

Even something as intrinsically personal as sex has been rational-ized and turned into a commodity, so that a casual reading of almost any glossy magazine will leave the impression that what one might imagine to be the most natural activity in the world simply cannot be enjoyed without a vast array of specialized sex toys, electrical vibrators, fancy condoms and instructional videos, not to mention techniques of such complexity that it seems something of a miracle that previous generations ever managed to reproduce themselves at all. Indeed, Ritzer highlights the way in which it is now possible to do all that – and more – 'without going through the muss and fuss of sexual intercourse', whether it be through phone lines or sites on the

World Wide Web that allow us to have 'virtual sex' with people we never meet, or through IVF procedures (which, in addition to their therapeutic use, are evidently becoming an increasingly popular choice among professional couples, who want to schedule the birth of their children to fit in with other demands of their rationalized lives).[19]

It would be easy to multiply examples of this phenomenon – and Ritzer does. They all have one thing in common: that a human quest becomes a bureaucratic procedure, and in the process what looks like rationality turns out to be shot through with flecks of the irrational. It is this kind of dichotomy which Ritzer aims to highlight, tracing its impact through many different aspects of contemporary life. In most areas, we accept it without question, resigning ourselves to the fact that this is just the way life is nowadays. But with a growing distrust of reason itself as a reliable way to understand the world, people are increasingly questioning where all this is leading us – especially in those parts of our lives over which we still have some control, namely our leisure interests, our activities when we are not at work. This is where I believe all this relates to the church, for if the church offers only the same things as the rationalized world of work, why should people who are oppressed elsewhere in their lives expect to find a resolution by joining the church? For many of today's post-modern people, afflicted by a high degree of social stratification in their everyday life, the church can often seem to be just more of the same, with (for example) its strict demarcation between clergy and laity, and little room for innovation or for tailoring its approach to individual needs. I remember sitting on a committee which was organizing a major European ecumenical gathering, and the person chairing it was concerned that we should ensure a substantial crowd would be present for the opening ceremonies. To a great extent I understood and shared his concern: since this event was likely to be featured in TV news bulletins, it was important to make it look good for the cameras, and not allow the Church to be portrayed as a dead or dying institution. He also had the added incentive of being the leader of a major British mainline denomination, and it was important for his Church to come out of this with an enhanced reputation – a motivation that I was less happy with, but still understood. But when he announced that 'We need pew fodder', his turn of phrase left me in no doubt at all that we were coming from quite different places. What he understood the purpose of the Church to be was not, to me, an attractive vision. Writing about life on the industrial assembly line in a McDonaldized world, Ritzer observes: 'Human beings, equipped with a wide array of skills and abilities, are asked to perform a limited number of highly simplified tasks over and over. Instead of expressing their human abilities . . . people are forced to deny their humanity and act in a robot-like manner. People do not express themselves . . . but rather deny themselves.'[20] Richard Münch offers a similar analysis when he writes that 'We are captured by the iron cage of a McDonaldized world and are cut off from any ties to the authentic world in which we would be able to take part in producing and reproducing a life that we would consider a good one.'[21] As I have talked to many people who would regard themselves as spiritual searchers (a term that is defined more exactly in chapter 4), that is precisely what they tell me about the church. Ironically, we Christians have talked and written more about the need for change and renewal during the second half of the twentieth century than at any other time in church history and, with one or two notable exceptions, it is hard to think of any previous comparable period when so little change has actually taken place. Our ways of being church at the start of the twenty-first century are virtually unchanged from what was going on in the nineteenth century.

We must avoid the temptation to overdramatize the situation, but could it be that we have allowed our churches and their structures to be taken over by the creeping rationalization of modernist culture, and we now find ourselves suffering all the drawbacks of that with very few of the advantages of it? Why else would we be so inflexible about relatively trivial things, insisting that practices and procedures have to be carried through even when there is no obvious need for them or purpose behind them? To give a simple example, in many churches it is still the practice to incorporate the giving of an offering in Sunday worship. There are good liturgical and theological reasons for doing so, and I have no quarrel at all with any of them. But in many churches I visit, I observe that almost nobody actually seems to put anything in the offering, and quite frequently it is only visitors who are left to do so – because the regular attenders are giving through direct payments from their bank accounts. Allegedly this is easier, more convenient, and so on (though it frequently seems to require yet another staff member in the church office to administer all the paperwork) – but in the process of adopting it, we can easily undermine one of the key purposes of worship, as a gifting of ourselves and our resources to the service of God. As a result, we end up with two rationalized systems, neither of which contributes directly to the spiritual purposes of the church: in terms of our worship, those who contribute through direct bank payments lose the ritual connection between worship and everyday life (for signing papers is a very individualistic, private activity) and, in terms of our evangelism, it must send out a very strange message to those who visit our churches if the very people who claim to be most committed never visibly put anything into the offering as it passes them by.

It is no coincidence that Ritzer chose 'McDonaldization' as the term that he thinks most aptly describes all this, for the fast food business has more than its fair share of apparently mindless operations that have to be gone through before the product is delivered to the customer. One only has to ask any young person who has worked in this industry, and they all have their favourite stories about the day when they used their brains to think of better ways to do things – only to be put in their place because that would infringe company policy. As a client, I find that there are some restaurants I always try and avoid whenever possible, because their procedures for getting the diner to the table with food set before them are so complicated and drawn out that they unnecessarily take up inordinate amounts of time. When it comes to food, we can readily appreciate the absurdity of the idea that there is only one way to do things. But there is a growing realization today that this applies to all sorts of other areas of our life as well, including especially personal growth and meaningful spirituality, neither of which can be easily quantified nor reduced to neat formulations. Is this one reason why people have lost interest in what the Church seems to offer?

3 THE CHURCH AND THE IRON CAGE

Though it was made long before the term 'McDonaldization' was coined as an appropriate way to describe the destructive and dehumanizing effects of social rationalization under the influence of modernist thinking, Terry Gilliam's 1985 movie *Brazil* still remains as one of the outstanding visual presentations of what can happen when people either accept, or find themselves powerless to oppose, mindless bureaucracy imposed upon them by a viciously destructive government. The film speaks with particular power into the British context, because that is where it is set. The 'Ministry of Information' which is at the centre of the spiralling vortex of inhumanity so vividly portrayed on the screen is depicted as a department of the Whitehall civil service, in which both government employees and the citizens whom they seek to control are uniformly destroyed by the creeping power of centralized systems.[1] When the film was first crafted, its bleak vision of a world without hope was too dark for the distributors, Universal Studios, who demanded that it be lightened up a little for release in the USA so as to be less grimly apocalyptic. As a result, the final scene was added, somewhat incongruously showing light shining through the dark clouds with which the director had originally intended it to end. However, no amount of cosmetic adjustments can hide the fact that its haunting images are too close to reality for comfort, and even in its edited version it still has to rank as one of the finest visual depictions of the 'iron cage' of McDonaldization that there has ever been.[2]

In relation to our theme in this chapter, the relevance of this movie is to be seen in the way the sadistic 'Ministry of Information' is portrayed. Naturally, it is located in a building that is itself a monument to modernity, with towering spires reaching up to the sky, and a surfeit of grand marble entrances, with guardians of the doors at all the key points, including a commissionaire at the main entrance, who may appear to occupy a menial position but, in truth, controls access to everything else. It is almost certainly not an accident that the architecture is very cathedral-like, for one of the first things the visitor sees on entering is an inscription which provides a kind of mission statement for the entire organization, 'the truth will make you free' – a slogan that combines a biblical text (John 8:32) with the objectives of Enlightenment rationalism, and ironically motivates the destruction of the very people it claims to serve. When I first saw this film, those were the key visual images that stood out for me, and encouraged me to explore more precisely the extent to which Ritzer's McDonaldization thesis can be applied to the Church. I did not have far to look before some of my worst fears were confirmed, and I found myself forced to face the uncomfortable possibility that this idea might not be as far-fetched as it seems. For when I then applied Ritzer's four key characteristics of the McDonaldization process – efficiency, calculability, predictability, and control – to the Church, I began to see some of the reasons why so many of today's people struggle so much with it.

Efficiency

Efficiency is not in itself a bad attribute, for it is just about identifying the best means to achieve a particular end. But in a society that has become over-rationalized, this searching for good ways is not something that is usually open to people to do for themselves. It has already been done by the system, which may well have institutionalized certain ways of doing things to the exclusion of any other possible options. This happens repeatedly in commercial organizations, where training in doing things in a particular way becomes part of an individual's socialization within the organization. Eventually it no longer matters whether a particular modus operandi is actually the most efficient: it just becomes the accepted – and essential – way of doing things for a particular group of people. Nor – contrary to popular perceptions – is it only, or mainly, older people who live this way. Younger people are particularly prone to it – not, I hasten to add, out of specific choice, but because society at large no longer provides them with worthwhile role models, which means that a major source of personal identity has come to be the adoption of an 'attitude' or visual appearance, doing things not because they are the best, but because loyalty to a particular image has been built up within the culture, which is difficult to question or reject. A good example would be the indiscriminate use of sex as a form of entertainment, which certainly pervades British youth culture (to a much greater extent than is the case in the USA), in spite of the fact that there are no obvious rational benefits at all, in terms of either short-term or long-term satisfaction, while there are clearly quantifiable dangers to both mental and physical health which can have long-term, even fatal, consequences. In order to maintain the illusion, it is important to perpetuate the notion that other ways of doing things are probably non-rational, and to be non-rational is always going to be less efficient.

It is not difficult to see signs of this approach within the Church. We love rationalized systems, and try to apply them to everything from our theology to the way we welcome visitors to our Sunday services. I have been writing this book during a period of study leave which has been spent away from my home environment, and which has meant that I have had the opportunity to visit several different churches incognito. While some sort of reception is, of course, always better than none, I have come away from too many churches feeling that I have been given the same sort of pre-packaged 'welcome' as I might expect in a fast-food outlet where the server will routinely enquire about my day, but really has no interest in either me or my life. As Ritzer incisively observes, such greetings amount to nothing more than that 'in a polite and ritualized way, they are really telling us to "get lost," to move on so someone else can be served.'[3]

For other evidences of the quick-fix pre-packaged 'church' we need go no further than the average Christian bookstore, where most of the stock is likely to be of this kind. There are 'how-to' books on every imaginable topic, including titles claiming to be able to teach us the 'ten steps to spiritual maturity', or how to be a successful parent in sixty minutes, while anyone looking for curriculum materials for Christian education is faced with a bewildering choice, all of them claiming to offer biblical truth and changed lifestyles in even more easily accessible bite-sized chunks than their competitors. Many churches are expending inordinate amounts of energy to ensure that their worship (by which they invariably mean singing or what some call 'music ministry') is carefully programmed and regulated. Alongside this there is a corresponding focus on appointing people to ever more narrowly defined ministry positions, building up extensive programmes, and ensuring that we have the right size of team to meet projected needs. American churches have always been much more programme-centred than British congregations, and in a society that is tolerant of a McDonaldized lifestyle that has worked reasonably well. In such a context, pre-packaged church can easily seem to be an attractive option: somebody else does the thinking for you, predigests it, and serves it up in an efficient manner. It is the spiritual equivalent of fast food, and unlike the home-prepared meal it requires no preparation, no cleaning up afterwards, and no involvement in cooking it. But – to continue the analogy – fast food comes in only very limited selections, and when the novelty of those wears off (and who wants to eat burgers for every meal?) then the majority of people look elsewhere, even if they do not seek out establishments that are paid-up members of the growing international 'Slow Food' movement.[4] Churches where everything is pre-packaged can often thrive for a while, but eventually they too lose their appeal. In any case, part of the emerging post-modern culture is a questioning, if not a rejection of such rationalized ways of doing things, and even those churches which have been successful through such strategies in the past are likely to find themselves struggling soon enough, so they are not going to be useful models for the rest of us to imitate.

Viewed purely in marketing terms, pre-packaged spirituality is no longer a premium product. It probably worked reasonably well in the years following the Great Depression, and after the end of the Second World War, when shortages of all kinds – not to mention the proclaimed benefits of emerging technologies – predisposed consumers to think that processed was best. I remember as a child in the 1950s, when frozen foods first came onto the market in Britain, my mother would buy products such as frozen peas and fish fingers, no doubt at much higher cost than their fresh equivalents – even though our home had neither refrigerator nor freezer at the time, and therefore we had to consume them immediately. That actually ran contrary to the intended purpose of frozen foods, which was their long storage life in appropriate conditions – but the fact that they were pre-packaged and ready-made was, at that time, a consideration that far outweighed any others.

Of course, being the church is not just about marketing, and a theology that comes pre-packaged, and in which there are no loose ends, is not true to life nor can it adequately reflect the richness of the gospel. Moreover, the key to efficiency in the business world is being able to process as many people as easily as possible. But Christian faith is not about processing people as if they were all peas in a pod. Life is messy – as increasing numbers of post-modern people are discovering for themselves. There is a lot of dirt which it will be impossible, and undesirable, to tie up in a neat package. Any kind of meaningful spirituality needs to take account of that, which means that Christians will fulfil their calling by guarding the integrity of the right questions, rather than handing out slick answers. In the process, we must of course take account of the accumulated wisdom and experience of those who have gone before us. But we can affirm and value all that without it becoming a straitjacket that restricts the spiritual explorations of our own generation.

Calculability

Calculability is about size and quantity and, in the case of fast food, there is usually an implication that the more of it there is, the better a meal the customer is getting. Again, the appeal of this can be located in the needs of people who lived through the Great Depression and the Second World War, for whom quantity was, if anything, even more important than efficiency. When Maxwell House instant coffee first came on the market, it was advertised as 'the cup that never runs out', which was good news for people accustomed only to shortages. Today, no one would dream of advertising coffee – of all things – in that way. There are now so many kinds of coffee available that people who rarely visit a coffee shop can be forgiven for not knowing how to make a choice on those occasions when they do. British people might think they already have too many different kinds on offer, but whenever I take British friends into a North American coffee shop I often find myself having to choose for them, because that is the only way they can cope with the enormous variety that is available. When I was a youth, churches would regularly commend themselves to their potential worshippers by offering the equivalent of 'the cup that never runs out', assuring people that not only would they be provided with a free seat, but there would also be a Bible and hymn-book thrown in. I can only suppose that, in that generation, these must have been incentives. Quantity was very important.

There is a widespread tendency today to equate quality with quantity in many different areas of life. In the context of food, they might indeed on some occasions be one and the same thing, for we do not eat fast food in order to savour the quality of the culinary experience, but to refuel our bodies for the next tasks ahead of us – and to do so as quickly as we can, quite possibly while literally driving to our next appointment. The same assumptions are made elsewhere. On television, the size of the audience dominates everything else, and as long as the ratings keep up quality is rarely an issue. In educational life, the value of academics is increasingly judged by reference to the number of papers or books they produce, or league tables of periodicals to which they contribute. As a result, there is a mad scramble to produce as much published work as possible, and the market is flooded with books that in more reflective times would never have seen the light of day. Christians are not immune from this obsession with numbers and quantity. Of course, numbers are not altogether useless as a means of assessing the Church's relevance to the spiritual search of our culture. Dying churches often resort to the 'quality not quantity' argument in order to justify their decline as providing evidence of their faithfulness. Numbers cannot tell us everything, but they do have a place in taking the spiritual temperature of our congregations, for a church with declining numbers will certainly be declining for a reason (though I am less certain that the reverse is necessarily true, that a growing church will automatically be one where something spiritually worthwhile is happening). But we do need to be aware of the limitations of numbers alone, for though they are the easiest way of measurement, they are a blunt instrument, and often have little to do with what is *really* happening. They can even mask the truth of a particular situation. Back in the 1970s and 1980s, the Church Growth Movement laid great stress on calculability as a key measure of spirituality.[5] But that is a connection that can rarely be made. The real question, even for growing churches, is not the numbers per se, but the realities which they represent. Most church growth currently taking place in Western culture is not actually church growth at all. To be sure, some congregations are growing, but when we ask where the additional people are coming from, in the vast majority of cases it turns out that they are being drawn from other churches, so that growth in one place automatically entails decline somewhere else. While there will of course be local variations, and exceptions that buck the trend, this must be overwhelmingly what is taking place in so-called growing churches today – otherwise, why has the total number of Christians as a percentage of the population not shown an increase, but has actually declined for the last thirty years, wherever we look in the Western world? Emphasis on quantification can encourage us to avoid the realities, and thereby skew the real picture of what is taking place.

Even in contexts where 'real growth' is taking place (by which I mean people coming to faith, or renewing a faith once lost), it is easy for concerns about calculability to result in the creation of dehumanizing structures. One of the encouraging signs in church life in England has to be the number of new churches (of all denominations) that are being planted (on the whole, the major denominations in Scotland and Wales have been less enthusiastic, if not overtly hostile to this strategy). A typical church plant almost always begins with people, rather than a building, though more often than not there comes a point where in order to be a 'proper' church a building is seen as desirable, if not essential. I recall the founder of what came to be a significant mega-church in the USA telling me how, with hindsight, he could see that this transition from people to building, while highly successful in one sense, had actually led to the spiritual diminution of the people because, as he succinctly expressed it, he had been forced to adopt a ministry style which was 'geared towards filling the building, instead of filling the people'. He had started with just seventeen people, and ended up with more than 3000, but in the process the church had become a depersonalized machine – against the self-consciously articulated theological aspirations of the original group, and without anyone really understanding what was happening until it was too late. Growth led to increased numbers, which required a bigger space to contain them, which called for fundraising and building projects, which necessitated a mortgage to pay for it all, which demanded efficient marketing and sales techniques to maximize the attendance in order to raise enough money to meet the payments, and on and on in a vicious spiral of cause and effect. When all of that came together, it created a system that, in terms of human relationships and real spiritual growth was pathologically self-destructive – but which was apparently necessary in order to maintain the trappings of 'success'. When I met him, the founding pastor of that church had left what was in effect his life's work (he had been at it for over twenty years), disillusioned by the monster he had helped to create, and feeling that his own spiritual energy had been sapped in the process. He had discovered the hard way the reality behind Ritzer's warning that we should 'avoid the routine and systematic use of McDonaldized systems' because 'habitual use [of them] is destructive to our physical and psychological well-being as well as to society as a whole.'[6]

This obsession with numbers can also work the opposite way around. I think of a city-centre church in Britain which had been struggling for years to maintain any sort of regular Sunday congregation. In reality, there was little chance it ever could attract a significant number on Sundays, as the immediate population base from which it had to draw was minimal. But it was in the heart of a prosperous business and shopping district, and the lay leaders of the church recognized that this was where they could make most impact, and took deliberate steps to turn themselves into a vibrant and attractive spiritual community Monday to Friday. They succeeded to a remarkable extent, and were able to identify specifically something like 2000 people who had regular contact with the church on this basis. Most of what took place midweek had an identifiably 'spiritual' core to it, so the church was not being used merely as a community centre, but by any definition would count as a worshipping and evangelizing centre. The denominational authorities, however, were unable to see this, because their regulations required that in order to be kept open a church must have a certain minimum number of regular Sunday worshippers, and a 'proper' church also needed to have a full-time minister – who, of course, would have nothing to do if there were no Sunday services, since that was the standard by which the nature of ministry was defined by the denomination in question. After a long struggle between the McDonaldized systems of the denomination and the spontaneous spirituality of the people, the system won, not least because it owned the premises. Calculability defined in a particularly sterile and irrelevant way strangled human and spiritual values, not to mention evangelistic opportunities.

An over-emphasis on what is quantifiable will generally hinder if not undermine personal and spiritual growth. Numbers certainly cannot be used to understand or interpret such qualities. Counting people should not be made a substitute for taking the risk to focus on discipleship, renewal and maturity. A more discerning question will be not, 'how many of us are there?' but 'how much like Christ have we become?' – remembering that Jesus himself left only eleven key disciples to change the world. If success comes to be equated with programmes (how many we have, for how many different groups, and so on), there is always going to be a danger that spirituality becomes confused with busyness, and instead of dealing with the *real* human issues, we create new programmes to mask our own ineffectiveness. A church that is dominated by programmes will inevitably become enslaved to calculability, because it is a key factor in running programmes: we always need to know when they will start and finish. Ironically, confusing quantity with quality at this level is likely to be evangelistically and spiritually self-defeating. Those who are serious about the spiritual quest are as likely to be impressed by the proliferation of services and meetings found in many churches as the sophisticated coffee drinker might be if offered a cup of lukewarm instant coffee. In relation to today's lifestyles, most churches just have far too many gatherings that they expect their people to attend, mid-week as well as at weekends. The difficulty felt by many people at this point is not so much about the amount of time that might be involved, as the quality of the experience in relation to the time they have invested. Time is actually one of the most valuable assets we have for the spiritual quest, and spiritual searchers are increasingly likely to sacrifice significant amounts of time in order to achieve their goal. If we take a look at the spiritual activities that do attract people today, they are things like vision quests, sweat lodges, and retreats – all of which demand a more relaxed attitude to time than a McDonaldized church culture is generally prepared to allow. Nor is this phenomenon restricted to the North American continent: the Samiye Ling Tibetan Buddhist monastery in south-west Scotland is oversubscribed for its silent and solitary retreats, which can last up to four years. How do churches which limit the scope of Christian worship to sixty minutes or less (even if it is repeated on several occasions in a week) expect to make any meaningful connection with people like this? And how do Christians who are impatient if a service lasts five minutes longer than they anticipated imagine that their 'spirituality' can possibly become an inspiration to those who take their own spiritual journey more seriously than that? Because of our commitment to this kind of calculability, many of our churches are simply not geared up to spend time either to explore God or to make meaningful connections with other Christians, let alone reach out to others who are searching for the meaning of life. It is the spiritual equivalent of the McDonaldized illusion that it is possible to get a lot of food for minimal expenditure.

Predictability

Of the four major traits of McDonaldization identified by Ritzer, this is the one which is most easily identified in the Church. Ritzer defines it in the following terms:

> In a rational society people prefer to know what to expect in all settings and at all times. They neither want nor expect surprises. . . . In order to ensure predictability over time and place, a rational society emphasizes such things as discipline, order, systematization, formalization, routine, consistency, and methodical operation. . . . It is these familiar and comfortable

rituals that make fast-food restaurants attractive to legions of people.[7]

Inevitably, it is only certain kinds of people who will feel 'familiar and comfortable' in this way, namely those who have been there before. The same factors as Ritzer highlights apply in the Church just as much as in fast-food outlets. Paradoxically, though, the predictability of what goes on in church is both a strength and a weakness. The security of what is predictable can indeed help people to feel safe – but the downside is that it all becomes routine. Moreover (and we will explore this more fully in the next chapter), it is only a particular type of person who is actually seeking that kind of security today. As a rough generalization we might say that those who are already in the Church are indeed people who, temperamentally, are attracted by predictability, while significant numbers of those who are not in the Church are actually repelled by it, because they like experimentation and change.

Pragmatically, the Church's love affair with this aspect of McDonaldization is a major stumbling block to effective evangelism in today's post-modern culture. It can easily encourage a lack of honesty within any given congregation. When I was discussing this question with a group of doctoral students at Fuller Seminary in California, they highlighted the way in which a desire for predictability can sometimes be used to stifle the healthy exchange of views. They pointed out to me how in many North American churches, it is taken for granted that certain political and theological views will be held by church members, and are therefore not discussed at all. For example, there might be an assumption that people in a particular church will all be pro-life, or will have a particular understanding of the New Age, or a specific view on biblical authority, or whatever. This is not a uniquely American phenomenon, as I have come across exactly the same expectation in British churches, usually related to the same kind of issues. I have also met people who have deliberately chosen to join a particular local church, or a specific denominational grouping, because they know that underlying assumptions are unlikely ever to be discussed, and they like to go with the attitude that says 'I believe the same as everybody else', because that way they are never going to be challenged.

Apart from the obvious practical handicap all this is imposing on effective mission among post-modern spiritual searchers, it also raises some theological issues as well, for the emphasis on predictability creates a constant pressure to homogenize all our under-standings of discipleship and lifestyle. There is inevitably a tempta-tion to process people so that they all turn out like clones of one another. The faith itself becomes predictable, and even experiences as personal and variable as conversion are forced into the same mould, so that in any given context one person's faith journey sounds much the same as another, because they have all been packaged to order, to fit some preconceived notion of how a 'true' conversion should be. Individuals hear of other people's experiences, and try and get the same for themselves, rather than living and believing in ways that are open to authentic (and potentially unique) experiences of the Spirit.[8] Educational and evangelistic programmes perpetuate this in such a way that, with only a modicum of experience, it is quite a simple matter to distinguish those who have filtered their spirituality through (for example) the Alpha course from others who have come through some other route such as Emmaus. Even theologians are not immune from this tendency, and the prescriptive nature of some theories of stages of faith is just a different form of the same desire for total predictability in the spiritual journey.[9] While they generally believe themselves to be light years away from approaches like Alpha, when I hear Christians who constantly analyse themselves in relation to faith development theory ('I'm mostly a stage four but I'm well on the way to making stage five') I must admit that I cannot tell the difference: they too are craving for a predictable form of belief that is every bit as circumscribed as the narrowest fundamentalism.

This same desire for predictability also frequently leads to the adoption of church programmes which attempt to 'imitate' other churches that are perceived as being particularly successful. The thinking is usually that by doing so, we can 'guarantee' the same growth and success as has occurred elsewhere: if we do things the same way as others, the same results will happen for us. This has been one of the major scourges of British church life over the last twenty years. If a church finds something that works for them, it is perfectly natural to want to share those insights with other people. That is how we encourage one another, and how we can learn from the experience of others. But once we start turning our faith stories into a package that can be sold to other people – as if God only works in this or that particular way – then the programme usually ends up being prescriptive, even if that was not the intention of the originators of it. It is not difficult to appreciate the commercial incentives for doing this, especially at a time when churches struggle to balance their books. But in reality, what is a good idea and culturally appropriate in one place is likely to be neither more nor less than that: a great idea in that place. It may not even be something that will work in the neighbouring community, because our social context is now so diverse that even a small town can contain several different subcultures, and the gospel needs to be contextualized in quite different ways in each of them. Of course we need to learn from the experiences of other Christians – their failures as well as their successes. But to make any real headway, we should not be copying others, but asking what we need to do in our own unique set of circumstances. In fact, a constant concern with shaping and packaging things can actually become a strategy for ensuring that nothing fundamental is going to change, because those who are recruited to run ready-made programmes are often the very ones who, with appropriate encouragement, might have had the energy and insight to create the experimental forms of worship and witness that could be transformational in their own local circumstances – if only all their time and enthusiasm was not being sapped with trying to adapt other people's ideas. It is easy to become so enamoured with what God has done somewhere else that we fail to discern what God might actually do in this place and at this time.

Mention of God (at last, some of you are no doubt thinking) reminds me that, in the end, Christian faith is supposed to be about the Other, and by definition therefore ought not to be predictable. Is it possible to have a world view – or a church structure – dominated by predictability without at the same time denying, or at least seriously jeopardizing, belief in a biblical God? It is certainly striking that all those spiritual paths that are now emerging in the West as serious alternatives to mainline Christian belief incorporate significant elements of the mystical, the numinous, the unpredictable, and the non-rational (which is not, of course, the same as the irrational). Arguably, the more rationalized everyday life has become, the more important it is for our inner lives to be focused on something mysterious. This would be consistent with the way that even ancient rituals which preserve this sense of mystery have an enormous and growing appeal.[10]

Control

This is Ritzer's fourth and final category. In some ways, I find it hard to regard as a separate concern, for issues of power and control are really the subtext that is running through all that has been reviewed here so far. We are constantly controlled at so many points of everyday life that it hardly seems necessary to list them all here. Not only fast-food outlets but also supermarkets exercise a rigid control over us when we visit them. The way lines are set up, to move us this way rather than that, the way goods are displayed on the shelves, the information about our personal habits surreptitiously obtained when we use 'loyalty cards' at the checkout – these are all examples of control as the underlying infrastructure which guarantees efficiency, calculability and predictability. Though shops pride themselves at providing us with a service, in reality we now do most of the work ourselves. In some places, we even scan the barcodes and work out our own prices, thereby allowing the supermarket owners to employ fewer checkout operators, and add to the efficiency of their business (less work and greater profits for them).

Many examples could be cited to illustrate the way in which Christians have sought to control spirituality. One of the most obvious, perhaps, is the way in which crusade evangelists throughout the twentieth century have given altar calls, which for those who responded then became the entry point into an extensive process of spiritual socialization and control not dissimilar to the McDonaldized way in which visitors to theme parks might be shepherded around the attractions. Indeed, the more one reflects on that comparison the more obvious the similarities become. Whereas the theme park has its 'cast members', the crusade has its 'counsellors' – the apparent image of supportive informality being, in both cases, a cover for their real purpose, which is to act as guards, ensuring that nothing takes place that might contradict the corporate objectives of the enterprise. Just as there is only one way to enjoy in safety the rides at a theme park, so there is only one way to make a commitment to Christ at a crusade meeting. Just as the theme park guests are forbidden to take their own food, these traditional forms of 'evangelism' take similar steps to ensure that only one kind of spiritual diet will be available. When people whom you have never seen before suddenly become intimate and personal, assuring you of their undying friendship, they might even have been trained at McDonald's. They have invariably been screened to ensure that, like their theme park counterparts, they will follow a certain dress code, speak a certain language, exhibit a particular demeanour, and give predetermined responses to questions. Like their secular equivalents, they too have their supervisors, who are there to check that no one violates the procedures, and to whom the counsellor who finds him or herself out of their depth can refer awkward clients. In some crusades I have observed, the comparison with the control methods of the theme park is complete down to the last detail, as 'converts' exit the venue through a bookstore or market-place selling all the themed items that they will need to com-memorate their visit (even, on occasion, including Bibles emblazoned with a photograph of the star of the show – not, of course, Jesus Christ, but the preacher!).[11]

That example of ecclesiastical control might seem so obvious (and ludicrous) that it is hardly necessary to highlight it. But there are also more insidious examples of the same trends in many churches that would have nothing to do with the kind of crusades I have just men-tioned. For example, in recent years, it has become trendy to try and encourage 'lay ministries'. That is of course a perfectly laudable con-cept, which is deeply rooted in the New Testament. But I wonder if much of it is not motivated by the same kind of McDonaldized think-ing (maximum efficiency at the lowest cost), rather than being founded on any genuine commitment to the promotion of personal wholeness and the acceptance of different gifts in the service of God's kingdom. In some churches 'lay ministry' seems to have become the ecclesiastical equivalent of filling your own grocery bags. It is cer-tainly striking that, for all our talk about releasing the gifts of the laity, most of our churches are only willing to release them to undertake the tasks that clergy would otherwise do, and if their innate gifts and talents are unconventional, we find it correspondingly difficult to change the system to create spaces for different things to happen. To confirm this, we need only to examine the various checklists and tests that are in common use to help people identify and define their spiritual gifts. While we say we are wanting to be sensitive to people's skills, and open to using them in the life of the church, the possible ministries that are on offer invariably have an over-emphasis on particular areas – all of them carefully chosen to ensure that we identify in other people only those gifts that are not going to challenge the position of the established leadership. The evolution of small groups in a church community – whether through deliberate 'cell church' strategies, or more informally – can also easily become just another control mechanism, unless such groups are allowed the space to develop as fully-functioning churches within themselves. Otherwise, they easily become shallow 'pseudo-communities', rigidly controlled by an agenda imposed from outside themselves (often out of fear that they will become centres from which the system can be challenged), rather than being allowed and encouraged to develop into open networks of mutual support, encouragement, and healing.[12] I am not advocating a free-for-all in the church, but there is a difference between control and accountability. All too often, we pay lip service to the ideals of diversity, when the truth is that we are only prepared to cope with a McDonaldized kind of difference – in much the same way as the market-place is increasingly turning ethnic foods into yet more rationalized restaurant chains,[13] or the New Age adopts non-Western spiritualities as 'a quintessential symbol of being chic . . . acquiring [them] as essential designer accessories [that] . . . can be consumed to alleviate spiritual boredom.'[14]

I have seen this happen so many times in churches of different traditions that I feel there is hardly any need to give more specific examples: churches appear to have more than their fair share of auto-crats and demagogues, concerned with keeping power and control in the right hands (their own). It is worth pointing out here that there is not a simple identification between control freaks and position in our inherited church hierarchies. Some of the most sensitive and open people I know are bishops and other senior church leaders, and some of the most power-hungry people I have encountered are lay leaders and local clergy. But it is at local level that so much damage is done not just to the Church's image, but also to the cause of the gospel – because this is where ordinary people experience church, and make their decisions about the possible relevance of Christian faith to their lives.

This issue of power and control is at the heart of all the other fac-tors that are at work in a McDonaldized style of being. Numbers become all-important to church leaders, especially in the American context where churches are self-consciously competing with one another for market share, because they endow clergy with status both in the local situation and also in wider denominational contexts. An over-emphasis on 'sound' theology is a manifestation of the same thing. It doesn't really matter here whether 'soundness' is defined by reference to a conservative or a more liberal theology – either way, it is about having control of spiritual processes, often backed up by putting questionable people through training programmes to re-educate them and get the 'right' result. Even good practices like setting goals for the church can easily become a subtle form of con-trol, by programming ourselves to accept certain specified results, and thereby not allowing space for something quite different.

This is a major challenge for all of us – myself included. It seems to be a natural human inclination to suppose that, if other people are to achieve personal maturity, meaningful spirituality, integrated growth and so on, that means they must end up being like we are. We too easily forget that a central element of the Christian faith is that God has created people in all their diversity – and that Jesus made weakness and vulnerability, not power and control, key characteristics for those who would be his disciples. The various themes to which Ritzer draws attention are all ways in which our culture believes it can measure 'success', but in the context of Christian spirituality that raises a further question about how we define success, for it has to be obvious that on these definitions Jesus could certainly not be considered to be a 'successful' person. We will return to this in a later chapter, because it goes to the heart of much that I want to say about the nature of an effective spiritual community for the twenty-first century.

Strengths and Weaknesses

I make no apology for presenting much of this in somewhat black and white terms. I have deliberately chosen to do so, in order to highlight some of the matters I believe we need to deal with. Ritzer's analysis of contemporary society can of course be questioned. For example, some aspects of what he calls McDonaldization have brought benefits to us, and continue to do so, though he never really explores them or recognizes them.[15] His use of a fast-food corporation as the key identifier of these trends makes the image as accessible as possible to a large number of people, but at the same time it tends to disparage the process in a way that would not have been the case had he chosen what might have been perceived as a more up-market product to serve as a model.[16]

In relation to church life, some of my earlier comments also need to be more carefully nuanced than they have been so far. For example, many churches are organizationally a mess, and could benefit from some consistent reflection on how to become more efficient at carrying through their mission. Learning from other churches is likely to be a valuable experience – though imitating them will not necessarily be. Predictability is not necessarily a bad thing, without qualification. In the words of an early advertising slogan used by the Holiday Inn hotel chain: 'The Best Surprise is No Surprise'. Few of us would be enthusiastic about international air travel without the predictability of safe transportation systems – and the same can be said about some aspects of the spiritual life. There is no point in constantly reinventing everything, and the predictability of rituals and liturgies can actually help people to focus on God, as well as providing a safe and familiar situation in which we can be challenged to new insights. By revisiting the same circumstances regularly, we can help people to hone their skills, and become better at doing things. In the context of healing, dealing with stress, or even regular prayer, there is a value in something that is predictable and predetermined, provided it does not become a Procrustean bed that inhibits new activities of the Spirit. Even control – with all its attendant dangers – is not uniformly a bad thing and some practices that have the initial appearance of being no more than forms of control can actually be turned around in such a way that they become a form of stability in an otherwise unpredictable world.[17] One of the consequences of the information age is that it creates uncertainty, so that we no longer even have access to basic knowledge such as what life skills it might be useful to have. Marriage is no longer for ever, and many different opportunities are open to us, with few people now able to assume that they will follow just one career path for life. In that context, part of the gospel will have to be to show people how they can take control of their own lives, and live responsibly in a world that – for all its systems and structures – is increasingly out of control in a moral and spiritual sense.

At the same time, we cannot escape the compelling logic of Ritzer's case, for the evidence is all around us in our daily lives. It is striking that neither in Ritzer's original work, nor (to my knowledge) in any of the literature to which his analysis has given rise has the Church featured in any significant way.[18] Maybe that omission is itself a statement about the Church's wider role in all this. For one might have thought that the Christian tradition – being concerned with ultimate values, and recognizing the importance of the spiritual as well as the physical – would have been a major opponent of the commodification of human life. In reality, nothing could be further from the truth, and while some may think it is going too far to suggest that the Church has actively promoted McDonaldization, it is certainly the case that it has done little to oppose it. Indeed, if Weber's original hypothesis is correct (and nobody has significantly undermined it), Christians (especially those in the Protestant Reformed tradition) need to take seriously the connections that he drew between the Protestant work ethic and the construction of the whole social edifice we now call modernity, and ask whether the Church is not in danger of being consumed by a social reality which was partly of its own making – and what we might now need to do if our faith is not to be rejected out of hand along with the culture in which it has hitherto felt most at home.

This is the point at which I would want to suggest that my application of the McDonaldization thesis to the Church needs to be allowed to modify the way in which Ritzer, along with both his supporters and detractors, have articulated it. There has been a good deal of debate as to whether the process of McDonaldization is to be located as a development within modernity or post-modernity. However, the ease with which the model can be applied to the Church challenges the assumption that this is the only cultural matrix within which it can be understood. Though globalization is widely imagined to be a recent development, made possible only by the emergence of technology and its associated communication tools, the reality is that the Church invented globalization long before anyone else was thinking of it. In the light of what we know and practise today, Christendom might not appear to have had the immediacy or apparent power of the media we now use, but in the context of its own day, it was comparatively at least as powerful as a multi-national corporation such as McDonald's, if not more so. As a matter of fact, many of the characteristics of what I have here identified as 'McDonaldization' in the Church can be traced back for centuries. By restricting his analysis to commercial and industrial concerns, Ritzer has missed, or masked, this historical dimension of the phenomenon which he so eloquently describes. In relation to the Church, the pressures of modernity have only heightened characteristics that were already there, which suggests that McDonaldization is not fully understood when it is located exclusively in the paradigm of cultural change from modernity to post-modernity. The roots of this tendency can more accurately be traced back to that combination of Greek rationality and Roman technological pragmatism that dominated the Hellenistic world at the time of the earliest Christians, and which was in time eagerly embraced by the Church, particularly after the conversion of Constantine in 312 AD. This realization is of particular significance in the context of the mission of the Church within contemporary Western culture, not least because of the fact that many of the spiritual solutions now being offered do actually go back as far as that period. I am thinking, for example, of the rapid rise of neo-paganism in recent years, and of increasing interest in the mystical and magical – all practices that were banished by the Graeco-Roman consensus, and which have been kept at the edges of Western life ever since. In terms of the Christian tradition, the tensions inherent in this can be characterized typologically as the differences between the Roman and Celtic ways of being Christian. Historically, these matters were apparently settled at the Synod of Whitby in 664 AD, but in reality the same arguments have never been laid to rest, and their resolution will now be quite central to the life and mission of the Church. We shall return to this theme in our final chapter.[19]

It might reasonably be asked why, if Ritzer's thesis proves to be less precise or comprehensive than he originally claimed it to be, it is still worth utilizing as a way of understanding some of the issues the Church now needs to address. The answer to that is really quite simple: it works. That is the one conclusion on which the vast majority of those who have commented on his original book are all agreed. Ritzer has been criticized for an over-dependence on the ideas of Weber, for appearing to be confused over whether McDonaldization is a product of modernity or post-modernity, for not taking sufficient account of the cultural dimensions of the lived experience of ordinary people, and for having developed a thesis that is not universally applicable to everything and everyone in all circumstances.[20] But despite all that, the model clearly captures some significant aspects of how people experience life today. It is what Peter Bilharz has described as 'a can opener',[21] and Ritzer himself characterizes his approach as 'not the end point, but rather the base on which others can extend our knowledge of the process'.[22]

Back to Practical Theology

Methodologically, that is how I perceive my own use of the thesis. It is essentially an invitation to think about some issues in relation to the life and mission of the Church. I am probably open to some of the same criticisms as Ritzer, in particular the claim that the thesis has no obvious or clearly articulated theoretical base.[23] I would argue that the notion that one needs first to develop a theoretical base as the foundation-stone of practical theology is a misunderstanding of the nature of the discipline, as I have already pointed out in chapter 1. That is not to say, though, that this approach is therefore cast adrift on an ocean of subjectivity and wishful thinking. It is, rather, an example of the kind of eclectic methodology which Alvin Gouldner once described as 'newspaper sociology' – as distinct from, say, historical sociology or cultural studies.[24] Those who read carefully will realize that this procedure does indeed incorporate a theoretical hypothesis, but not one that is expressed in the kind of abstractions that would

easily be recognized by the Cartesian autonomous rational individual. On the contrary, the embodiment of the argument in concrete
life experiences is not only essential to the process of articulating and
expanding the idea, but is itself part of the thesis that is being
advanced. This is just a different way of articulating Browning's argument regarding the nature of theology, that 'We never really move
from theory to practice . . . Theory is always embedded in practice.'[25]
Using a different image, Browning also distinguished between the
kind of practical theology that resembles single frames from a movie,
which operates by 'stopping a moving picture to examine the frames
one at a time', and the sort that proceeds by 'assembling with artistic
flourish the entire reel, coordinating it with sound and light, and
letting it play.'[26] The way I am approaching the subject, letting the reel
play is going to be far more important than examining the frames one
at a time.

Though, as I have explained, I am wanting to be rather cautious
about Ritzer's location of the rise of McDonaldization exclusively
within the cultural paradigm shift from modernity to post-
modernity, I can see well enough that, in missiological terms, this is
probably the key issue that today's Christians need to engage with. It
can hardly be coincidental that the eclipsing of modernity (more
accurately, the surfacing of significant disquiet about and within it)
has been accompanied by a corresponding decline in the influence
and credibility of the Churches, for there has been a symbiotic relationship between the two for centuries. While it is easy with the
benefit of hindsight to imagine that the Church somehow allowed
itself to be taken over by ostensibly 'secular' forces within the emerging culture, as James Beckford has pointed out the reality was more
complex than that:

> . . . the cultural and political impetus towards modernization
> had religious roots in aspects of Protestantism which found
> protection and encouragement in some powerful sections of
> British society and, eventually, in some statutory and quasi-
> official parts of the British state. . . . It would therefore be quite
> wrong to evoke the image of a battle between organized
> religion and the forces of modernization in the UK. It was not
> even a question of 'concessions' by religion to modernity.
> Rather, by the early-20th century, there was a progressive, but
> not always smooth, convergence of interests between many
> religious, scientific, economic and political interests under the

active patronage of the state . . . very few mainstream religious organizations in the UK have actively tried to impede the growing dominance of science and technology over social life.[27]

The one thing I would want to modify in that position is the way in which (in common with most sociologists) Beckford takes it for granted that Protestantism is the only strand of Christianity to exhibit these rationalizing features. We should not forget that the Enlightenment nostrums which provided the underlying rationale for modernity were, to a considerable extent, an expression of the very same world view as that held by the ancient Greeks, and it is therefore not difficult to draw a clear line of cultural continuity and development not only from the Reformation to the emergence of the modern world, but also further back from Hellenistic culture to Christendom, and the Renaissance. Nevertheless, our immediate concern is clearly with the more recent periods, for with the evident collapse of the kind of secular society which modernist theorists dreamed about, the Church is increasingly in danger of being left high and dry as one of the last bastions of modernity. In organizational terms, it is arguable that the mainline denominations are already the last modernist, Victorian bureaucracies that are left.[28] That is likely to be problematic enough. But merely addressing the difficulty as an organizational matter will solve nothing: those Churches that have sought to do so through the selective introduction of contemporary management techniques into their operational structures have not noticeably stemmed their decline. Indeed, such attempts may even have accelerated it, for 'Routinization has within it the idea of lifelessness – people moving from one task to the next without any joy or spirit. Many churches have been void of joy and spirit due to the routinization of their church life.'[29] In discussions of social rationalization, the similarity between aspects of church life and what Ritzer has now called 'McDonaldization' was observed as long ago as 1978.[30] But while social scientists might be content with concluding that there is little to choose between the 'rituals' of the fast-food business and what goes on in the Church, for Christians the underlying issue is a much tougher one that will demand a degree of honesty that we have not historically tended to be capable of. Quite simply, we seem to have ended up with a secular Church in a spiritual society. How we might understand that, and find the resources to deal with it, will need to occupy our attention for much of the rest of this book.

4 WHOM ARE WE TRYING TO REACH?

If my analysis of our contemporary predicament is anywhere near correct, the Church today not only faces some hard challenges, but is also presented with some incredible opportunities. On the one hand is the inescapable fact that, throughout the Western world, the Church as we know it is in decline. On the other, there is the equally incontrovertible fact that we live in a time when the overt search for spiritual meaning has never been more intense than it is now. Thirty years ago, when I was a student, it looked as if the Church's credibility in the world at large might falter because of what seemed to be the unstoppable march of scientific rationalism. This was right in the middle of the Cold War period, when in many intellectual circles in Britain it was trendy to embrace the Marxist ideology represented by the Soviet empire. Indeed, some eminent British academics actively worked as Soviet agents, and sought to recruit their students and colleagues to the same cause. Many more took it for granted that, insofar as there might be anything of value anywhere in the world, the mechanistic and atheistic world view represented by communism was probably where it was going to be found. It was decidedly unfashionable to believe in any kind of spiritual reality, and students with religious beliefs took it for granted that their professors would give them a hard time – an expectation that was invariably well grounded. At the same time, many people of my generation had the sense that something big was in the process of happening. For this was also the time at which we began to discover that the search for meaning and personal wholeness was not necessarily going to be fulfilled through the inherited systems handed down from previous generations.[1] For many, this came through the emergence of pop music, with its rhythms and cadences that – by comparison with the works of classical composers, or even the popular music of the early twentieth century – seemed more primal and unstructured, but which for that very reason resonated within our souls and touched parts of our being that more conventional music never did.[2] For others, especially in the USA, it was the Vietnam War which high-lighted the bankruptcy of the inherited system, as the most powerful nation in the world found itself in a no-win situation, and yet seemed incapable of doing anything about it, while the brightest and best of two nations did their utmost to annihilate one another. It was no coincidence that it was the maverick Richard Nixon who eventually succeeded in extrapolating America from that conflict, for it required somebody who was prepared to do things differently, to step outside the existing paradigms – a habit which later, of course, led to his downfall. In the same period, the Civil Rights Movement created and led by Dr Martin Luther King Jr was, in its own way, highlighting the same problem. It was a rationalized view of the human race that had created slavery in the first place, and though that had in theory been abolished long before, no amount of legislation seemed to make a practical difference: it required a change of hearts and minds, and the embracing of a different way of being that would integrate Americans of African and Caucasian ethnicity as genuine partners. The 1970s and 1980s saw a similar need for a paradigm shift in relation to the place of women and men as equal partners. With the benefit of hind-sight, we can now see that all these issues were interconnected, and together ensured that the world at the start of the twenty-first century would be radically different from what it had been just fifty years before. The emergence of new scientific paradigms had already placed serious question marks against a mechanistic world view, and it was inevitable that in due time the one culture that was most obviously based on it would itself implode and disintegrate – as it did in spectacular fashion throughout Eastern Europe in the early 1990s.

For most of the second half of the twentieth century, the Church generally had an ambivalent attitude to the cultural changes that were taking place. As a teenager in the 1960s, I remember church leaders railing against the Beatles and other emerging pop groups and giving young people stern warnings about the dangers of listen-ing to their music, let alone going to their concerts or adopting their dress styles – and that was even before John Lennon had made his famous claim that 'we're bigger than Jesus now'. In a more sinister vein, I also recall a missionary from South Africa visiting my home town and reporting on the work of the churches there, warmly extolling the virtues of what I later came to realize was the apartheid system, and roundly condemning the activities of people like Nelson Mandela or Martin Luther King. Those two particular examples would not generally reflect Christian opinion today (though had I chosen to mention equality between women and men it might be a different story), but the same kind of love-hate relationship with the culture still pervades many churches and para-church organizations. People of my generation are now leaders in the Churches – that is, those of us who have stayed, for huge numbers of our contemporaries left, precisely because they were unable to reconcile what was presented to them as 'real' by the Church, and what they knew from their life experience to make sense and provide them with meaning. There is no doubt that those who were born in the period between the end of the Second World War and up to about 1960 (the 'baby boomers') were almost literally born at the cultural turning of the tide. The ways of being that had been inspired by the ideology of the Enlightenment, and translated into everyday lifestyles through the development of industrialization, were in the process of being eclipsed and replaced by something which was not altogether clear at the time (nor is it yet), but which was obviously going to operate on different assumptions than almost anything that had gone before. As more information about atrocities such as the Holocaust came to light, and we became aware of what industrialization could do (for the murder of Jews and others by the Nazis was a highly rationalized industrial process), it became obvious that the human race could not survive for long without a radical paradigm shift. This has not, however, been a universally held conclusion within this generation, and it seems to me that much of the present predicament faced by the Churches can be traced directly to the personal insecurity of many who are now in positions of leadership. Though social analysts habitually assign baby boomers to specific birth dates (typically 1943–60), things are not quite so self-contained. People of this generation are not as undifferentiated as that. Being born on the knife-edge between the two world views of modernity and what we now call postmodernity inevitably meant that some would fall off on the postmodern side, while others certainly fell off on the side of modernity. I was definitely one of the former, and so I am not well placed to understand how and why others of roughly the same age as myself should still be locked into the mindset of modernity. Perhaps it is something to do with temperament and personality types, though that is just a hunch, for I know of no research that has ever addressed this question. But one thing that does seem clear to me is that, by and large, the Church has embraced those who espouse modernity, and to a greater or lesser degree does not really know how to relate to those whose more natural way of being is the post-modern style. I remember some years ago being at a conference at which a leading English evangelical theologian took me on one side and, in a way that I'm sure she meant to be benevolent and helpful, expressed a genuine regret that I had found only limited acceptance in the circles in which she moved, telling me that because of my eclectic views I was perceived as being 'a very dangerous person' (her exact words). I smiled politely, but reflected afterwards that there was no way I could be any different than I am, and fitting into the rationalized schema of theological modernity – whether evangelical, liberal, or anything else – was not for me. I could have done it, of course, and in some ways my life may well have been a good deal easier if I had – but I would have denied my own essential being in the process. I mention this not to disparage the person in question (who has, in her own way, made a significant contribution to the life of the English churches), but to highlight what seems to me to be a major challenge for the Church in terms of effective evangelism among those people of my own generation who feel at ease in the post-modern paradigm, not to mention those who are younger, who have known nothing else. A key characteristic of post-moderns is that we do not like to be pigeonholed. We have learned that life is a lot more complex than that, and to reduce to a series of predictable rational categories the rich variety of our experience (of God, I would say, as well as of other people) is too restrictive and inauthentic. This is part of what Ritzer means by 'the iron cage of McDonaldization', and if it is problematic for increasing numbers of people when they encounter it in everyday life, it is no less so in relation to the Church. It will not be the way in which we can reach and challenge either those who already regard themselves as happily post-modern, or the generations yet to come – all of whom will be.

If the situation were quite that simple, it ought to be a straight-forward business for us now to reinvent the Church in a way that will not only enable today's people to hear the gospel but also to find a supportive community in which they might embrace its radical challenge and then go on to share the good news with others. For what kind of social organization would eagerly embrace ways of being that can only guarantee its own inevitable extinction? But in the case of the Church, that is not the whole story. While the churches as we know them are increasingly irrelevant to the spiritual concerns of growing numbers of people, they clearly do help some people in their spiritual quest, otherwise presumably they would attract even fewer people than they do now (and we should not forget that, despite all the decline, regular attendance at British churches still exceeds attendance at spectator sports events, while in many parts of the US churchgoing is still a cultural norm). Rather than putting ourselves down, as Christians tend to do, we should be applauding at least that achievement: that, after two or three centuries of sustained ideological attack on the very possibility of religious belief, our forebears succeeded in handing on to us a Church that not only survives, but within the narrow parameters of its own particular kind of people, is even thriving. In the English churches, for example, the numbers of older people attending church actually increased in the period from 1989 to 1998, in a way that roughly corresponded to the rising numbers of older people in the general population. In some ways, that could be interpreted as an encouraging sign.[3] It is, however, only half the story, for we should also be asking ourselves what kind of Church we are going to hand on to the generations that will come after us. In some local situations, churches have moved beyond the point where that is a sensible question, for they have already become the exclusive preserve of those who are middle-aged to elderly. In many more, Christian parents struggle to empower even their own children to continue with meaningful faith into adult life. This can be not only a personal tragedy for families who find themselves in this situation, but also raises a major question with regard to evangelism. For if those brought up in the Church (who presumably know it better than most) find that it fails to provide them with spiritual direction, how can we with any sort of integrity invite others to come and join us?

All these factors come together to suggest that there will be no one simple and universally applicable way in which we can reshape our churches to face the challenges of changing culture. There will be different solutions for different circumstances, and in many cases there will even be multiple relevant solutions within the same set of circumstances. For it seems obvious to me that much of our problem stems from the fact that, for the most part, the ways of being church that we now have match the concerns of only a certain kind of person, at a time when the culture is more openly diverse than it has ever been.[4] In order to unpack some of the implications of this cultural diversity, it will be worthwhile taking time here to remind ourselves of the kinds of people whom we need to reach, and their different lifestyles and concerns in relation to the discontinuities of life that we have already identified in a previous chapter. My analysis of them will be somewhat eclectic, for good reasons. Traditional methodologies of classifying people according to social and economic status are increasingly irrelevant for understanding the spiritual yearnings of people today. There is simply not the same correlation between earning capacity and church commitment that there once was. While church leaders can regularly be heard bemoaning the fact that the churches have become middle class, I believe things are infinitely more complex than that analysis would suggest. Both in Britain and the USA, some of the most prosperous and flourishing churches are firmly rooted among working-class people, of different ethnicities. Though I do believe that inherited middle-class values are part of the Church's problem (and we will return to that in the final chapter), a more useful way of understanding people in relation to the mission of the Church will be to try and identify how they are dealing with the rationalization and apparent meaninglessness of life. I think of this as a cultural and missiological analysis more than anything else, and on this basis I want to suggest that we can identify at least seven distinct groups to whom the Church will need to relate if it is to fulfil its evangelistic mandate. While some of them – such as the secularists – are violently opposed to Christian faith and values, and others – such as the corporate achievers or the apathetic – will be difficult to reach, in principle there will for each of them be a way of being church which will offer them the realistic possibility of encountering the gospel in a form that will be able to challenge them to a life of serious discipleship.[5]

The Desperate Poor
One of the consequences of the rapid social change that has taken place in recent decades has been a dramatic increase in the numbers of people who are living in poverty. The gap between those who have and those who have not has widened, and visibly so, with the streets of Western cities now filled with homeless beggars to an extent that our grandparents would not have believed possible. Moreover, the desperate poor find their possibilities for personal fulfilment are affected by the same trends to McDonaldization as do those who are in employment. For example, an able-bodied beggar on the streets of India (a country that, in real terms, is much poorer than either Britain or the USA) can take any number of initiatives in order to enhance his or her lifestyle. To Westerners, the opportunities may seem trivial, but a person who takes a wooden box to a street corner, containing tools for cleaning shoes or crafting household utensils or items of clothing, is afforded a dignity that is denied their Western counterparts, who

would not be able to be proactive in this way without work permits, trading permits, registration with government bodies, and all the other paraphernalia of the modernist rationalized state. This is one of the reasons why some of the most severe marginalization anywhere in the world is now in so-called developed countries. Of course there are other factors contributing to this. Quite often there is an ethnic component. In the USA, for instance, because of slavery very few African-Americans were ever able to share in the social and economic benefits of the industrial revolution. Because of the location of their homes, in inner-city areas with outdated and inefficient phone systems, they are now losing out on the benefits of the computer revolution as well. Similar disadvantages are faced by the indigenous people of Australia, or by immigrants in Britain who were never able to learn English and therefore missed out on the economic growth of the post-war boom years, and whose children and grandchildren still frequently suffer as a result of that disadvantage. Other significant groupings among the desperate poor now include people struggling with various mental health problems, who have no resources of their own with which to fund appropriate treatment, and find that the State has little interest in them unless they behave in ways that suggest they might be a danger to other people.

The Christian message has a good deal to say about the responsibilities of those who are better off in relation to such people, and the Churches (especially in Britain and Australasia) have not been slow to recognize that, and to take every opportunity to encourage their governments to adopt policies that might begin to address this significant issue. But justified concern for such injustice has often seemed to lead to a feeling of helplessness among Christians, because they have not been able to transform their worshipping communities into 'churches for the poor'. The truth is that, without radical change, most churches never will become accessible to the poor. They never have been throughout the rest of history, except arguably in the feudal societies of the Middle Ages when church attendance was integrated into other aspects of daily life as part of the prevailing economic and class structure. A similar pattern still persists in some parts of the American Deep South, but the poor have virtually never been a part of the Church in the West since the onset of mass industrialization in the nineteenth century and the urbanization which that created. That is not to say that Christians have not made a difference in the past. They have. The Salvation Army is perhaps the best example of all, but other Churches including the Methodist Church which was William Booth's original spiritual home also made a significant contribution during the late nineteenth and early twentieth centuries to the educational, as well as the spiritual life and prospects of poor people throughout Britain. In west and central Scotland the many independent missions that grew up among industrial workers in the early twentieth century also made significant contributions to the social cohesiveness of those communities. Because of their theology, which gave a high status to lay leadership, they became places where working people who were quite literally cogs in an industrial machine during the working week could find themselves valued as people of significance on Sundays, in congregations where their insights into the gospel were every bit as welcome as the pronouncements of those with a formal theological education. Indeed, they were often more welcome, as they spoke from the heart and with a deep understanding of the social realities faced by others in their neighbourhood. To a lesser extent (for they were more dominated by the professional and managerial classes), the Plymouth Brethren offered the same opportunities for advancement to the poor of their day. But – and this brings me to the point I want to make – the mainstream Churches have virtually never been able to relate to the poor in any significant and long-lasting way. There have been exceptions, some of them striking in both their originality and their accomplishments. In the Scottish context, it was the work of George Macleod, while a parish minister in an industrial area of Glasgow, that led to the founding of the Iona Community in the mid-twentieth century. But all these movements have been the vision of inspired individuals, who in one way or another needed to step outside the mainstream in order to minister effectively alongside the poor. The same pattern has generally been repeated in the USA, where the churches that can make a difference in ghettoes and among ethnic minorities (who, in that context, are to a large extent coterminous with the urban poor) are independent congregations led by those with a specific calling and vision for such circumstances.[6] The conclusion seems inescapable: without some radical change, the average church will not be able to reach the desperate poor in our culture. Perhaps a majority of Christians will simply need to accept that specialist ministries may do the best job, and be prepared to support them with all the resources they can (spiritual as well as financial) – though if we are prepared for more radical solutions to our predicament, it is not impossible to imagine a way of being church that can empower the poor while also offering creative spiritual solutions for the problems faced by people in other sections of our culture.

The Hedonists

Much the same thing might be said of a second group who can also be easily identified. For huge numbers of people deal with the discontinuities and pressures of life today just by partying at every possible opportunity. These people live for themselves. For some, it may be an unconscious adoption of society's prevailing values, while others are just taking advantage of the increased permissiveness of the culture, and grasping the opportunity to make their own choices and assert their own individual rights.

Though working-class life has often been characterized by a tension between hedonistic behaviour on the one hand and deep religious commitments on the other, the kind of party-going lifestyles now emerging have quite a different character from those embraced by people who in the past might have been seriously drunk on Saturday nights and then would go to church to express repentance the next morning. In traditional socio-economic terms, the people I am thinking of here are a much more diverse group, and include some who are rich as well as those on more moderate incomes. Some undoubtedly have a conscious intention to put themselves first, though far more of them (and this is a group who are predominantly, though not exclusively, in their twenties and thirties) find that the realities of life are just too painful to deal with head on. Others are disillusioned with the breakdown of a prior belief system. But all of them would empathize with the sentiments expressed in Douglas Coupland's book *Life after God*, when he comments that: 'though we took a billion different paths to get where we went, our lives oddly ended up in the same sort of non-place.'[7] They can cope only by escaping from it all, and are likely to spend every spare moment in activities that will anaesthetize them to the pain. They might even be damaging their health and shortening their life expectancy in the process: it has been known for a long time that there is a connection between hedonistic escapism through alcohol and mortality rates in places like Moscow, and recent studies in the UK have shown a similar correlation between weekend party-going and sudden, unexpected deaths from heart failure.[8] Apart from the pressures of a McDonaldized society which we all face, many of these people have suffered their own personal traumas, related to the kind of fragmented and broken family backgrounds they have endured. For generations, values – including notions of spirituality and models for personal identity – have been handed on from parents to children, but for young people who have spent their formative years in a sequence of different homes, discovering and defining a meaningful adult identity can be a highly problematic process. Huge numbers of young adults find themselves confused and cynical – not out of choice, but more by default because there seem to be no other options open to them.

While I was writing this book, I attended a conference in Hollywood which brought together a group of movie-makers, story-tellers, and theologians to look at the question of image in relation to contemporary films and the emerging culture. As part of that, a group of young adults shared some of their concerns.[9] They were from different ethnic and social backgrounds, and included middle-class kids as well as some who had become entangled with the gang culture of Los Angeles. But they all brought the same message, which was not only simple and stark, but alarming and challenging. They told us that we have corporately so effectively ridiculed the possibility of finding appropriate role models that, in the words of one participant, 'We no longer have any idea what reality actually is.' Another reported how he had been told in high school that it was important not to have role models: not only was this a sign of personal weakness (individuality being all important), but since we all know that even famous achievers fail and make mistakes, there is no point in having anyone to admire. The trend for deconstructing everyone and everything has left us with no heroes to follow, and so most young people are more likely to know what is no longer worth believing in, than to have a positive and clear idea of what they do actually believe. When they search for some pointers toward images that might help to form identity, all that seems to be available is a combination of music videos and advertising, which can provide nothing more substantial than an 'attitude' or 'aura' to imitate, which in turn can be used to determine what is 'cool' or 'not cool'.

These are not my words: even where I have not inserted quotation marks, I have reflected the terminology used by young people who knew what they were talking about, because this had been their experience. Is it any wonder that increasing numbers of people find the human journey too painful to contemplate, and instead adopt a hedonistic lifestyle on the assumption that, in the midst of the pain, we need to grab whatever chance of happiness we can – however fleeting that may be? Once we are left only with ourselves, our soul begins to fragment, for we need relationships with others in order to be human. A lifestyle of raves and parties may not be relational in any deeply satisfying sense, but at least there will be a large number of other people there at the same time and place. Considering the enormous numbers of people who search for transcendence in this way, the Church has paid remarkably little attention to how it might reach them. The time of day at which such events take place may be one reason, for most of it happens in the middle of the night. It is a lifestyle which, following a hard week at work, typically includes an early meal on Friday evening, then maybe going to the cinema or a show at 9.30 or 10.00 p.m., followed by a party or a rave, which might last till 2 or 3 o'clock the next morning – a process that will be repeated the next day (Saturday), with Sunday being spent recovering from it all in order to be up for work on Monday morning.

Like the poor, the party-goers have always been with us, and they too have virtually never been a part of the church. One of the reasons for this is that, by definition, this kind of anarchic behaviour is a way of expressing contempt for the control and oppression that people feel they are experiencing in so much of life today. By becoming almost different personalities at weekends, people find an inner strength to be able to cope with the rigid structures within which they find themselves enmeshed the rest of the week. In the words of John Street, 'In taking pleasure, we grasp what is ours alone, and we deny the right of the greedy and the powerful to some part of ourselves.'[10] For that very reason these people are unlikely to be reached by the churches we now have, for they themselves can often seem like representatives of the dominant social order, and therefore part of the problem, not part of its resolution. If these people are to hear the gospel in relevant ways, it will require visionary and inspired Christians who are prepared to step outside the existing paradigms. It is easy for the Church to criticize such apparently excessive behaviour, without realizing that this is all part of a discourse of protest, and in the deepest sense is an expression of personal and corporate anguish. As Douglas Coupland perceptively noted in his novel *Generation X*, which documents the search for meaning by three young people who have taken time out to reflect on such things:

> the carapace of coolness is too much for Claire . . . She breaks
> the silence by saying that it's not healthy to live life as a
> succession of isolated little cool moments. "Either our lives

become stories, or there's just no way to get through them." I agree. Dag agrees. We know that this is why the three of us left our lives behind and came to the desert – to tell stories and to make our own lives worthwhile tales in the process.[11]

Unless Christians engage with these underlying concerns, they will have nothing to say to such people. In addition, an effective spirituality for those attracted to the hedonistic lifestyle will need to be an embodied spirituality, which can understand play as worship, and see God's kingdom as a party (both very scriptural notions). Almost by definition, therefore, they will not be reached by a church that meets in a traditional way on Sunday mornings. Indeed, in the first instance they will probably not be reached by a church which meets during the day at all.

The Traditionalists

Though futurists tend to underplay their significance, a large number of people fall into this category. I have called them traditionalists because most of the other available terminology could be misleading and imply negative connotations which I wish to avoid. These are people who are fundamentally happy with where they are now. There is not a lot they would want to change. In that sense, they are culturally conservative, but merely labelling them 'conservative' would be an inadequate way of understanding what it is that makes them tick. Their world revolves around the people and places which are physically accessible to them – family and local community – both of which are likely to be placed in the broader context of their nation, of whose heritage they are more likely to be proud than to be cynical. They represent the kind of oral culture in which, as Walter Ong has noticed, people do not so much live in the past, as use the stories and memories of the past in order to serve the present.[12] Concern for what is traditional becomes a way of understanding where one fits into the grand scheme of things, especially for people who often feel their inherited ways are under threat all the time. Sociologically, traditionalists may include a preponderance of working class or blue-collar workers, people who are not desperately poor but are none the less struggling to make ends meet on a daily basis. But this is not an economic category as such, and many upwardly mobile and so-called middle-class people are also traditionalists in the sense that I am using the term here. They live for their immediate surroundings, rather than concerning themselves with making history or changing the world. In fact, they would be uneasy if the world did change in any significant way. Their world revolves around their family, and one of the most important values is a sense of continuity within this context, maybe with different generations of the same family attending the same schools, and sometimes following one another into the same jobs. For the same reason, local shops (in Britain) and (in the US) small neighbourhood cafes will always be more important to these people than glamorous shopping malls or trendy eating places.

There are detailed differences in traditionalist lifestyles, depending on whether they are urban or rural, and to some extent there are differences between the way this outlook on life manifests itself in, for example, Britain, the USA, and Australia. But both regional and national variations are fewer than we might expect, and in all three countries these people are the backbone of the culture. With their adherence to traditional family values, and their loyalty to national institutions, others may regard them as overly sentimental, even jingoistic, but they are tough and hard working. Most people of this kind are not going to be social activists, and may even espouse values which others who consider themselves to be better informed will regard as incoherent and incompatible. For example, in Britain, many of the strongest supporters of the monarchy are to be found among immigrant communities from the colonies of the former British empire. More liberal thinkers are puzzled by this, for these were the very people who ostensibly suffered most from Western colonialism and empire-building. But their view of the nation is family-oriented, and the royal family is a natural part of that network: the family from whom others take their meaning. Though traditionalists might appear to have a conservative social and moral bent, this derives not from a political or moral ideology as such, but again more from the circumstances of family life. They will be flexible and support people who seem important to them, even when they transgress what might look to the outsider to be important ethical rules.

These are the people who have been most misunderstood by both politicians and church leaders. British political parties in particular (more so than in the USA and Australia) regularly present their manifestos as a programme for dismantling this traditionalist lifestyle, in the mistaken belief that people will be happy to be 'rescued' from this way of being. In the 1950s and 1960s, British town planners demolished whole areas that were home to such communities, imagining that their inhabitants would welcome it. They never did, and as a result of the enforced dislocation many in this group found themselves with disintegrating lives, and some drifted towards marginal criminality. The Church makes the same mistake, and when Christian clergy and others with a higher education end up working in churches comprised of such people they can find it hard to handle what, to them, looks like fundamentalism but which in reality is a different style of community life, this time focused around the Bible. This explains why it is important to such people to know who is 'in' and who is 'out' – not as a matter of great theological moment, but in relation to the question of community identity. This can be very mystifying to people who have been theologically trained, and who assume that their literate way of conceptualizing things is somehow the 'right' way to think and speak – instead of recognizing it for what it is, namely the discourse of those who hold the power in our culture. Christians, of all people, should never forget what the Bishop of Avila, speaking on behalf of the philosopher Antonio de Nebrija, told Queen Isabella of Spain as long ago as the fifteenth century: 'language is the perfect instrument of empire'.[13] Ignorance of this is a key reason why so many enthusiastic young clergy have been destroyed in parishes with a preponderance of working-class traditionalists, and also goes a long way towards explaining why churches have found it so difficult to establish or maintain a meaningful presence in areas of urban deprivation, whether they be inner-city ghettoes or their edge-of-town equivalents. It also explains why apparently 'fundamentalist' churches seem to thrive in such places – though this is usually less related to their theology as such, and is more directly connected to their awareness of the importance of rituals of gathering, their recognition of the spirituality of a particular place, and their understanding of the significance of the kind of community celebration that will help to consolidate group identity. For the same reasons, groups that practise adult baptism and emphasize its function as a rite of passage tend to make more progress overall in such communities than do those who are exclusively paedobaptists – and in this latter grouping, those ministers who refuse baptism to children on the basis of their assessment of the perceived absence of faith in their families are likely to be completely misunderstood here.

For traditionalists, church programmes – whether growth strategies based on models derived from corporate management, or instructional models related to conventional formulations of systematic theology – will have little appeal. The spoken word, coming straight from the heart of the speaker, sharing personal stories of faith, will always win hands down over abstract theorizing. It is no coincidence that the African-American style of preaching, with its interactive sharing and questioning, its vivid illustrations and stories taken from real life as well as the Bible, its high entertainment value, and its direct and specific challenge to action, is at its best among these people. It would be hard to think of a comparable phenomenon in traditional British churches, though the increasing attractiveness of English black-led churches to white people has to be connected to this question of style. Ironically, when churches with this kind of 'traditional' style become successful, they very often then feel that they need to conform to the habits of apparently more established and mainline churches – as a result of which they easily find themselves enmeshed in the same spiral of decline, because they only end up alienating the very people whom they were best equipped to reach and serve.

The Spiritual Searchers

If the traditionalists often have a philosophy of self-denial, the people I have called spiritual searchers can undoubtedly be characterized as motivated by a desire for self-fulfilment. Whereas the existence of the three groups mentioned so far can be traced back over a fairly long period historically, this way of being seems to be more closely identified with the opportunities afforded by post-modern culture. In describing these people as spiritual searchers, I am not meaning to imply that none of the others might also be engaged in a search for some kind of ultimate meaning. But these are the ones who are most likely to name their search, and while those who are traditionalists will tend to define meaning in terms of finding answers to life's questions, for this significant group the search itself is likely to be the all-important thing.

Who are these people? In the course of writing this book, I found myself one Saturday at the beach in Santa Monica, southern California. I went partly for recreation (a day off), and partly to take some exercise. As my wife and I were rollerblading along the extensive cycle track, which stretches for several miles (that was the exercise part), we stopped for a rest at one point and sat on a seat alongside a much older man, who immediately introduced himself and, after exchanging a few pleasantries, launched completely unselfconsciously into giving us an account of his spiritual philosophy for life. David (for that was his name) was in his late seventies, and what he said was as succinct an account of the shift from modernity to post-modernity as I have ever heard. He never mentioned Ritzer or McDonaldization, but his life story centred around the unsatisfactoriness of rationalized living, at the end of which he said, 'I think we really need to put reason in its place, and live more directly from the heart', adding that 'rationality is good for making grocery lists so you don't forget things, but it's a very bad guide to relationships, and even worse for the spiritual life.' He then proceeded to tell us where he would search for spiritual meaning, mentioning in passing trips to some of the great sacred sites of Europe and South America, and the inspiration he had found in various metaphysical books such as *A Course in Miracles*[14] and *The Celestine Prophecy*.[15] But he especially singled out a community in Arizona, where he likes to spend time dancing, singing, listening to and telling stories. He was the kind of person who would probably have shared all this with absolutely anybody who was willing to listen, though he made it clear that since we were from Scotland, and therefore Celtic people, in his eyes that endowed us with a particular spiritual credibility and worthiness.

Church people, both in Britain and America, are inclined to hear such stories with a good deal of cynicism because, as they constantly tell me, they never meet people like that. That is because most Christians spend too much time in the church, and not enough engaging with people in the wider culture. For conversations like that are by no means unique to southern California. Perhaps they would be less likely to happen at the beach in Britain, but that is only because of the climate. At the average cocktail party in Britain, the people I meet would have felt completely at home with David – and could even have taught him a thing or two.[16] For this seems to be where one large section of the professional middle classes throughout Western culture now find themselves. I hesitate to apply the label 'new age' to this group without further definition, though that is certainly one way of understanding them.[17] More generally, they are people who feel at home in a post-modern setting, and are comfortable with the image-dominated culture which is now the norm. In his study of the influence of television on cultural identity, Gregor T. Goethals identified something with which David, and others like him, would feel totally at home: 'Through song, dance, and story-telling, people identify with their society.'[18]

While of course all the other groups mentioned here are important in terms of the Church's mission, this one is probably the most crucial of all, both because of its numerical size and also because of its influence in the wider culture. It is not a generational group per se, but most baby boomers fit in here, as also, to one degree or another, do individuals from all younger generations and, as my encounter with David showed, even much older people as well. Sociologically, these are the very people who, thirty years ago, would have been pillars of the churches. They are movers and shakers in their local communities. They are the ones who organize campaigns and petitions, usually through single-issue pressure groups and networks of an informal kind. They have a suspicion of organized bureaucracy, which means they will rarely run for election to local councils (the traditionalists and secularists being the ones most evidently attracted by that – something that for the searchers merely confirms their prejudices that our inherited institutions are no longer working). For similar reasons, such people are unlikely to be attracted to the church which, as they see it, has become a place with too much religion and too little spirituality. They will probably not know exactly what they mean by 'spirituality', but one of the ways it will be contrasted with 'religion' will be as an all-embracing reality that can give meaning to the whole of life. Whereas church will be perceived as something that happens once or twice a week in organized services, their spiritual search will be concerned to find something that will be holistic, affecting not just an hour or two on Sundays but the rest of the week as well. Christians might reasonably protest that this is a misunderstanding of what church is supposed to be about, and that the gospel is nothing if not a radical lifestyle for every day, but that will cut no ice with the searchers, who see little evidence of that in the life of Christian people. For them, the main difficulty with the Church is just its irrelevance: it has lost the ability to speak to them. They are not noticeably anti-Christian – indeed, many of them have a quiet sense of regret that the Church no longer works for them in the way it apparently did for their parents and grandparents. It is just that what they see of Church fails to connect with their experience of life.

Those who do take the time to explore more carefully what today's Church can offer will often conclude that it is an unfriendly place for those with a genuine concern for the spiritual search. Things that seem trivial to Christians can assume larger proportions for the searchers. For example, I have often been quizzed by these people about the apparent lack of gravity with which Christians approach their faith. Why do we mostly read the Bible only in short sections, when we say it is the most important book in the world? If that was true, would we not take it more seriously? For people who are prepared to re-educate themselves to a completely different way of thinking in order to wrestle with texts like *A Course in Miracles*, Christians can seem extraordinarily casual about the Bible. For similar reasons, efforts to update worship – especially music – can seem childish and lacking in conviction. Structurally, too, the Church is likely to come across as an obsessively patriarchal institution, with no real place for women, and too much top-down control being exercised by leaders (whether they be men or women). The absence of any recognition that there is a feminine side to being – let alone to God – alienates both women and men who are spiritual searchers.

These people are not extremists, still less anarchists. Of all the groups mentioned so far, they are the ones who take their responsibilities to future generations the most seriously. They are likely to be self-consciously intentional about the way they conceive and nurture their children, and will take specific steps to ensure that they become balanced and well-developed individuals. They are fully aware of the disintegration and fragmentation of Western culture, and want to do something about it. Values are important, though not the 'family values' typical of the traditionalists, who are more likely to be looked down on with contempt as cultural dinosaurs. While they will pride themselves on being open-minded and tolerant, the tolerance of spiritual searchers will not extend to people who see things differently in a more conservative way – something that will be a two-way process, because the traditionalists, for their part, will often be vigorously opposed to the lifestyle of the searchers. Paradoxically, searchers will most likely be working hard to establish moral norms for themselves and their children, though in the absence of acceptable ready-made models of either values or spirituality, they will tend to create their own spirituality and value system, using whatever materials they can find.[19]

These people are nonconformists, but not in the traditional sense of that word. Their way of being is a radical departure from all previous generations, and from all other groupings in today's cultural context. They learn by experimentation, and have a deep desire to try everything at least once. They are as likely to be attracted by noise and excitement as they are by silence and mystery – just so long as they can do it all for themselves. Intuition and emotion (what feels right) is more important than discipline and reason. Yet alongside this there is frequently a deep desire to learn in the company of others who are on the same kind of journey – not in the sense of uncovering abstract propositional ideas about the meaning of life, but rather by sharing stories and learning from one another's experiences. Leith Anderson's comment exactly captures the mood of these spiritual searchers: 'The old paradigm taught that if you have the right teaching, you will experience God. The new paradigm says that if you experience God, you will have the right teaching.'[20] The Church's inability to relate to this group of people is probably the single most significant reason for the circumstances in which we now find ourselves, and unless and until we are able to reimagine the Church in ways that will relate to their deep desire to find meaning and direction in life, the decline of recent years will undoubtedly continue.

The Corporate Achievers

In the past, these people have been the mainstay of mainline British churches, and still are in many American congregations. They are people whose lives are dominated by their career. In this respect they are different from the traditionalists who, when they have regular employment, see it only as a means to an end, and find their true identity in the local community and through family connections. They are also different from the spiritual searchers who, though they might be high-flying career people, nevertheless do not see corporate achievement as the goal of life, and may well choose to abandon a predictable career path in order to enhance other areas of their lives, especially where relationships are involved.

Since by definition there will always only be a few successful people who make it to the top, most corporate achievers will not be achievers at all (at least not by their own standards). They will more likely be constantly striving to improve themselves. In the process they may have to project a particular image of 'success' in their lifestyle, living beyond their means in a way designed to tell their neighbours that they have actually made it, and intended to let their employers know that they could cope with the trappings of success, if only they were given the right promotion. To say that this leads to a lonely and fragmented lifestyle is perhaps merely to state the obvious. Though ostensibly driven by an insistent individualism, in which their ability to reach their full potential depends only on themselves and their own inner resources, such people paradoxically often end up with little sense of self worth or individual identity, both of them having been sacrificed to the corporate image and the constant striving for 'success'. There is probably more genuine loneliness among these people than in any of the other groups discussed here, and because competitive individualism inevitably leads to the destruction of the social side of the self, they find relationships difficult – whether on a personal basis in the home and wider family, or in terms of any kind of social consciousness that assumes we might need one another in order to create a balanced and harmonious society. Of all the groups identified here, these people are the ones most likely to feel thoroughly at home in a McDonaldized world. Indeed, they are probably going to extend its influence well beyond their professional activities, in such a way that they endanger their own humanity. Part of the reason why they can find relationships difficult is their tendency to rationalize and categorize everyone in terms of the opportunities they present for the marketing of their product, whatever that may be. People are understood and valued only insofar as they can be fitted into the McDonaldized mindset which corporate achievers tend to accept as their fundamental world view. The emphasis on activism in the market-place, engendered by a culture in which value is assigned not on the basis of who you are, but in relation to what you do, only serves to heighten the sense of fragmentation between the public and private aspects of life felt by people in this situation. The truth is that the whole of life simply cannot be grounded on a philosophy of winning and getting to the top, which means that the only way such people can have any kind of humane experience will be through maintaining a rigid separation between their public image and their private life. Those who fail to do so eventually find their personal relationships disintegrating, especially if their spouses or other significant persons do not share the same McDonaldized outlook on life. This is one of the key features that distinguishes corporate achievers from spiritual searchers: while members of both groups might easily be found in the same types of professional employment, the searchers would never internalize commercial values in this kind of way. The idea that there might be a dichotomy between the private and the public aspects of their lives would, for the searchers, be anathema: unlike the achievers, they are constantly looking for ways in which their personal values and public face can be harmonized into a non-conflicting holistic lifestyle.

Insofar as spirituality relates to this way of being, it tends to be used, like everything else, in a purely functional way. Because it is directly related to the public image of corporate achievers, conventional religious observance is likely to be more acceptable than anything smacking of spiritual enthusiasm. This is the civility of middle-class religion, and its persistence has contributed significantly to the downfall of the mainline denominations everywhere. Those of us who are involved with such churches (and I include myself in here) have been far too complacent in voting people like this onto church boards and committees, and when they have got there we have been far too reticent in challenging their outlook and motivation. It is one of the root causes of nominal and inactive church membership, and the dominance of such people in positions of leadership is in turn a major reason why so many congregations find it impossible to change in such a way that they might begin to relate to those other groups in the community which we have already discussed. If we want to know why our churches have become so McDonaldized, we need look no further than the kind of people we have historically placed in positions of lay leadership: far too often they have been appointed not for their spiritual competence, but for the image which they seek to project in the corporate world. Not only have they sometimes used the church in order to enhance their status in that world, but they have also brought the philosophy of the corporate enterprise into the church. Perhaps the most obvious evidence of that is the way that so many churches have been persuaded to bring their congregational life into line with the latest management techniques from the world of business. But that is not the most damaging aspect of all this, for theologically the idea that personal worth and value is something to be worked for is the very opposite of the gospel, and (to use a biblical metaphor) constitutes a kind of secularized works-righteousness in which individuals have only themselves to blame if they hit difficulties in life – something which not only undermines the capacity of the church to be a caring community, but which for that very reason alienates those who have not bought into that particular world view. While its most obvious and eloquent expression is to be found in the outlook of the so-called Word-Faith teachings of people like E.W. Kenyon, Kenneth Copeland, Kenneth Hagin, and their associates,[21] most churches would find it a sobering exercise to examine the extent to which all this has influenced the way they operate. Commenting on people like this, Tex Sample observes that they are 'the most difficult to reach and move in a liberative and transformative direction'.[22] If they are indeed entrenched in the leadership structures of the mainline churches, this can explain a lot.

The Secularists

Statistically, this is a relatively small group, though it is far from unimportant. Not only are these people the ones who are least likely to be able to hear the gospel, but they are also highly influential. Peter Berger describes them as constituting 'a globalized *elite* culture'.[23] They are generally people with higher education, academics and other high-flying professionals, especially in the humanities, and they are, in effect, the only group now left who still self-consciously defend the conventional 'liberal' beliefs of an Enlightenment world view. Because of the kind of positions they occupy, they play a large part in determining the officially sanctioned definitions of reality and meaning that are reflected in the Western education system, in the media and in certain sections of government. They form a very powerful subculture of people who, for the most part, speak only to others like themselves, wherever they might travel around the world. They are the people who find it hard to believe – let alone understand – the enormous explosion of spiritual concern that is taking place throughout the world today, simply because they do not belong to the popular culture where this is happening, and on those occasions when they do encounter it they refuse to take it seriously. In their world, the secularization thesis (that the progress of modernity will inevitably annihilate spirituality) still holds good, because in their limited circles that is exactly what has happened.

The Church has suffered more than it realizes from the influence of this group. From about the 1940s to the mid-1980s, church leaders expended much energy in the futile effort to try and appease such people, largely because of their influence in public life. Not infrequently, church leaders who should have known better actually joined forces with them, and in the process underplayed the spiritual dimensions of the gospel in favour of presenting the Christian faith as some kind of programme of social improvement or personal therapy. Of course, as a holistic message Christianity includes all that, and more besides. But the one-sided emphasis of the middle years of the twentieth century left the Western Churches ill-equipped to know how to relate to the new popular spirituality of more recent times.[24] At worst, it has engendered a perception among the people I am calling spiritual searchers that the Church has nothing to offer them, and might even be the very last place anyone should expect to find God.

At the same time, church leaders who earlier attempted some accommodation with the secularists correctly understood that, if there is a real threat to the Church and the gospel, this is the direction from which it will come. For twenty-five years I taught in a British university which was dominated from top to bottom by people like this, and their absolute determination to destroy the Christian faith has to be seen to be believed – as also do the small-minded and petty ways in which they often go about it, something which gives me confidence that they are unlikely to succeed. While remaining convinced advocates of modernity at heart (this is what gives them their position of social privilege), secularists often adopt selected aspects of post-modern thinking. In particular, deconstruction has become a favoured weapon, because it can so easily be used to highlight the failures and weaknesses of previous generations of Christians, who can be ridiculed as imperialist collaborators, playing power games with truth in order to establish their own supremacy. I have no desire to deny or minimize the mistakes made by some of my Christian forebears – in fact, I think we ought now to be taking active steps to correct and apologize for them. But when I read the vitriolic attacks mounted by such people against what they regard as the self-conscious power games of previous generations, I am tempted to respond in a less than dispassionate way, by referring to the popular saying that 'it takes one to recognize one'. Though secularists present themselves as the upholders of democracy (which presumably explains how they have managed to keep their dominant position in the Western establishment), the way in which they define freedom as only being the freedom to be like them is, in practice, a denial of the very thing they claim to cherish. In the words of Ziauddin Sardar, this outlook 'offers not dissent but the orthodoxy of doubt, the dogma of moral relativism and the creed of triumphant secularism. It is as liberating as the torture gadgetry of the Spanish Inquisition.'[25] Moreover, it offers a jaundiced and one-sided view of both history and human nature. The idea that Christians are to blame for all the wrong that is in the world overplays the religious dimensions of Western imperialism by conveniently choosing to ignore contrary movements, both in the Bible and in colonial history, while the notion that people are motivated only by a desire for power presents a cynical disembodied view of human nature that is not only unsubstantiated, but also does not ring true to the experience of most people, who do indeed see themselves as people with potential for good, even if they do not always achieve their ambitions in that respect. Moreover, according to Sardar (whose book will repay closer attention in this connection), not only do such secular élitists pose a particular threat to the Church, but they are also at the vanguard of the continued exploitation of other world cultures.

Can such people be reached with the transforming power of the gospel? Of course, but we should not build our expectations too highly, for these are people whose world view takes its shape from their prior rejection of the gospel, and who are therefore quite unlike most people in the other categories defined here, who have often never effectively heard it.

The Apathetic

I have placed this category last, but it probably represents a significant number of people. In fact, it may not be a category of the same order as the other six – and I certainly do not use the term 'apathetic' in any pejorative sense. But the fact is that there are many people who simply do not give any thought at all to the big issues connected with meaning and identity. Their lives seem to centre around what other people might regard as trivialities. For example, I have a friend whose husband has never in all his life had an interest in church, or indeed in anything else that might relate to a grand vision for life. His life consists of a series of very stereotyped and predictable patterns. He gets structure from daily rituals that cannot be interrupted – activities like walking the dog, working in his shed, even having a smoke at certain times and not others. His weekly pattern is fixed in such a way that, though he has a lot of free time, he must do things in the same order every week, and the schedule cannot be varied even though, on the face of it, it would create no particular inconvenience to do so. Naturally, discontinuities and major questions do intrude into the lives of such people from time to time, with the deaths of friends or relatives, the breakdown of relationships and so on. But they never seem to mean anything, and their consequences are soon buried in the details of everyday life. These people often live for their work – not in the same way as the corporate achievers, for ambition as such rarely seems to feature – but more because it provides a rhythm to life. Keeping busy and occupied is important, and in that sense these people are almost the exact opposite of the spiritual searchers. They might be superstitious, but that is the closest they are likely to come to anything that could be labelled as 'spiritual'. When challenged about the possibility of some other dimension to life, they will tend to accept the positions espoused by the secularists – not because they necessarily believe them, still less because they have thought about them, but it just becomes one other way of avoiding further engagement with such matters. James Redfield captures the mood of such people perfectly: 'they use their routine to distract themselves, to reduce life to only its practical considerations. And they do this to avoid recalling how uncertain they are about why they live.'[26]

There may be some parallels here with those I have called hedonists, for in both cases there is often an underlying sense of pain and hurt, and an inability or unwillingness to deal with that in any overt sense. Avoidance is the easiest strategy, and Church will be only one aspect of contemporary life with which they struggle to relate. They are likely to be just as negative and cynical about politics, which (like the Church) will be regarded as irrelevant. This makes such people very difficult to reach in a transformational way, especially those in this group who are older, who tend to have no aspirations about anything, and to be generally pessimistic about the possibility of anything great and good ever happening in the world – and even if it does, it will still be none of their business. As the father of one of the characters in Douglas Coupland's *Microserfs* puts it: 'As you get older, the bottom line becomes to survive as best you can.'[27] Apathetic people are by no means limited only to the general population, and are likely to be found in most churches, especially the mainline denominations. When they are present in any numbers they, together with the corporate achievers, probably constitute the majority of nominal Christians – people who belong, but with no significant level of commitment. As in the rest of life, their church connections have no meaning beyond themselves.[28]

Addressing Personal Needs

I am not claiming that these seven categories exhaust all that might be said about the changing shape of Western culture today. Nor do I wish to argue for some kind of strict demarcation between them. For example, there is a clear overlap between the hedonists, the corporate achievers, and the secularists, for many of these last two groups are hedonists in their private lives while presenting an entirely different public image. Most of those who constitute the desperate poor belong also to the group I have called traditionalists, many of whom, in turn, while not desperately poor in the sense of being homeless, are nevertheless at the bottom of the social scale. As young people from traditionalist families gain higher education, they often move away from their roots and join the corporate achievers – they are less likely to join the spiritual searchers. Occasionally, corporate achievers, faced with the impossibility of getting what they want from that lifestyle, give up the effort – and when that happens, they are most likely to join the hedonists or the apathetic. And so on. For some people, the move from one group to another might reflect different stages of life. It would also be possible to argue that these groups reflect different aspects of cultural change, with the traditionalists feeling more at home with a pre-modern world view, the corporate achievers and secularists representing modernity, and the spiritual searchers and hedonists being thoroughly post-modern – while the poor, as always, are not fully integrated into the culture at all, and the apathetic are, well, apathetic.

For all these reasons, I need to use these designations rather flexibly. But that does not undermine their usefulness as a typology for our purposes here. It may well be the case that people can and do move from one to the other. That is the nature of contemporary life. Just as we no longer need to be imprisoned within the social class of our birth, so it is also possible to mix and match our underlying outlook on life. Surprisingly few do, however, which is why I believe that this way of looking at the people whom the Church is trying to reach will help to throw into a sharper focus some of the challenges we now face. Who are the people who are most commonly found in the Church as it is? As I have already indicated, the desperate poor and the hedonists are virtually never there, while the secularists exclude themselves by definition. But the spiritual searchers are hard to find as well. In fact, most churches have only traditionalists and corporate achievers in them, with perhaps some of the apathetic round the fringes – and that is just as true of independent churches as it is of traditional mainline denominations. To a large extent, this is a reflection of the kind of people who are now in pastoral leadership, who (depending on their own disposition) feel most comfortable among traditionalists or achievers. But the irony is that we are not really very good at reaching these people either, for by no means all traditionalists and corporate achievers are in the churches. There seems to be an intuitive recognition of this, for just about every recent development in evangelism has been aimed at these two groups, particularly the corporate achievers. The Willow Creek model of seeker services trades on the individualism and privatism of these people, by offering them a context in which they can explore aspects of Christian faith in the same way as they might seek out information on a business competitor, by attending trade promotions or presentations in an anonymous capacity, and then retreating to the privacy of their own inner lives in order to deal with what they have learned. The Alpha Course appeals to the need of such people to categorize everything, and provides them with a theology of simple cause and effect whose outcome can be catalogued in much the same way as one might predict yearly profits on a balance sheet, even down to being able to tell them in advance on which week of the course they can expect to receive the Holy Spirit. The 'purpose-driven church' popularized as a result of the achievements of Rick Warren and the Saddleback Community Church in southern California is clearly the sort of atmosphere in which upwardly mobile corporate achievers would feel at home, because much of the thinking behind it came from the world of business in the first place.

I mention these examples not to denigrate them, but rather to point out that, insofar as we manifest any concern at all for the unchurched, much of our effort seems to go into reaching only one kind of person. Who cares about the hedonists, or the traditionalists? And who knows how to engage with the spiritual searchers or the apathetic? It might be argued that the traditionalists, by definition, will be satisfied with traditional churches – were it not for the fact that these people find church no more attractive, as a group, than do the others. We clearly need to find ways of reinventing the Church that will help to relate the gospel to the family and community orientation of such people, not to mention their predilection for oral communication over against bookishness. The same is true of the spiritual searchers, who will simply not be reached by the churches we now have. Perhaps surprisingly, one of the aspects that alienates both these groups is the bookish way in which things are done in church, with too much emphasis on a style of academic theological discourse which divorces spirituality from everyday life. They are not interested in the traditional deductive approach to faith (or to anything else, for that matter). The thinking-leads-to-doing way is not only culturally alien to these people, but also leads to the kind of formality and predictability which they find hard to match with the rest of their experience of life. Paradoxically, of course, that is the very style that commends approaches such as the Alpha Course to other types of people. But this is not the only characteristic that traditionalists and spiritual searchers share in common. Both groups are profoundly hungry for meaningful relationships, and in that context are also likely to be willing to make themselves available for social action, certainly within their own communities. They are also likely to feel more at home exploring ultimate meanings through their own shared stories of faith than through propositional truth claims of one sort or another. If the apathetic can be touched in some way, they too can find meaning in the same kind of context.

Given the seeming incompatibility of the concerns and needs of these various groups, can we imagine a way of being church that will be able to encompass them all? To some extent that will depend on how flexible we are with our imagination, though there is one event of recent years that has highlighted quite clearly some of the possibilities. I refer to the extensive public response (not only in Britain, but throughout the world) to the death of Diana, Princess of Wales, in August 1997. Shrines were constructed by the most unexpected people in the most unlikely places, rituals were invented by groups of the population who were well beyond the reach of any of the churches, and I have no doubt whatever that, for those capable of seeing it, the many spontaneous expressions of popular spirituality exhibited on that occasion provide some key insights into the kind of questions raised in this book. I have already written at considerable length about that, and I will resist the temptation to repeat it all here.[29] But in relation to this immediate discussion, it is striking that Princess Diana's death seemed to unite all my population groups, except two: the apathetic and the corporate achievers (unless we were to include the marketing of souvenirs). The desperate poor saw Diana as a person who cared about people like them, indeed as a person whom some of them knew, for they told stories of how she had taken her two sons on working visits to shelters for the homeless and destitute in inner-city London. The hedonists also mourned her passing, for they saw her as one of them – a tragic figure for whom life was too painful, and therefore never-ending parties, constant sex and fun were the only transcendent possibilities left. The spiritual searchers saw her as a campaigner for key concerns of the kind of single-issue pressure groups they love – and a 'spiritual' person as well, who was not afraid to speak of visits to mediums, or indeed of her previous deeds in past lives. The traditionalists for their part loved her because she was royal, and also because through the television she had visited all their homes, and was in a real sense 'one of the family'. Even secularists took part in the rituals, despite feeling that much of it was ultimately meaningless. No doubt some corporate achievers also felt deeply, but as a group they were the ones who questioned the public response most cynically. Perhaps that also explains why the churches were, to a considerable extent, caught unawares by it all, and were unable to see the longer-term implications for effective worship and evangelism.

We should not forget that the gospel always brings radical challenge to change, and different types of people will no doubt need to hear different challenges. The desperate poor might need to be challenged to realize that they can be empowered to take control of their lives, through the healing power of Christ and the support of other people. The hedonists may need to be challenged about the selfishness of their lifestyle and their responsibility for their own well-being. Some traditionalists will need to be challenged about racism, which is endemic in many of their communities. The spiritual searchers may need to learn that being rational is also part of being human, and that the acceptance of diversity will have to include benevolence towards people they do not actually like. The corporate achievers will need to be shaken out of their individualistic and competitive attitudes, which make them incapable of understanding the importance of a communal dimension to life. The secularists will need to be reminded that being spiritual is not a dysfunctional condition, though that alone will hardly win them to faith. And the apathetic will need to be inspired and enthused with the discovery that life can be more exciting and meaningful when lived in partnership with others. But can all these people groups be reached together? A long tradition of thinking about evangelism says that this is a futile undertaking, and that the Church should self-consciously choose to operate only in clearly defined homogeneous units. Not everyone has accepted that as a theoretical principle, though those who have opposed it most vociferously have conveniently ignored the fact that almost all our churches already are homogeneous units, created by one sort of person for others who are like them. The kind of categorization I have outlined here could be used to reinforce the homogeneous unit principle, and of course I am perfectly well aware of the fact that my effort to put people in boxes and label them in this way can easily be criticized as just another form of the McDonaldization about which I have complained in the previous chapter. That will always be a danger with any form of rational thinking. Still, the differences between these categories do seem to exist, and there is no point in denying that. Different churches will find it is possible to move forward at different speeds and with different groups of people, but we should never lose sight of the fact that our ultimate goal has to be to move on from tolerating diversity, to actively promoting reconciliation. If the Church replicates the fragmentation that is in the world already, it does not deserve to have a future. Ritzer has been criticized – fairly, in my opinion – for his generally bleak outlook, which seems to envisage a future that is even more constricting to the human spirit than the past and the present. That is perhaps the inevitable conclusion of an intellectual analysis with no spirituality to undergird it. As a Christian, I find it a contradiction in terms to also be a pessimist. The gospel is not just about challenge and change but about empowerment and new life, which means that while we need to be realistic about the situation in which we now find ourselves, we need to look at all these boxes as flexible spaces, places from which we will need to be liberated if we are to fulfil the purpose of God in our lives. The lines are there, even in their most threatening form ('the iron cage'), but we must learn how to think and act outside of them. That may actually be easier than we imagine, but only if we are prepared to take a long hard look at ourselves, and then step out with faith to occupy spaces that may turn out to be risky.

5 CELEBRATING THE FAITH

Worship is at the centre of Christian faith. Indeed, it is at the centre of all authentic spirituality, right across the world and in all religious traditions. The people I have described as 'spiritual searchers' may speak more naturally of looking for intrinsic values that will infuse meaning into the whole of life, but their definition of 'spirituality' invariably includes something akin to ritual and liturgy, both of which have historically been prominent in Christian worship. Since worship is also fundamental to being human, it would seem to be an obvious point at which the Church's life might most readily intersect in creative and evangelizing ways with the concerns of those who have yet to encounter the gospel in a form they are able to hear. What is obvious, however, has also become increasingly problematic. For one thing, those who find the Church no longer speaks to them regularly identify what we do in worship as a major stumbling-block. In addition to that, whenever churches begin to wonder how they might renew the faith of their own members, as well as reach out to others, it appears that worship is more likely to become a source of conflict than an effective way forward. As I speak with both clergy and lay people, of many different denominations and all around the world, it sometimes seems that no one is totally happy with what we now do. There are many reasons for this, and the exact way in which this discomfort manifests itself varies from one tradition to another. But we cannot afford to ignore the impact that negative experiences of worship are having in relation to our mission in the world and, more broadly, the future chances of survival for the Church in many parts of the West. Insofar as people still visit our churches on a casual basis (something that happens more in North America than it now does in Britain), such a person is more likely to encounter worship than anything else, and it ought to be a cause for concern when they go away unsatisfied. It should be an even greater concern to us when the children of believers, who have more experience of the Church's worship life than most, decide in early teenage – or even before –

that it no longer speaks to them. The truth is, though, even more challenging than that, for huge numbers of regular adult worshippers also seem to be bored out of their minds by what goes on in a typical service. All of this raises a crucial question, for if worship does not 'work' for large numbers of those who regularly participate in the life of the Church, not only is that going to sap our own spiritual vitality, but it will also ensure that we have little confidence in inviting others to join us.

Worship Wars

It is easy to find scapegoats to blame for all this, and most of us do. Clergy are criticized for being aloof and boring, out of touch with the concerns of ordinary people. The criticism is often true, but not necessarily deserved, because many clergy are themselves victims of their theological education at this point, and have never been shown how to be effective leaders of people – often because their professors did not know themselves, or because the curriculum majored on narrowly-defined textual studies at the expense of praxis. Moreover, what they have been taught, with its particular cognitive and pro-positional style, sometimes looks as if it might have been designed for the express purpose of ensuring that none except their own kind will be able to relate to what they have to say. I have a good deal of sympathy for those who give up a significant part of their lives to undertake courses in theology – often at great financial expense to themselves – only to find that at the end of it all they are still not equipped in the people skills that will always be at the heart of any effective ministry.[1]

Given the pressures that many clergy are under, it is not surprising that, for their part, some of them continually carp on about lay leaders as the ones who are holding back progress. Sometimes they do, but again it is not as simple as it can be made to look. For where do lay people learn their models of what it means to be church? The answer has to be from generations of clergy whom they have known. If congregational leadership degenerates into a power struggle between different interest groups, one reason for that is to be found in the style of leadership consistently exhibited by many clergy, which admires power and control and marginalizes more collabora-tive ways of doing things. And so it goes on . . . traditional choirs and their leaders blame those who like contemporary music, the contemporary musicians blame the organist, the organist becomes defensive about participation by informal and 'non-professional' music groups – until eventually everybody thinks someone else is responsible for everything, and the congregation becomes, at best, dysfunctional, if not self-destructive. Tragically, these so-called 'worship wars' have become so commonplace that there is no need to elaborate any further on them here.

But there is one underlying reality to all of this, which is directly connected to our central theme. For the arguments about worship highlight, perhaps more clearly than any other aspect of church life, the way in which Christians have – sometimes unwittingly – allowed themselves to be taken over by the kind of ideology that Ritzer has identified as McDonaldization. Just as human lifestyles became factory-oriented in the period following the Industrial Revolution, with meaning coming to be defined in ever more narrowly mechanistic terms, so the Church also adopted many of the same characteristics, becoming mechanical and predictable. Whether that predictability centred around the Eucharist (as in the broad catholic tradition) or preaching (as in Reformed Protestantism) seems to have made little real difference, for our eager embrace of rationalized ways to worship has led to the unexpected ecumenical consequence that we are now all wrestling with the same problems – a coincidence that, if handled creatively, could also offer us a significant opportunity, for if we can all manage to learn from one another's experiences instead of addressing only our own constituencies we might yet move forward in ways that will build up the body of believers, and create safe spaces in which others might be invited to follow Jesus.

In his book *The Reinvention of Work*, Matthew Fox identifies seven key features of much inherited church life which he believes can be directly traced to the uncritical way in which Christians have accepted the secularizing influences of modernist culture.[2] They are worth some consideration, not only because they seem to me to be an accurate reflection of where we now find ourselves, but also because they help us to see that worship wars in which there must be winners and losers are a waste of time. In attacking one another, as if worship was just a power struggle over personal preferences, we are addressing the wrong questions. The things we now struggle with are related both to cultural change and also to significant theological values, and both of those are much bigger than any of us, either individually or corporately, and the challenges posed within that dual frame of reference will therefore require for their satisfactory resolution a far more comprehensive renewal of church life than the kind of in-house arguments about new music or revised liturgies which, for the most part, have dominated the discussion so far. Fox makes the following points, which I will set out as a series of questions:

■ Under the influences of a mechanistic age, did even our rituals come to be machine-like – mechanical and lacking spirit and prayerfulness?

■ In a world view which understood the cosmos and the world of nature to be inanimate and without ultimate purpose, was it inevitable that people would become satisfied with rituals that were also inanimate and without ultimate purpose? 'Did enduring the sheer boredom of ritual become a virtue in our soulless universe?'[3]

■ In a world view where matter consists only of inert atoms, has inertness been hallowed in such a way that church leaders have been trained to think that they themselves ought to be bland and colourless, rather than lively and enthusiastic? Fox may sound extreme when he claims that 'Seminary training of our would-be worship leaders today is more attuned to inertness than to spirit making, to memorized prayers rather than to prayers from the heart, to reading texts rather than to celebrating holy passion and pathos.'[4] Unfortunately, however, I know the world of theological colleges and seminaries too well from the inside to be even tempted to disagree with that. This is too close for comfort to the standard models of clergy training that have been taken for granted throughout Britain, the USA, Australasia, and other places to which our ways of doing things have been exported.[5]

■ If the earth itself is lifeless, does that lead to a form of worship that has no place for anything earthy, especially not our bodies? Again, Fox hits the nail right on the head when he comments that, with the exception of African-American churches (to which I would also add Hispanic churches in the US, indigenous churches in places like Africa and South America, and Afro-Caribbean churches in the UK), 'there is no place in liturgy for moving the body, there is no dance, and there is no sweat. The benches are screwed eternally to the floor to prevent our bodies from moving and coming alive.'[6]

■ In a world view where the cosmos lacks spontaneity and freedom, do rituals inevitably reflect the same outlook, 'determined by books, laws, committees'?[7]

■ Has modernity encouraged the dominance of a form of church architecture which sets worshippers up only as spectators, creating spaces where distance, and not participation, is a central value?

■ Is all this based on an Enlightenment-inspired view of God as 'the supreme engineer or mathematician, pronouncing eternal, absolute, unvarying laws' and therefore requiring to be worshipped in the same kind of rationalized forms?[8]

Fox has of course made a reputation for himself by raising such critical questions about the Church's current beliefs and practices. His tendency to sketch a larger-than-life picture of things has often given his critics more justification for dismissing his opinions than they deserve.[9] The observations just enumerated all contain an element of calculated hyperbole, for not all worship that took place during the period of modernity was like this. But the general point is well established, and the overall world-view assumptions of the last several centuries have had more impact than we realize on what now goes on in our churches. In particular, I doubt whether anyone could plausibly question what to me is the obvious fact that in all our traditions worshippers have consistently been cast in the role of passive spectators, and places and spaces for worship have been defined by reference to the rationalized categories of Newtonian science.

Creating Spaces for Worship

The importance of space in relation to worship has been well discussed among liturgists for much of the twentieth century, but with a few notable exceptions we have generally been either unable or unwilling to do much about it. The debates of the mid twentieth century about the design and structure of church sanctuaries mostly centred around furnishings, and arguments about whether the pulpit should be central (as in the classical Reformed tradition) or whether table, pulpit and baptistery should be given equal prominence.[10] While some aspects of that debate may still be relevant, more recent theological reflection on the nature of the church has moved well beyond such discussions about church furniture. For both those models assumed that worship was, in effect, something to be 'conducted' by ministers and other professionals. Theologically, that understanding of the community of faith has been superseded by a renewed understanding of the role of the whole church, and a rediscovery of a very simple ancient truth: that liturgy is 'the work of the people' (the literal meaning of the Greek word *leitourgia*).[11] Our practice however has not caught up with our theology, largely because we have continued to do theology on the deductive Enlightenment-inspired reflection-followed-by-action pattern, rather than the practice-reflection-action pattern advocated here. That lack of coherence seems to have resulted in only marginal adjustments to our forms of worship, which frequently amount to little more than lay people being brought in to do the same things that ministers once did, no doubt because that has required only minimal disruption to the status quo, and no attention at all to the question of space in worship.

If it is true that 'the medium is the message', then it is certainly the case that the space in which community celebration takes place not only bears its own witness to the underlying realities of our beliefs, but also in many ways serves to define and determine them. While the concept of 'space' for worship can have several connotations, not all of them necessarily related to the physical space of buildings, it will not be inappropriate to begin our exploration of this question through consideration of the physical spaces in which Christians typically gather for corporate worship. The truth is that the external space does, to a very large extent, determine the personal internal space within which the worshippers can encounter God. In the long-established cultures of Europe, space for (and, therefore, the meaning of) Christian worship is often determined by the Gothic style of church building, with long narrow transepts, probably with columns or pillars. That kind of space can only give out one message: that worship is about formality and hierarchy. But other styles have their own message. Some of the Protestant Reformers may have thought they were returning worship to the people after what they regarded as centuries of abuse derived from the Constantinian and medieval model, but they merely perpetuated the existing spectator mentality, and replaced the kind of theatrical space which facilitated the medieval mass by an educational space which focused on the preaching of sermons.[12] When evangelism came to be defined as a separate activity from worship and celebration, different sorts of space were created, mostly based on secular entertainment models. Early twentieth-century Protestant churches were regularly built to look like Victorian concert halls, with the pulpit and pipe organ as the dominant visual elements in much the same way as theatres of that time had organs alongside a podium for the master of ceremonies. More recently, newer Protestant churches (especially independents and mega-churches, who ironically often claim to be most concerned about recognizing worship as the work of the people) have created sanctuaries that can only be intended to be entertainment spaces, complete with stages, lighting, and even theatre-style seats.

The discussion of space for celebration might seem to be an unexpected intrusion into this book, but it actually goes to the heart of our concerns, and is of central importance to our renewed mission in the culture of post-modernity. When the meeting place of the British parliament, the House of Commons, was being refurbished after the Second World War, Sir Winston Churchill commented that, 'We shape our buildings and ever after they shape us.' Space will actually be a key factor in any rethinking of effective mission in today's world, and we need to learn to be far more intentional than we have sometimes been about the kind of space in which we gather. Many congregations, of course, find themselves saddled with buildings that they cannot significantly change, certainly not in terms of their fundamental structures. This is especially the case with historic buildings, which governments invariably wish to be preserved in their 'original' condition, at least in terms of their external appearance. But the shell of a building is not the same as the space in which the community of God's people meet, and in the vast majority of cases it is not difficult to change that. All churches have regular opportunities to redesign their space, if only because buildings require renovation from time to time. It is a serious mistake for this to be limited to repainting and decorating what is already there. If we are indeed in the process of becoming the people whom God wants us to be, then any work in a building should be used as an opportunity for rethinking our mission – asking who we now are as the community of faith, what changes have taken place in our spirituality since the last time the place was redesigned, and using that to help determine what kind of space will empower us to celebrate that evolving reality, as well as portraying it effectively to those whom we want to reach with the gospel. If we fail to take all that seriously, we can end up in theological contradictions, and with styles of gathering that actually deny what we wish to affirm.

At a very obvious level, a minister wishing to empower his or her congregation to take seriously their own calling as the people of God, equipping them to make a distinctive contribution to the corporate life of the body of Christ, whether in worship or witness, simply cannot do it by preaching sermons from a pulpit. By definition, the body language of the space is saying that the person who stands behind (or sometimes in) the pulpit is more knowledgeable, more powerful and generally better equipped than those who merely sit and listen. The contradiction is too loud for anything to be accomplished that way, and regardless of all our good intentions the message from the space will always overpower the message delivered in words. I remember reading a story in one of Sigmund Freud's books in which he describes a therapy session with a woman who declared undying and faithful love for her husband, but who throughout the session played with her wedding band, slipping it on and off her finger – an action which he discovered more truly reflected the reality than her spoken words. A similar thing is happening when, from a position of strength, we attempt to encourage Christian people to discover and use their own ministries. Trying to enable a church to break out of the iron cage of McDonaldization in a space that is itself the cage simply will not work. It is also worth reflecting on the fact that having a beautiful building does not necessarily translate into having an appropriate space for worship. I recall a church in the UK which embarked on an ambitious renovation project of its building, and spent a great deal of money in the process. A small and enthusiastic group of men (no women) from the church were appointed to oversee it, which they did with considerable devotion and commitment. But they were all engineers! Their main concern was for structural matters, and to them (and the architect) good design was about making the place look like a 'real' church. They produced what they were aiming for, and the refurbished building was admired far and wide as a model of how an old building might be restored. But when the community of faith then tried to worship in this space, all kinds of tensions began to surface. For the people themselves had, as a group, moved on in their self-understanding. They were developing a vision of themselves as a dynamic, active, moving group of God's people – whereas their splendid building told them only to be spectators. They found that, to be who they wanted to be – who they felt they were – they had to work against the building, not with it. Some of those who had overseen the project concluded that their hard work over a period of several years was not truly appreciated, and left the church. That was just one consequence, for arguments about worship that ought to have been settled at the outset then rumbled on for years afterwards, in a way that was ultimately detrimental to the continuing life of the congregation. Overall, the Roman Catholic Church seems to have dealt with this issue more effectively than Protestants, and in the time since the Second Vatican Council (which was of course thirty years ago, and therefore hardly recent!) there has been a good deal of intentionality in addressing this matter of appropriate spaces for worship – with what (to me) is the ironic result that a tradition which still preserves more hierarchical structure than most is frequently better able to equip all of God's people than other denominations who claim to have been trying to do that very thing for centuries![13]

This question of space is not related only to big questions about the shape of buildings. Many Protestant churches in particular are so lacking in open floor space that anything other than a clergy-centred event requires contorted convolutions and furniture movements. The provision of adequate room for weddings and funerals is regularly accomplished only by moving items of furniture, sometimes even the communion table, while baptisms are often done in a corner, and even when they are at the front of a church there are frequently no clear sight-lines from the congregation. At some points in the church year, things can become hopelessly crowded, as they do in many churches during Advent, with Christmas trees, advent crowns, decorations, gifts, and more. I remember once leading a weekend workshop in an Anglican church where the altar was placed right behind a pillar, and all around it were heaps of old bicycles, making the whole place look like a disorganized junk yard. While that was no doubt an extreme example (and the bicycles were not a permanent feature, but were being collected for some charitable cause), this kind of situation enhances the impression that worship is about mumbo-jumbo done in a hidden – even secretive – way by those in the know, rather than something that is open and welcoming. It is significant that of the five liturgical spaces identified by James F. White as being essential to good worship, two of them (congregational space and movement space) are concerned with the ways people relate to one another.[14] Imagine the difference for a wedding, a funeral, and a baptism if people are able to gather round the central players, the wedding couple surrounded by their friends, the body of a loved one literally embraced by the circle of mourners, the person being baptized encircled by those already in the community of faith. That is how we humans most naturally arrange ourselves at significant times, thereby creating a space that bestows more dignity on the occasion as well as providing more opportunity for natural interaction (not to mention easy access for the disabled).

There is a tendency to deal with this question of the McDonaldization of space for worship only by reference to seats, rather than space as more widely understood. Pews in particular have become a favourite bête noir for many. As a late medieval invention, there can be no doubt that they were introduced into church buildings as a way of ensuring that there would be a strict demarcation between clergy and laity. Aidan Kavanagh has it right when he comments that 'Pews, which entered liturgical space only recently, nail the assembly down, proclaiming that the liturgy is not a common action but a preachment perpetrated upon the seated, an ecclesiastical opera done by virtuosi for a paying audience. Pews distance the congregation, disenfranchise the faithful, and rend the assembly.'[15] It stands to reason that we will never create community in a place where we spend most of the time looking at the backs of other people's heads. But the pews per se are not to blame for that. Most churches which replace pews with chairs still put them in lines, so that little has changed in terms of the worship space. Though I think my personal preference would ultimately be for comfortable well-upholstered chairs to be part of the furnishings of a worship space, I would not wish to dismiss pews outright. For example, a pew is, by definition, a seat where we sit alongside other people, whereas an individual chair is just that – an individual space that can easily be understood as a statement about the value of individualism in worship. Comfort is often cited as a reason for getting rid of pews, but in many instances churches replace uncomfortable pews with uncomfortable chairs, which leaves me wondering if the desire to change the furnishings is not related to our cultural individualism to a much greater extent than we even realize. Pews do not need to have the kind of restricted leg-room found in the worst kind of economy air travel, nor do they need to be set out in rigidly straight lines, nor to be designed with seat and back at the kind of angle that seems as if it was deliberately calculated to induce muscular and spinal fatigue. That kind of seating seems to be a peculiarly British preference, for most American churches have pews that overcome all those problems, with well-designed upholstery set at a sensible angle, often in a semi-circular format to ensure good sight-lines, and invariably with enough space between rows for people to move easily where they are, or to move out of their seats altogether into larger spaces without feeling they are inconveniencing others. Many of our perceived seating problems are first and foremost matters of design.

A more important question of space and seating relates to how seating and space are used. It is a well-established fact that straight lines of seats, whether pews or chairs, discourage interaction. This is sociofugal space, and is the kind of seating that might be used in a place where interaction is either inappropriate or not very likely. A

theatre, or an airport lounge, or other waiting spaces will typically
have this kind of seating, and when people are given a free choice of
where to sit (as they would be in a church as opposed to, say, a
theatre with seat allocations), this layout invariably drives people to
the edges, whether that be the back of the sanctuary or the ends of
rows. No one likes to sit in a place where they might feel trapped. The
opposite of this is the sociopetal use of space, which is the way we do
things at home. Even the most dysfunctional family would be unlikely to set the furniture out in rows. The dining table has chairs
grouped around it, and a lounge room has chairs and sofas assembled
in a way that focuses attention on the centre of the space. This type of
arrangement is also common in places like bars, or hotel foyers,
because it brings people together, and is welcoming and community-
building. Such considerations should always have been theologically
important in the context of the church, but at a time when increasing
numbers of people in our culture are looking for a place to belong, it
will be suicidal for us to ignore it any longer. I remember going to a
Taizé service in a church that must have been big enough to hold 2000
people – but with only a handful in attendance, and every one of
them sitting in a different place entirely detached from everyone else,
it was about as far removed from the genuine Taizé experience as you
could imagine. Far from finding myself included within a community of God's people, it was for me a dehumanizing experience, more
like being placed in solitary confinement – something that is used as
a last resort in the punishment of offenders precisely because it is a
form of being that we know to be so contrary to the deepest needs of
the human spirit that we presume no one will want to repeat the
experience, even in jail. Yet in some of our churches, we do it all the
time! The solitary experience has even been promoted as the way to
reach so-called seekers, and entire models of church have been
patterned around it. Western individualism has never been given a
divine mandate, and a church that panders to it is denying the gospel
more effectively than it knows. By way of contrast, I visited with the
leaders of a church in Los Angeles who have established an exceed-
ingly successful outreach programme, not only among those I have
called traditionalists and spiritual searchers, but also with the hedonists, who are a very difficult group to reach. They hit on the secret of
success quite literally by accident, as they were planning a 'seeker-
friendly service' using one of the ready-made models from elsewhere,
and the senior pastor invited a member of the congregation to 'make
the building welcoming'. What he had in mind was a little tidying up

of the entrance, maybe a few extra lights, some floral displays, and so on. What he found when he arrived for the service was that the woman he had asked to do the job had taken him at his word, and the entire church had been remodelled so as to be more welcoming. She had assembled a collection of sofas and easy chairs borrowed from her friends, and the main sanctuary had been entirely cleared of the traditional rows of seats, in place of which was a series of round tables, accommodating maybe a dozen people at each. Because the leaders arrived too close to the time of the event, there was no way they could restore 'normality' to the church building – which was just as well, for they soon realized that this was exactly what they needed if they were to be able to relate effectively to one another, let alone to the people they were seeking to reach from outside. They have never returned to the old format, and regularly gather in the same way for worship, not only with tables but with an open space in the middle. No doubt that helps to explain why people like the hedonists who spend much of their time at parties and in nightclubs find it such an easy place to relate to. But there is challenge in there too, and I can say from personal experience that celebrating the Eucharist while seated round a meal table is a very different experience altogether from what more usually happens in all our traditions.

The McDonaldization of the Liturgy

Mindless McDonaldization is not limited to the way we use space in our church buildings. The sacraments – of all things – have fallen victim to the same rationalizing treatment. The imagery of fast food is more apposite than many of us would like to admit when it comes to the ways we celebrate the Eucharist, with individual cups holding a specialized form of drink known as 'communion wine' (bottles of which often carry a health warning against using it as a regular drink because it is effectively a manufactured chemical soup!). When these cups are disposable, and when the bread is likewise reduced to a substance that looks and tastes like disks of soft plastic (as it tends to be in churches with a higher liturgical tradition than those which use individual cups), or even minuscule cubes of real bread, their inadequacy as appropriate symbols for the body and blood of Christ should be obvious.[16] If we have become so enslaved to efficiency, calculability, and predictability that we have allowed our love affair with rationalization to deprive even this central aspect of worship of any obvious visual symbolism or signification, who knows what we might do with other elements of the faith? If the gospel is reduced to the miserable categories of our fast-food throwaway society, why should we expect that people who are already feeling oppressed by those very things in their everyday lives will come to us in their search for genuine spiritual nourishment?

In too many instances, the way the Church has come to celebrate even central parts of the faith has all the characteristics of what Weber called 'mechanized petrification'.[17] Lest this seems too harsh and cynical a judgement, I hasten to point out that the connection between the celebration of the sacrament and McDonaldization has not gone unnoticed by others. In a report originally issued in 1978 under the title *Environment and Art in Catholic Worship*, the Committee on the Liturgy of the National Conference of Catholic Bishops of the USA traced a direct connection between the two: 'Liturgy has suffered historically from a kind of minimalism and *an overriding concern for efficiency* . . . As our symbols tended in practice to shrivel up and petrify, *they became much more manageable and efficient*.'[18] Notice there the specific mention of efficiency in the context of a smoothly managed operation. Nor is the Eucharist the only sacrament to have suffered in this way. We have mostly done the same thing with the other major gospel sacrament, namely baptism. Under the influence of modernity, baptismal fonts were reduced to insignificant pieces of furniture, devoid of any obvious connection with water. Methodist liturgist James F. White cynically, but accurately, reminds us of the consequences of that: 'The baptismal fonts we have in many Protestant churches . . . are an outward and visible witness that baptism has been a short and insignificant ceremony performed from a bowl tucked out of sight most of the time.'[19] In this respect, Anabaptists have done no better than those who baptize infants, for their baptisteries – though larger – are frequently hidden beneath the floor, or just become ugly and dangerous eyesores collecting dust. The US Catholic bishops once again have their finger on the pulse of our culture, as well as a good sense of theological perspective, with their recommendation that 'immersion is the fuller and more appropriate symbolic action in baptism'[20] – a recommendation which they back up with the provision of relevant information about the construction of fonts which will embody that ideal, including interesting comments about the value of running water over against a stagnant pool, so as to reflect the reality of new life, movement, and celebration which are intrinsic to a fully biblical understanding of baptism itself. In the past, we have wasted too much time and energy debating who should be baptized, while ignoring the far more important aspects of its theological and symbolic signification. Far from supporting an understanding of baptism that is rooted in God's overwhelmingly generous love, the use of small quantities of still water actually serves as a symbol of a God who is tight-fisted – another striking case of the words we speak saying one thing ('God's grace is never-ending'), and the symbolism saying the opposite ('Just don't expect too much of it'). It is impossible and pointless to try and establish a verbal orthodoxy when it is accompanied by a visual heresy.

There are no winners and losers here: all our traditions face exactly similar challenges in relation to authentic and meaningful worship for today's people. It is not even a question of our lack of faith or inattentiveness to the demands of the gospel. To quote once more from *Environment and Art in Catholic Worship*: 'A culture which is oriented to efficiency and production has made us insensitive to the symbolic function of persons and things . . .'[21] Of course, there is more to it than that, and it would be disingenuous not to recognize that there is a history behind much of this and the way in which Protestants chose to reject the symbolic and representational, out of fear that it might become a focus for idolatry, inevitably led to an over-emphasis on the spoken word. Different traditions have reached their own conclusions on this ever since the time of the Reformation. The Orthodox tradition, Roman Catholics and Lutherans still recognize that the spiritual can be expressed through the material, notwithstanding past abuses, while the Reformed Churches (a term I am using somewhat loosely to include Presbyterians, Congregationalists, Baptists, Methodists, and others such the Quakers and Salvation Army who share much of the practice, if not the theology) have generally been more cynical about the very possibility of what is material serving as a vehicle for what is spiritual – while Anglicans appear somewhat ambivalent, for different sections of that communion take different approaches. In many instances, especially within the Reformed tradition, what happened in reality was frequently little more than the replacement of an idolatrous worship of the visual by idolatrous reverencing of what was written and aural. Though this clearly matched (and was no doubt inspired by) the dominant ideologies of the day, notably Neoplatonism and the rising tide of modernity, Lutheranism managed to escape the worst excesses of this theological imbalance by supplementing the visual worship of the Eucharist with the spoken word in terms of prayers, the reading of Scripture, and so on. But other sections of the Church lost sight of the materiality of spirituality, and not surprisingly also became increasingly disconnected from fundamental Christian doctrines of creation and incarnation, with the result that worship became more and more disembodied, and in some instances amounted to a pragmatic (if not theological) denial of the incarnation.

As long ago as the middle of the twentieth century, Paul Tillich highlighted the potential weakness of this emphasis in the context of cultural change following the Second World War, with his warning that 'Protestantism is a highly intellectualized religion. The minister's gown of today is the professor's gown of the Middle Ages ... But professors are intellectual authorities ... This sort of authority is the exact opposite of the kind that is sought by the disintegrated masses . . .'[22] He naturally wrote of what he knew, for he was himself a Protestant. But while the Roman Catholic Church has undoubtedly succeeded in avoiding some of the worst ravages of modernity, in the report already mentioned the US bishops repeatedly highlight the fact that they too are wrestling with the same issues as the Protestant tradition: 'In view of our culture's emphasis on reason, it is critically important for the Church to reemphasize a more total approach to the human person by opening up and developing the non-rational elements of liturgical celebration: the concerns for feelings of conversion, support, joy, repentance, trust, love, memory, movement, gesture, wonder.'[23] It is important for us to be aware of the historical currents that have made us who we are today. It is equally important for us not to engage in cynical deconstruction of the past. The heroes of past generations were human, just as we are. They had some brilliant insights, and they made some dreadful mistakes. Indeed, their brilliant insights sometimes gave rise to what can now look like their mistakes. At the time of the Reformation, the invention of the printing press was creating a massive paradigm shift in favour of the written word, and it was part of the genius of the reformers that they were aware of that, and were bold enough to relate their theology to it. In the longer term, we can now appreciate that in the process some significant aspects of traditional Christian belief and practice were lost. As Gordon Donaldson has put it, for the majority of people even at that time, 'the more intellectual appeal of the sermon must have seemed a cold and comfortless novelty, and a God who no longer was brought down from heaven to be adored on the altar must have seemed a remote deity with whom it was harder to communicate.'[24] No doubt we will make similar mistakes in our generation, and for that reason alone we ought not to condemn our forebears unthinkingly. The fact that we share the same strengths and weaknesses ought to remind us that theology is never done in abstraction, but always in the context of a historical situation. In the present cultural circumstance, we do well to remember that when we allow the concerns of one context to become determinative for later situations, that is itself idolatry, and invariably leads to the spiritual stagnation of a faith that is meant to be living and dynamic. We all bring our own baggage to the theological task, just as our predecessors did – and in moving on from here it is more important that we recognize the needs of the present and (insofar as we are able to discern them) of the future, rather than dismissing with contempt the accomplishments of the past. We can no longer live as if this was the sixteenth century, and when we do we are not actually being faithful to our forebears at all, for they consciously contextualized Christian faith for their own culture. Our tendency to preserve what they did has been one of our perennial problems, and a key contributing factor to turning our churches into museums rather than places of genuine prayer. Nowhere does the gospel call us to be curators of antiquities. By the same token, given the ethnic and other diversities present in Western society today, we can hardly expect to come up with some cure-all prescription that can be applied universally and indiscriminately to address the problems the Church now faces in relation to cultural change in general and post-modernity in particular.

This is the point at which I part company with the prescription offered by Matthew Fox, who seems to believe that worship will be renewed through being realigned to the emerging scientific world view of so-called new science. There is no doubt that recent discoveries in physics are demonstrating that the world, and our experience of it, is far more complex than the Newtonian paradigm allowed, with many more dimensions of existence than has hitherto been imagined. But to base our theology on today's science seems to me to be no more profitable than it was for our predecessors to adopt the ideological criteria of their day. I want to go back even further, to our biblical roots, and ask what resources we might find there for helping to address today's questions. In a previous book, I proposed a definition of worship which many others have found helpful in thinking through this issue in relation to post-modern culture: worship is 'All that we are, responding to all that God is.'[25] In line with this understanding, Robert Webber writes that 'In worship [Gospel] truths are not only said, they are sung, danced, dramatized, and seen through art.'[26] That sounds fine, until we realize it is not true. For the most part, dance, dramatization, and art in all its forms are not what most people think of when they reflect on their experience of worship. On the contrary, the vast majority of churches still tend to place most emphasis on textual and auditory aspects of worship. I am not wishing to deny that these are important, but I am very clearly wanting to say that they are by no means a reflection of biblical worship in all its rich variety. In the rest of this chapter, and the next two, I therefore want to explore some non-textual and non-auditory aspects of worship, not because texts and words are unimportant, but because we already know rather a lot about them and it is the other expressions we need to reflect on now.

Movement in Worship

In *The Spectacle of Worship in a Wired World* – in my opinion, one of the most outstanding recent books on worship and culture – Tex Sample correctly identifies the embodiment of culture as a major element in the shift from modernity to post-modernity, and overall the most significant of all the challenges facing the Church and its traditional practices. He argues that the way people today bond with one another and express their commitment is quite different from what it was even as recently as the middle decades of the twentieth century, and identifies 'the practices of spectacle, performance, soul music, and dance' as central to what is going on, if not necessarily the whole picture. Through stories and reflections (the whole book is a model of how to do practical theology), Sample draws out the implications of all this for the Church, and in relation to worship concludes that 'people must be given permission to move . . . The worship of the future will involve congregational dance. It can be learned and can be a significant way to glorify God. It will, of course, need to be indigenous to the people involved.'[27] This conclusion is especially significant, because it is the judgement not of a trendy post-modern person, but of an experienced theologian in good standing with a mainline denomination, whose reputation is unassailable and has been earned over a lifetime.

If Descartes' dictum 'I think, therefore I am' could define human nature during the period of modernity, then 'I move, therefore I am' might well be an appropriate way to describe today's people, who find themselves intuitively moving to the beat of (their kind of) music in a way that would not have been true of previous generations. Those I have called hedonists are most obviously at home in such a cultural setting, but they are not the only ones: traditionalists and spiritual searchers also live happily in this world, as do the desperate poor. We therefore ignore it at our peril in any talk of worship as evangelism. Some will find it surprising to learn that there is no shortage of biblical materials which relate directly and specifically to this very theme in connection with worship. Indeed, the sheer quantity and diversity of texts related to movement in worship only serves to underline the extent to which contemporary worship has moved away from the historic roots of Christian faith and celebration. Though most of its advocates probably feel a need to justify dance or movement as a part of authentic Christian celebration, it was for centuries at the heart of the Christian tradition. Not only has liturgy always included – indeed focused on – movement (often associated with song and music), but symbolic movement is an intrinsic part of human culture all over the world. In one way, it is the most obvious of all the arts, for it requires no materials apart from the one thing we all have: a body. Dance expresses something very fundamental about being human, and is a vehicle through which we intuitively learn more about ourselves than we thought possible.

It is just a little over ten years ago that I discovered this for myself. My wife and I had been invited to spend six weeks in Australia, working ecumenically with the churches there on themes related to the renewal of worship. At the time, we had both recently become aware of the power of movement in evangelistic contexts, through a major ecumenical celebration we had helped to organize in Scotland.[28] We were convinced that this was something we needed to share with Christians in Australia – but whereas Olive, my wife, had explored it all in a practical way, I had not. Like many men – especially church men – I thought it was a good idea, but only in a theoretical sort of way and just so long as somebody else would take responsibility for it. I had even attended a few workshops which Olive had been running, but I had always managed to contrive to find something else to do (usually something that needed to be done, such as providing the music, making cups of coffee, or whatever). I ought not to have been, but I was surprised when, in the course of our planning for the Australian workshops, she pointed out to me that I could no longer stand on the sidelines. If there were only two of us in the team, then we both had to be wholeheartedly in it – and that meant I would have to participate fully and actively. I managed to agree to all this without actually practising anything specific before we left the UK, so my first active participation in dance in worship was on the other side of the world from my home base. The fact that I was prepared to experiment with movement in worship where I thought nobody would know me, rather than at home, probably said something quite significant about me at that point in my life. It was only later that I realized how ridiculous even that was, for the reality was the exact opposite of what I imagined, since what the two of us were doing was highly publicized everywhere we went! Olive was generous to me, and my starting point was in a circle dance, so I was not alone. Moreover, this was no supercharged emotional atmosphere, nor was it done to throbbing musical beat, nor was it charismatic in any sectarian sense of the word (the series was sponsored by the World Council of Churches, which more or less guaranteed it was entirely mainline Protestant clergy, with a sprinkling of Roman Catholics). In fact, we were a collection of diverse individuals, whose feet were not always in step, and who were struggling to find ways of worshipping that would be faithful to the gospel and relevant to our culture. So I was totally unprepared for the sheer power of this form of movement in a context of worship and spiritual questing. For me, it was quite literally a discovery of dimensions of myself that I did not know of, and the combination of body, mind, and spirit united turned out to be not only much greater than the sum of the individual components, but to be quite transformational. As a group, we certainly had fun, but we also found ourselves relating to different parts of the human personality than had usually been the case in what we knew of worship. Moreover, in the process we found ourselves becoming a completely different kind of group, connected in a deep way not only with each other but even with the cosmos itself. It was a transcendent moment, an experience which took us beyond ourselves and into a different level of being. Had I known then what I know now, none of this would have struck me as at all unusual. Not only is dance profoundly theological (a circle dance being a living statement of God's immanence, while a line dance speaks of God's transcendence), but the healing power of dance is also well documented.[29] Indeed, as long ago as 1978, J.G. Davies who was professor of theology at the University of Birmingham (and well ahead of his time, though often regarded as quirky and eccentric) had commended dance in worship for this very reason, insisting that unlike a word-based theology which 'passes from premises to conclusions and expresses rationality', 'In dance we discover what we as physical beings can and will do. . . . Dancing itself is not an amusing distraction . . . it is an exploration, a voyage of discovery.'[30] For me, though, it was only when I came across a statement by Lucian of Samosata (a lawyer in Antioch, 125–90 AD) that I discovered a way of expressing exactly how I had felt during that Australian trip: 'those who sketch the truest history of dancing would tell you that in the first generation of all things the dance grew up, appearing together with ancient Love. In fact, the circling motion of the stars and their intertwining with the fixed planets . . . are signs of the primeval dance.'[31]

This notion that dance is a way of moving in time with creative love, and therefore a primal expression of our personal connection with God, is reflected in the Hebrew Scriptures, where dance is assumed to be an integral part not only of everyday life (as in Ecclesiastes 3:4), but also of regular worship, where its highly developed state can be judged from the surprisingly large number of technical choreographic terms that are used to describe it.[32] In the historical context of ancient Israel, dance – both religious and otherwise – was commonplace, and was no doubt adopted from the practices of other peoples along with the style and design of houses, utensils, and other arts and crafts. There is ample evidence of the ways in which Israel took over religious practices from the surrounding culture, though these were invariably adapted and rewritten so as to emphasize Israel's distinctive faith in Yahweh as the God of history and ethics, in contrast to the underlying fertility motifs that dominated other traditions whose practices were rooted in the ongoing cycles of nature. The dominant theme is not the rejection of culture, but its redemption, and this certainly happened in relation to the ways faith was celebrated in regular worship.

Just about all Old Testament references to dancing are found in a context of worship, to such an extent that when worship is mentioned without specific reference to dancing, its presence can almost certainly be taken for granted. In fact, the same Hebrew words can mean both 'rejoice' and 'dance', and the same is true in Aramaic.[33] In view of its many detailed regulations about the conduct of worship, some find it odd that the Torah contains no mention of movement in worship. But when we examine these regulations, they typically deal with aspects of worship that were unique to Israel, or given a unique interpretation, whereas dance would have been taken for granted in the cultural environment. It also probably fell into the category of litany (the framework of worship), rather than being a specifically designated action such as sacrifice. The Law contains no instructions for prayer either, whereas the litanies of the book of Psalms have plenty of references to both prayer and dance. In any case, as we shall see, the kind of dance reflected in the Old Testament was not choreographed or performance dance (the sort for which detailed instructions are necessary), but was almost exclusively spontaneous folk dance, the kind of thing the whole community could engage in together.[34]

Tex Sample proposes that this is the kind of movement which we need to explore in making worship accessible to today's spiritual searchers, and my own conclusions point very much in the same direction. It will therefore be worthwhile taking a little more time here to explore the various categories that can be identified in the sort of celebratory dance that features in biblical worship.[35] Community celebrations, whether national or local, feature prominently as occasions for dance. In the nature of things, they focused on military victories over enemies, and therefore might seem to be not specifically related to worship, though that argument is somewhat undermined by the way in which the final editors of the Hebrew Bible regarded all such events as indicative of God's goodness towards, and care for, the people. Responses to that would, by definition, be regarded as worship. Examples of such occasions would be the dance of Miriam after the passage of the Red Sea (Exodus 15:20–1), and the celebration of Jephthah's victory over the Ammonites (Judges 11:34) or of the achievements of Saul and David (1 Samuel 18:6, 30:16). The intrinsic value of dance as an expression of spirituality is underlined by the prophets, for whom dance is a sign of hope, of national celebrations yet to come.[36]

Dance on national occasions was not limited to military successes. David, for instance, was 'whirling before Yahweh with all his might' when the Ark entered Jerusalem (2 Samuel 6:14–15). Elsewhere in the Bible, individual dance as performance invariably leads to disaster,[37] which may explain why there is emphasis here on this as a dance for God, and not a performance by David. Indeed, the statement that 'David and all the house of Israel brought up the ark of the Lord with shouting, and with the sound of the trumpet' almost certainly implies a more broadly-based community activity. This particular story is instructive because David's wife Michal reprimanded him for dancing with such vigour, and the editor of 2 Samuel linked her spiritual narrowness at this point to her inability to have children, thereby expressing a clear approval for the kind of physical exuberance demonstrated by David. The distinction between performance dance and community celebration implied here is something we shall need to pick up later in our reflections on how these scriptural resources might be used in today's Church. Dance also features in a context of personal and family celebration (e.g. Song of Solomon 2:8, 6:13, 7:1ff.; Psalm 45:15–16; 1 Maccabees 9:37–9), as well as being an integral part of the prophetic experience of the Spirit (1 Samuel 10:5–7). But by far the most extensive collection of materials relates to dance as a part of regular temple worship.

Even a casual acquaintance with the liturgical resources of the Old Testament shows that biblical worship was very much a multimedia experience, and in that respect was quite different from what most of us are familiar with today. Music features prominently (Psalm 22:3), often combined with movement, both individual (Psalm 63:5) and corporate (Psalm 42:4), and there are also references to choirs (1 Chronicles 15:16–24, 16:4–7; Ezra 2:40–2) and a very varied collection of musical instruments: tambourines, harps, lyres, trumpets, rattles, horns, flutes, cymbals (2 Samuel 6:5; Psalms 43:4, 68:25, 81:1–3, 98:4–6, 150:3–5; Isaiah 30:29; 1 Chronicles 25:1–5). Singing itself often appears as a dramatic performance (Psalms 42:5, 11; 43:5; 46:7, 11).

Movement and dance take at least three different forms in worship. There are references to free dance, sometimes connected to specific themes such as forgiveness or thanksgiving (e.g. Psalm 26:6), though more often of a general nature (e.g. Psalms 149:3, 150:4). There are even more passages containing both accounts of and general directions for processional movement of one sort and another (e.g. Psalm 42:4, 48:12–14), including examples of community dance using props and taking place inside the temple courts around its various altars (e.g. Psalm 118:19, 26–7). There are also examples of the use of dance as a form of symbolic re-enactment of key aspects of Israel's beliefs. A favourite theme in this connection was the celebration of God's work in creation (e.g. Psalms 46, 66, 74), one of the most detailed examples of this being Psalm 68, which describes a procession with the Ark and the celebration of God's enthronement in the temple. Most of these psalms are similar to religious songs and dances found in Canaanite and other cultures, which were evidently adapted so as to become vehicles for the celebration of Israel's own distinctive faith. Other passages show historical events being celebrated in the same way (e.g. Passover, Exodus 12:21–8), and the Feast of Tabernacles came to have a particularly strong association with dance as a part of worship. Many scholars connect the various psalms that celebrate God in creation, and others like Psalm 118, with this festival, which was celebrated as an autumnal harvest festival, and therefore strongly rooted in the agrarian culture of Palestine, but historicized in such a way as to preserve the overtone of connections with the world of nature, while also drawing attention to the story of how Israel's ancestors had journeyed through the wilderness of Sinai before finding a place to inhabit. As we might expect with a harvest festival, it is consistently depicted as an occasion to be marked with great exuberance (Exodus 23:16; Deuteronomy 16:13–14; Nehemiah 8:14; Leviticus 23:42–3) and if, as many think, the reference in Judges 21:19–23 to 'Yahweh's feast held every year at Shiloh' is to the celebration of Tabernacles, then group dancing is specifically connected to it. That was certainly the image projected by the rabbis of a later period, who report that

> It was said that the gladness there was above everything.
> Pious men danced with torches in their hands and sang songs
> of joy and praise, while the Levites played all sorts of instruments. The dance drew crowds of spectators for whom grandstands had been erected. It did not end until the morning
> at a given sign, when water from the spring of Shiloh was
> poured over the altar.[38]

By New Testament times, the temple was no longer the central focus for Jewish worship, largely due to the fact that most Jewish people no longer lived within easy travelling distance of Jerusalem. Sometime during the two or three centuries preceding the Christian era, the synagogue had emerged in order to meet the need for a more locally accessible resource, first in the communities of the Diaspora, but then eventually synagogues were also built in Palestine itself. For historical reasons related to the perceived uniqueness of the temple in Jerusalem, the synagogues had to create their own forms of worship, which were generally more focused on word than on ritual and action. But it would be a mistake to imagine that the spectacle and colour so evident in the temple simply disappeared from the synagogue communities. For synagogues served a dual purpose, as a cultural resource centre for the Jewish style of life, as well as a place for worship. All the major festivals were still celebrated there as part of the community's cultural heritage, with the traditional singing and dancing. Of course, that way of expressing things by distinguishing the various functions of the synagogue would have been alien to the ancient mentality, which had a holistic perception that did not separate out the sacred from the secular as readily as post-Enlightenment Christians tend to do.[39] Quite apart from that, though, the entire question of the relationship of the worship of the earliest churches to the life of the synagogues is far more uncertain than previous generations of scholars imagined it to be. The fact is that we have considerably less hard evidence about Jewish worship in the period of the New Testament than was once supposed. In this connection, Paul F. Bradshaw correctly points out that 'Too often in the past over-confident assertions have been made about the nature of Christian worship in the first century on the basis of false assumptions and methods or of dogmatic rather than historical criteria.'[40]

While the Old Testament and Jewish background will naturally be important, Christians will want to know especially what kind of resources we might find in the New Testament and the practice of the earliest churches. The first Christian believers had a complicated love-hate relationship with Judaism and the synagogues. On the one hand, their style of gathering was rooted in what I have called here the synagogue as worship centre, though at the same time they mostly wanted to reject the practices that could be found in the synagogue as cultural centre (especially things like circumcision and Sabbath observance). In addition, during the first century they were operating within a very specific social context, which inevitably constrained their possibilities at many points, including worship. Unlike Judaism, they were not at this time a *religio licita* within the Roman empire, which sometimes required them to meet in secret to avoid persecution, and in that context presumably it would be necessary to adopt a less than exuberant style of celebration. Even when persecution was not an everyday reality, there was generally a lack of available space, for though they met in Roman villas, which could be quite extensive as dwellings, there would be no open spaces even remotely comparable in size with the courts of the Jerusalem temple, or indeed temples constructed to honour other deities around the Roman world. In addition, one of the Church's major competitors in the religious market-place of the day was the cluster of cults generally known as the Mystery Religions, and they frequently accorded a high priority to mystical and sensual experience, sometimes expressed through passionate and unashamedly sexual dance. All these factors conspired together to ensure that we have less direct evidence for dance – or music, for that matter – in the very earliest Christian worship than perhaps we would like. There is no denying that movement in worship does not feature strongly in the New Testament – though, I would wish to add, neither do many of the other practices which we now take for granted, including the preaching of sermons as we know them.[41] However, when we understand all these factors in a wider context, the scarcity of information is nothing like as crucial as it can be made to seem. There can be no question that traditional Jewish worship formed the basis for Christian worship, though this was not taken over uncritically, and the New Testament authors have no hesitation in rewriting the agenda by explicitly rejecting some previously central elements, such as sacrifice (Hebrews 9), priesthood (Hebrews 7:11–28), and circumcision (Acts 15 etc.), as well as other traditional ceremonies (Colossians 2:16–23). It is therefore reasonable to assume that other aspects of the inherited pattern of worship (including music, dance, the reading of the Scriptures, and prayer) were to be continued. Of course, some Christians have argued that everything relating to Old Testament worship is to be rejected. But those who present this case most force-fully actually weaken their argument by then basing their own understandings of authentic Christian worship on the synagogue. On the one hand, this is an institution which (unlike traditional temple worship) had absolutely no scriptural mandate at all, and on the other it is often presented as having been only a worship centre, and not a cultural centre. When shorn of its cultural purposes, the image of synagogue life perpetuated by Western Protestants turns out to fit remarkably well into the paradigm of modernity, with emphasis on reading, reflection, and other passive modes of learning – which pre-sumably explains its popularity as a model for Christian worship among people who themselves favour precisely those things.[42]

In addition, there are of course some New Testament passages that do imply the inclusion of music and song in Christian worship (Colossians 3:16; Ephesians 5:19–20; 1 Corinthians 14:26), while movement in worship is specifically recommended in 1 Timothy 2:8, thereby demonstrating that the body was clearly regarded as an appropriate vehicle for spiritual expression – a point that is also made in passages such as Romans 12:1 and, in a different way, 1 Corinthians 6:19–20. There is also the fact that in Aramaic, like Hebrew, the same word could mean both 'rejoice' and 'dance' – and so phrases that have conventionally been translated as 'rejoice in the Spirit' might just as easily have meant 'dance in the Spirit'.[43] Quite apart from this, though, is the underlying logic of those truths that were central to the beliefs of the earliest Christians, not only the incarnation, which demands some kind of embodied spirituality, but also the resurrec-tion of Jesus. As J.G. Davies has observed, 'a church which believes in the resurrection of the body cannot rest content with a life style that deadens the body.'[44] In the absence of evidence to the contrary, it is far safer to assume that dance and movement were not rejected, but were taken for granted as part of a holistic spirituality. Jesus' story of the Prodigal Son implies as much (Luke 15:25), while the fact that other passages mention the possibility of dance being used for unworthy purposes must mean that it had a legitimate place in the life of the earliest Christian communities (e.g. Matthew 11:16–17; Mark 6:17–28; Luke 6:23; 1 Corinthians 10:7). In each of these instances, it is not the dance itself that is condemned, but the way it was misused. Like any other good gift of God, dance – even in worship – can easily be corrupted.

Notwithstanding some erudite studies which have claimed to be able to discern extensive liturgical traditions within the New Testament, the reality is that we know very little specific detail about how the first generation of Christians worshipped.[45] There is far more evidence for the following centuries, and here we find significant continuity with the Old Testament traditions, not least in the form of some striking references to the place of dance in both worship and theology. Chrysostom (AD 386), for instance, referred to David's dance as a model of 'dance to the glory of God' (*Proaem in Pss*), though he emphasized that Christians should 'dance with the angels . . . spiritual dances which are . . . most modest' and which would be different from the 'unseemly notions' of pagan ceremonies (*On the Resurrection of Lazarus* i). Others also expressed a clear concern for Christian dance to be of a different character from the dance of pagan religious rituals. Gregory Nazianzus (AD 369) advised the emperor Julian not to indulge in 'the dissolute dances of Herodias and the pagans', but to 'perform the dances of king David before the ark; dance to the honour of God . . . [this is] worthy of an emperor and a Christian.'[46] Ambrose of Milan (AD 339–97), commenting on Luke 7:23, emphasized the importance of the physical and spiritual being brought together, as a natural expression and extension of one another.[47]

Others highlight dance as a part of the life of heaven,[48] while Tertullian links upper-body movements with prayer (*On Prayer* XIV), to which Clement of Alexandria added foot movements (*Stromata*). Eusebius connected dancing with hymns (*Ecclesiastical History* iii.22), while Theodoret described how the Christians of Antioch 'danced not only in the churches and in the assemblies of the martyrs, but also proclaimed the victory of the cross even in the theatres' (*History of the Church* III.xxviii).

The disappearance of dance – as of other forms of spontaneous worship – was part of the institutionalization of the Church, with the consequent need for control to be vested in the hands of powerful hierarchies. Under the influence of a vigorous Platonic world view – which in any case marginalized the material (and, therefore, the physical and bodily) – Christian faith and celebration was gradually reduced to cognitive categories, thereby ensuring that only those with education could hold power, and in the process marginalizing the poor, as well as women, and setting the Church on a downward spiral of rationalism and suspicion of all things natural, which came to full fruition in the period after the Enlightenment. One of the challenges we face today in recreating space for people to express themselves in the worship of God is that we do not allow this itself to become yet another form of control. From its beginnings in the Hebrew Scriptures, right through to the early Christian centuries, authentic movement in worship was the work of the people. Dance as the people's work will always be dangerous for those who like power, because by definition it is a symbol of power shared among people: power with, not power held over, others. Though he had never heard of the idea that worship might be 'McDonaldized', J.G. Davies again went to the heart of the challenge we must face with his observation that all this 'raises a serious question mark against the continuation of largely cerebral forms as well as querying the production of fixed orders that allow for no creative freedom such as dance requires and expresses'.[49]

For our worship and evangelism today to be faithful to the gospel, it is important that what we do should have continuity with our roots. It is easy enough to think of ways in which we can throw off the shackles of McDonaldization, but it is important to have some strength of conviction behind it, rather than merely following the latest trendy idea. In terms of our worship, there are plenty of biblical resources that can help us to see how we might yet recover more open-ended ways of celebration that will have theological integrity as well as missiological relevance. I am not claiming that the rediscovery of movement is the only thing we need to do, but I believe it is a pivotal topic, and both our evangelism and our community building will make little progress unless we go back to our roots at this point. We will return to some practical concerns in the final chapter, but first we must move on to ask what other scriptural models might be available to help us develop a more spontaneous way of allowing the gospel's prophetic, radical, and challenging voice to be heard in today's culture.

6 PROPHETIC GIFTS

Once we begin to view our biblical roots through the spectacles of the challenge now placed before us by the emergence of post-modern culture, it is surprising how many points of convergence there are – by which I mean, insights that are as old as the earliest strands of the Judeo-Christian tradition, and yet which look as if they could have been tailor-made for the circumstances in which we now find ourselves. The prevalence of dance is one example of something that is intrinsic to the biblical revelation, and yet directly relevant to today's concerns for effective worship and witness. Drama is another one. If dance is a way in which the embodied human person can be caught up into the celebration of God's glory that, according to Scripture, is never-ending in the heavenly realm, drama provides a vehicle through which we might be challenged to a more radical discipleship and style of life that will reflect the values of the gospel and will contribute to the establishment of God's kingdom so that, in the words of the Lord's Prayer, God's will might be done 'on earth as it is in heaven' (Matthew 6:10).

Some surprising parts of the Bible can be understood as dramatic performance in the broadest sense. The sacrificial system of worship as practised in the Jerusalem temple is unlikely to strike many Christians today as an attractive form of spirituality. Though we do it all the time for food, the whole idea of killing animals as part of some religious rite is alien and abhorrent to most of us. Of course, if animals were slaughtered for food not in an abattoir, but in full view of us all, we might well feel the same unease about that as well. Anthropologists have struggled to understand what is going on in sacrificial worship – for it is still a feature of many religious systems today, and is by no means restricted to the practices of ancient Israel. Throughout the world, it seems to be a way of both symbolizing and reinforcing the underlying realities of life, of dealing with the discontinuities and contradictions and restoring the balance of relationships between God and people.[1] In this respect, sacrifice was essentially a dramatization of the significant elements of Israel's faith, and the slaughter of animals (along with the offering of crops and other inanimate objects) was a way of portraying those beliefs, as something created by God was offered to God, and then (in most sacrificial offerings) was returned to the people as a symbol of the renewed community they enjoyed with one another in the presence of God.[2] A closer reading of the Hebrew Scriptures will show that all the significant components of Israelite faith were celebrated in much the same way, with matters of theological moment consistently presented and celebrated through dramatic presentations of one sort or another. The Sabbath day, for example, with its very distinctive sets of actions that were allowed or prohibited, was a celebration of God's work in creation, while other significant events were also marked by acted-out symbolism. At the time of Passover, which was the annual feast celebrating the escape of the slaves from Egypt, the worshippers dressed in the same way, and used the same props as the original slaves had done in the story in Exodus 12:11. A similar thing happened at the Feast of Tabernacles, which came to be connected with Israel's early wilderness wanderings, and which was marked by the building of outdoor shelters and reliving the events of that particular historical episode (Leviticus 23:39–43). All the Old Testament festivals had this strongly dramatic element within them. Drama was a way of ensuring that belief was always tangible, and would never become a collection of abstract propositions. It also made it easy for events that otherwise might have been a remote memory to be applied as a living reality to the lives of all subsequent generations. The embodiment of the story through this kind of physical representation was not an optional extra to be added, or not, according to the personal preferences of individual worshippers. On the contrary, without this there could be no authentic retelling of the story of redemption.

We find exactly the same phenomenon at the centre of the New Testament. The incarnation itself is the most powerful and significant drama of all. Indeed, the notion of word becoming flesh is a very appropriate definition of what good drama truly is. Later on, Jesus' actions at the Last Supper, and the subsequent regular celebration of that in the Eucharist, all constituted drama in every sense of the word, along with baptism – as we have already noted in the previous chapter. These, and other aspects of the life of the earliest Christian communities, continually used dramatic devices to represent and celebrate faith in a way that kept the realities real for ordinary people.

In the process, their very centrality provokes and challenges today's Church in relation to our ongoing commitment of faithfulness to the gospel.

Dramatists, Mime Artists and Prophetic Witness

These dramatic dimensions to the Bible – though in practice frequently overlooked – have been sufficiently well documented by others that it is not necessary to say more about them here. But when we begin to look more closely at the scriptural records, some highly distinctive forms of drama take centre stage at significant points of the narrative. The work of the prophets, for example, cannot be adequately understood apart from this perspective. Because we have only the written accounts of some of their sayings, we easily imagine that they must have been speakers, and probably also writers. The truth is quite different, and we know for certain that, for the most part, they were not literary people, for none of them wrote in their entirety the books that now bear their names, and the majority of them wrote down nothing at all. Such evidence as we do have shows that those who did write things regarded this as a secondary form of communication, to be used only in times of emergency – as when Jeremiah, in fear for his life, had his friend Baruch write his messages down and then read them out in public (Jeremiah 36:1–32). But in normal times, the prophets were invariably relational communicators, for whom 'body language' was not an optional addition, but an integral part of their style. In some cases, their body language constituted the entirety of their message, as with the prophets mentioned in 1 Samuel 10:1–13, who apparently spoke no words, yet still managed to inspire Saul for his task as Israel's first king. While that particular blend of music, dance, and mystical energy is not the most characteristic form of prophetic message in the Hebrew Scriptures, even the so-called preaching prophets regularly delivered their messages in dramatic form, especially through the use of what today we would call mime – the one form of drama that is arguably the least prescriptive of all and which, because it often has no words, depends on those who see it to draw their own conclusions about its meaning and message. The fact that this open-ended form of drama is the one most regularly used in the Bible is of considerable interest in the context of post-modern culture, for it holds out the possibility of enabling us to avoid the problems of McDonaldization while at the same time not losing the cutting-edge of prophetic communication. For this reason alone, it will repay more detailed attention. In fact, as we shall see, some of the most effective and powerful prophetic Christian communicators throughout the centuries have known this.

Mime has a number of similarities with other art forms, and because I wish to distinguish it from dance on the one hand and clowning on the other, it will be worthwhile laying out a few definitions here. A typical dictionary definition regards it as 'a performing art in which characters are mimicked or ideas and moods conveyed by means of facial expressions, gestures, and the like, without the use of words',[3] though a more specialist definition might include statements such as 'the art of recreating the world by moving and positioning the human body', 'the art of creating the illusion of reality', 'the art of imagining the world together with others'.[4] A simpler way of thinking of it would be to regard mime as a particular kind of gesture. Gestures come in different styles. Some are capacities we are born with – like laughing or crying. Others – such as sitting or walking – we need to learn. Yet others are cultural gestures, like hugging, waving and greeting, or sticking our thumbs up – and some might mean different things in different cultural contexts (e.g. holding two fingers up). In this context, mimetic gestures can be thought of as movements that copy life in some way, in order to recreate and redirect it (a meaning that, as we shall note shortly, has close connections with the Hebrew concept of *dabhar*, the 'word'). The value of mime in terms of communication cannot be underestimated. Albert Mehrabian's research discovered that only 7 per cent of the impact of any message comes through the spoken words, and that 38 per cent comes from what he called vocal signals (tone of voice and so on), while a massive 55 per cent depends on non-verbal signals (body language).[5] The homespun wisdom of a traditional (and no doubt ancient) Chinese proverb expresses the same truth more memorably: 'I hear – I forget, I see – I understand, I do – I remember.' But even Aquinas recognized the truth of all this, acknowledging that '[the emotions] are more effectively aroused by things seen than by things heard'.[6]

Long before the researches of modern communication specialists, the people of Bible times had intuitively discovered the power of mimetic gesture, and the regularity with which it had entered everyday life highlights its importance. Some mimetic gestures feature so often that we can read the Bible almost without noticing them, and certainly without fully appreciating their significance. People clap their hands to represent triumph (Isaiah 55:12; Psalm 47:1), they lift their hands in praise (Psalms 28:2, 63:4, 119:48, 134:2, 141:2, 143:6), or bow to show humility (Psalms 72:9, 95:6). In order to pay attention to God, they might lift their head (Psalm 24:7), or kneel to pray (Psalms 95:6, 145:21, 34:1, 63:4, 72:15 – where the Hebrew term *barak* occurs, meaning 'to kneel expectantly in an act of blessing'). Laughing with joy (Genesis 21:6; Psalm 126:2), washing feet as a form of service (Luke 7:44; 1 Timothy 5:10; John 13:4–14; Genesis 19:2) – these are all mimed actions, along with the sharing of communion as a sign of fellowship (Matthew 26:26; Mark 14:22). In the same category we might place being baptized as a sign of new life (Acts 2:38; Romans 6:3; Colossians 2:12; 1 Peter 3:21), taking off one's shoes to show openness to God (Exodus 3:5; 2 Samuel 15:30), tearing one's clothes in mourning (Joshua 7:6; 1 Samuel 4:12; Lamentations 2:10; Revelation 18:19), or beating the chest in sorrow (Luke 18:13). The same mimetic actions could be either praiseworthy or signs of insincerity, as with pouring dust on the head to express inadequacy (Joshua 7:6; 1 Samuel 4:12; Lamentations 2:10; Revelation 18:19) – an action which, in the context of ostentatious fasting, Jesus dismisses as mere 'play acting' (the underlying meaning of the Greek word 'hypocrite' in Matthew 6:16, the use of which underlines the appropriateness of regarding all these gestures as a kind of formal mime).

Beyond this, however, there are at least forty examples of the use of mime as performance in the Bible. Ezekiel is perhaps the foremost mime of all, for the simple reason that he was dumb for much of his ministry (Ezekiel 3:26). A typical example of his use of this form of communication would be in 4:1–3, which describes how he drew a sketch of the city of Jerusalem on a brick, and using this model enacted a military attack on it, finally placing an iron pan or plate over it to illustrate its remoteness from God. Ezekiel 4:4–8 describes another mime which involved him lying on the ground tied up in strong ropes, while 5:1–4 tells how he shaved himself in an especially flamboyant gesture, using not a razor but a sword – and then completed his performance by weighing his hair and burning some of it in a fire. There are many other examples of similar things throughout Ezekiel's ministry (6:1–14, 7:23–7, 12:1–26, 20:45–9, 21:1–12, 24:1–27, 32:17–21, 37:1–25). Jeremiah was another one for whom mime was obviously a favourite form of communication, using all kinds of props, including loincloths (13:1–14), pottery (18:1–19:15), goblets of wine (25:15–36), stones (43:6–13), and scrolls (51:62–4). One mime, involving a yoke, spoke so powerfully to those who saw it that it led to a physical confrontation with another prophet by the name of Hananiah (27:1–28:17). Other biblical mimes incorporated the destruction of clothing (1 Kings 11:30–40), the shooting of arrows (2 Kings 13:15–19), the stripping off of clothes (Isaiah 20:1–6), even perhaps (depending on one's interpretation of the story in Hosea 1:1–3:5) a long sequence in a prophet's life. The book of Jonah can also be understood in a similar way as a story intended to be performed drama, though in that case the spoken dialogue must have been more central – while the book of Job represents a different form of drama, in which the mimetic element has been almost entirely displaced by the spoken dialogue (though it is still present).

Mime also appears in the New Testament. According to some, the application of the term 'signs' to Jesus' miracles in the Gospel of John indicates that they were intended to have a mimetic character. Certainly, other episodes from the Gospels, such as the cleansing of the temple (Mark 11:15–17; John 2:13–16), the dramatic entry into Jerusalem and cursing of the fig tree (Mark 11:1–14), and the meeting with the couple at Emmaus (Luke 24:28–35) – as well as the last supper – all contain mimetic elements. Other New Testament examples may be found in Acts 21:10–13 and Revelation 18:21.

Some passages also refer to the use of mime (as distinct from dance) in the context of worship. Psalm 149:6–9 describes a mime in which the worshippers took a two-edged sword and symbolically re-enacted God's victories over their enemies – a type of mime which was common also among the ancient Egyptians, Greeks, and Romans, especially as a way of welcoming victorious warriors when they returned home. Besides the dance of celebration, Miriam's joyful expression of praise also incorporated a mime portraying how the victory had been won by God (Exodus 15:20–1). There are other examples of the same combination of mime and dance in Judges 21:21 and 1 Samuel 18:6–7, 21:11 and 29:5.

Given the complexity of some of these mimes, they cannot have been purely spontaneous, but must have been carefully choreographed and rehearsed, and some passages do indeed provide clear evidence of that (e.g. 2 Kings 13:14–19; Ezekiel 4:1–7:27). Words might be spoken either before or after a mime (occasionally at the same time, as in Acts 21:10–13), though it is Hosea who integrates the prophetic use of mime into something like a theology of divine revelation. Hosea 12:10 lists three ways in which this prophet understood God's message being communicated to the people. First is the spoken word (*dabhar*), a term which in Hebrew implies a speaking that is far more dynamic and full of cosmic energy than the kind of disembodied words we have become accustomed to encountering in post-Enlightenment culture. Alongside that, Hosea mentions the vision that is seen (*hazon* – an obvious reference to some kind of mystical spiritual experience), and then finally is an acted out drama (*damah*). Bible translators have typically represented these with terms that can easily be domesticated within the world of literature and conventional verbal expression, no doubt reflecting their own experience and presuppositions about appropriate forms of religious discourse. *Dabhar* has frequently become merely 'words' in the sense of propositional statements, while a favourite translation of *hazon* is 'revelation' and *damah* has even been understood as 'parable'. None of these renderings are wholly inaccurate (for example, good drama can indeed serve as a parable), but the overall impact has been to conceal the dynamic nature of prophetic communication behind a protective wall of bookish ways of doing things. The three media mentioned in this text are clearly intended to be different, though complementary, forms of communication. Since creativity is at the centre of God's being, it is only to be expected that whenever God communicates it will be with creative diversity. When the diversity intended by the Creator has been subtly homogenized to become only word-based, why are we surprised that we are struggling to share the gospel in ways that will be heard by humankind in all their God-given variance? The rediscovery of these two non-verbal forms needs to be a priority if we are to restore biblical wholeness to our witness today.

From its earliest days, the Church operated in a culture with a rich theatrical tradition. Along with other forms of performance art, mime was very popular in the Roman empire, not least because of its ability to transcend language and cultural barriers and therefore bring a degree of coherence to what was a very diverse grouping of nations and peoples. Mime artists could as easily be found on the streets as in the homes of their rich patrons, and in some ways they served as the popular newscasters of their day. They not only drew attention to what was going on, but they also (and especially) used their art to 'imitate life' (the meaning of the Greek word *mimesis*), presenting exaggerated images as a way of exploring what was going on, and exposing the hypocrisies and inconsistencies that have always been part of human behaviour, especially in public life. The traditional deities of Greece and Rome had always been regarded as fair game for this kind of parody, and once Christian beliefs began to permeate society they were used in this way too. Because so many aspects of church life were themselves dramatic, it was not difficult to send them up, and baptisms, the Eucharist, healings and exorcisms were favourite themes, along with arguments among prominent Christians about doctrinal issues that were no doubt important to the protagonists but could seem trivial and irrelevant to others in the cultural mainstream. In the period before the conversion of Constantine, mimes who became Christians often found themselves uniquely placed to challenge the underlying world view of the political system. During the reign of Diocletian (245–313 AD) there was a concerted effort to crush the Church. Christians were dismissed from the emperor's staff, church buildings were destroyed, Christian leaders were imprisoned, and all Christians were required to offer sacrifices to him and his own favourite deities.

The most significant prophetic challenges to this policy came from mimes. In 287 AD, at Antinoe in Egypt, the local prefect, Arianus, declared that all visitors must sacrifice to the local gods, or be put to death. For everyone apart from Christians, this was no problem, so when a faint-hearted deacon arrived there he knew what the consequences would be if he followed his conscience. In an effort to avoid having to make a public stand, he hired a famous mime by the name of Philemon to do it for him. Philemon dressed up as if he was the deacon, and then just as he was about to make the sacrifice, he was stopped in his tracks by a vision in which he saw Jesus. The crowd had no idea this had taken place, of course, so when he announced that he was a Christian and therefore would not offer the sacrifice, no one was surprised: they all thought he was the deacon anyway, and that was exactly what they expected. But then Philemon revealed his true identity, and no one knew what to do – for (in the light of his unexpected encounter with Christ) he now refused to sacrifice even as himself. Offers of money, love, fame and fortune made no difference. But Philemon was joking no longer, and he was put to death (along with the deacon), using his final words to remind the crowd of his theatrical background and his previous willingness to ridicule Christian faith: 'You laughed at those comic blows then, but the angels wept. Now, then, it is only fair that your tears should not weigh against the joy which the angels feel at my salvation.'[7]

A similar story is told of a later occasion in 302 AD, when Diocletian returned to Rome having won great victories, and again took steps to banish the Christians. This time he went in person to the theatre to see a famous mime called Genesius who was to satirize the Christian faith. As part of his act, Genesius mimed a mock baptism, but in the process of doing so, he too had a vision of Jesus, and his make-believe baptism became, in effect, a real one. An emperor who had hired a mime to mock the Christians ended up being ridiculed himself, and what was intended to be an attack on the Church turned out to be a powerful presentation of the gospel. As a result, Genesius was tortured and executed, as were a significant number of other mimes during these early centuries.[8] When Theoderet wrote of mimes who 'came upon the stage and suddenly entered into the ranks of the martyrs, gaining the victory and seizing the crown . . .', these were the people he had in mind.[9] Other mime martyrs known to us by name were Gelasiunus (297), Ardalio (298), Porphyrius (362) and Masculas (486). The prophetic ministry has always been a dangerous business. Some church leaders regularly used mime in evangelism, and Gregory of Nazianzus (329–90) wrote scripts to be used in this context. But there were others who used mime in the service of heterodox theologies – Arius of Alexandria (260–336) presented a mime of the crucifixion, while the Gnostic *Acts of John* mentions mimes of the last supper – and this was one of the factors that eventually led to its demise.

Clowns and Martyrs

Though clearly using mime skills, characters like Philemon and Genesius are better understood as early examples of Christian clowns. The two forms of communication are in any case closely related, and both of them are exaggerated ways of reflecting life and commenting on it. But there are some differences. The mime is most usually a figure of serious challenge, who may highlight a problem without necessarily offering a way in which it might be resolved. The prophets of the Old Testament often used mime in this way, as a medium for announcing judgement rather than a way of holding out salvation. Clowning more often combines the two, and without losing the prophetic cutting-edge of mime, is a medium of both challenge and salvation, confronting people with the reality of themselves, but then lifting them up and moving them on to a more hopeful way of being. Clowns also do it all with fun and humour. Whereas a mime can remain detached from the situation being addressed, the clown cannot fail to be involved, addressing issues through laughter and in a spirit of personal openness and vulnerability. The mime is more likely to present a minimalist message, while clowning offers a bigger picture, using colour and broad brush strokes (literally as well as metaphorically) in ways that open up spaces for people's own imaginations to find solutions to their predicament.

It will be worth pursuing this theme a little further, for humour is likely to be one of those other things we need to rediscover and use as part of our celebrating and witnessing to Christian faith in post-modern culture. Properly understood, and placed within a context of biblical models, I believe this can be one of the most powerful expressions of a relevant spirituality for today. As J.G. Davies observed more than twenty years ago, 'Comedy in its highest form is a search for and a discovery of truth.'[10] I have already said something about my own personal connection to this form of Christian ministry in the first chapter of this book, where I set out my methodology, so its inclusion here needs no further justification from me. It will, however, be worthwhile engaging in some theological reflection on the meaning and significance of clowning in relation to effective mission with those who have not yet heard the story of Jesus. In doing so I make no special claims for this over and above other forms of creative communication. But it fulfils the criteria already identified as being essential to sharing faith in today's world: it is both human and humane, in every sense of those words, it is biblical, with a profound spiritual message, it is traditional in that it relates to ancient church practices, and it is open-ended, allowing space for people to respond for themselves, in their own time and place, to the gospel.

If we are to empower people in the spiritual search today, we need to find vehicles that will allow us to be real about ourselves. Humour is one way of doing that, especially when we are enabled to laugh at ourselves, for by doing so we accept the fact that we are part-hero and part-fool, part-success and part-failure. Good clowning sets these two worlds against each other, and in the process provides new insight into the deeper significance of what is real and meaningful. It gives a sense of balance between success and failure, and thereby offers the possibility of a starting point for renewal. It can also be a way of dealing with apparent powerlessness, for both individuals and whole societies. During the final days of communist government in Poland in the late 1980s, thousands of people took to the streets of Warsaw every night – dressed as clowns. They were well aware of the possibility of a violent crackdown on their activities, so they did nothing that could reasonably be interpreted as political provocation. There were no speeches or political rallies, for that would only have invoked the kind of backlash they sought to avoid. All they did was walk about the streets dressed as clowns for two or three hours each night, before returning to their homes. The use of such festivity as a form of social protest can be traced back at least as far as the Middle Ages,[11] and for the Polish protesters it was a powerful means of dealing with their own internal oppression, while at the same time highlighting the weakness of the communist regime. For what kind of government could possibly be intimidated by a crowd of people dressed in funny clothes? How could anyone justify arresting, or even opposing, such people? Yet their continued presence, highlighting the absurdity of a political system that was indeed unsettled by such behaviour, was one of the most powerful of all expressions of public opposition at that time and, together with other factors, played its part in securing the downfall of communism not only there but throughout the east of Europe.

Wherever we look, the Old Testament is full of this kind of humour, even at points in the narrative which we might be inclined to regard as very serious.[12] The exodus story starts with Moses at the burning bush, an episode that is shot through with humour, whether it be the revelation of God's name as 'I am who I am' (something that Moses could only imagine must be some kind of joke), or the preposterous idea that a person who is unable to speak even to save himself should be appointed as spokesperson for the Almighty (Exodus 3:1–4:17). Before that, the stories of Genesis had already displayed the same sense of humour. Noah received instructions to build a big boat miles away from any water (Genesis 6:11–9:29). What kind of God would suggest such a thing – and what kind of person would think it made sense to do it? Only a clown! Even Abraham and Sarah, when the greatest miracle of their entire lives was announced to them (they were going to have a child, even though he was a hundred years old and she was ninety) – instead of treating it with great seriousness and reverence, as people might be expected to do in the face of such a divinely gifted wonder, they laughed and then ended up calling the child 'laughter' (the literal meaning of the name 'Isaac', Genesis 18:9–15). Other stories displaying an unexpected twist of humour include the account of how Balaam was supposed to be a seer, and therefore highly knowledgeable about most things – but he ended up learning the most important lesson of his life from his ass (Numbers 22:7–35). Then there was Gideon, who went into battle against the Midianites but left his weapons behind and equipped his soldiers only with clay pots, horns, and fiery torches (Judges 7:1–23). They smashed their pots, blew their horns, shone their lights, and overcame their enemies – but the funniest thing of all is that everyone knows they would have been certain to lose if they had gone into a regular battle!

We have already noticed the way the prophets used mime, but they also incorporated humour not only into their messages, but also in their lifestyles. They ate bugs (Mark 1:6) and hid under bushes (Jonah 4:6–8); Isaiah walked around naked for three years (Isaiah 20:2–3); Jeremiah smashed pots (Jeremiah 19:1–13) and wore a yoke on his neck (Jeremiah 28:10–16); Hosea married a prostitute, who then went back to work in the brothel – and he ended up having to pay to spend time with his own wife! Ezekiel cooked his food over a fire fuelled with human dung (Ezekiel 4:12), and regularly saw skeletons moving, and wheels spinning in the air. He even ate a copy of the Bible (Ezekiel 3:1–3). Then there is the story of Jonah, who tried to escape his calling only to be eaten by a fish – and not just eaten, but subsequently thrown up. They even died in crazy ways: Jeremiah was thrown into a cesspool, then kidnapped and taken to Egypt (Jeremiah 38:1–13, 43:1–13); Isaiah was sawn in half; John the Baptist lost his head over a dance; and Ezekiel just volatilized. Mark Liebenow's comment on all this is itself a humour-laden understatement: 'These are not normal people, not sensible like you and me . . . Are these nice, sane people?'[13]

The same streak of humour runs throughout the New Testament as well. Think of Jesus' choice of disciples, headed up by Peter, who was an unpredictable person if ever there was one – yet Jesus gave him a name like 'Rock', and then said in effect, 'This is the kind of unreliable person on whom I will build my church' (Matthew 16:13–20). If Jesus had no sense of humour, he would never have done that sort of thing. The same playfulness appears with more sinister consequences in his choice of Judas, who was a known Zealot (revolutionary) and whose surname 'Iscariot' actually meant something like 'the dagger man' – yet Jesus made him treasurer to the disciples, and then seemed surprised when he betrayed him! Douglas Adams points out how throughout his ministry Jesus is regularly portrayed in a classical clown mode, juxtaposing completely different worlds alongside each other. At the very beginning of Matthew's Gospel, even his genealogy is a joke: Matthew clearly wanted to persuade his readers that Jesus was the Son of God, yet when he listed his forebears they turned out to be not the great and the good, but a collection of prostitutes, murderers and criminals (Matthew 1:1–17). What can be made to look like serious theological discussions about topics such as the meaning of Messiahship are also shot through with decidedly comic elements.

As a figure of weakness, Jesus is completely incongruous as the Son of God and Messiah, who was supposed to be powerful and all conquering. Moreover, the way the disciples engage with Jesus over this has many of the traits of classic comedy, with Peter invariably playing the straight guy who asks all the questions that the others want to ask, but don't know how to.

There are other stories in the Gospels which display this same comic quality. For example, on one occasion Jesus was asked a very serious question about adultery (for the woman at the centre of it, it was literally a matter of life and death) – and he responded by drawing pictures on the ground (John 8:2–11). When confronted with another serious matter, this time about the payment of taxes, he replied by sending a disciple off to get a coin from the mouth of a fish (Matthew 17:24–7). Who but a clown would do that? Towards the end of the story, he entered Jerusalem in what was, in effect, his coronation parade, the time when the messianic king would come to claim his heritage – and he did it on a donkey, which was not even his own (Mark 11:1–11). The Passion story itself has the same tragi-comic character, as Pilate asks him about truth, and he is led to the cross dressed up like a king, where a placard says he is one, even though he isn't – and then the prime witnesses of his resurrection are all women, the one group whom nobody in the ancient world would be likely to believe.

In his teaching also, Jesus continually used techniques that are typical of serious clowning, by poking fun at pompous people who took themselves too seriously, and always taking examples that sounded either unlikely or impossible and wondering what the world might be like if things were different, and if the rules worked some other way. Much of Jesus' humour depended on word plays in Aramaic, which do not always readily translate either into another language or another culture. Imagery that clearly invokes humour would include the idea of the first being last (Mark 9:35), the yoke as a symbol of freedom (Matthew 11:29), the blind leading the blind (Luke 6:39), and the prospect of God's kingdom being like something as insignificant as a mustard seed (Mark 4:30–1) rather than something reliable like, say, a cedar of Lebanon. There are also those passages which envisage someone with a plank in their eye trying to see to remove a speck (Matthew 7:1–5), or a camel managing to squeeze through the eye of a needle (Mark 10:25), not to mention the idea that pearls might be given to pigs (Matthew 7:6 – but who would do it anyway, especially in a Jewish culture?), or of turning the other cheek, carrying a stranger's bags an extra mile (Matthew 5:39–42), becoming like children (Mark 10:15), or getting born again (John 3:1–10 – no wonder Nicodemus had no idea what he was talking about). Even apparently serious parables like the Good Samaritan can be full of humour, for it is a typical comic good-news/bad-news scenario: there is good news (help is coming), but the bad news is that the help is from someone whom the hearers are not going to like – and it only gets worse when the person who started it all by asking the question, 'who is my neighbour?' learns that in order to be part of God's kingdom it is the unacceptable person whom he needs to imitate (Luke 10:29–37). Summing up all this humour in the Gospels, Liebenow observed that

> Parables were never intended to be instruction manuals . . .
> They were intended to confuse the rational. Those who intend to understand God rationally are doomed to failure, for God is not rational. . . . We have to learn to react from feeling, rather than from thought. It is only through living the parables that we can come to understand them.[14]

This is classic clowning.

Even Paul, who is often thought of as too serious for his own good, shared Jesus' concern for encouraging people not to take themselves too seriously, and he did so with humour. His style certainly has more dry humour than we find in the Gospels, as for example when he recommends that those who were wondering whether or not they should be circumcised should, instead of merely removing little bits of their penis, go ahead and remove the whole lot, castrate themselves, and thereby solve the problem once and for all (Galatians 5:7–12). A humorous image with more universal appeal is probably the picture used in 1 Corinthians 12, of human body parts walking about and talking to each other, which is pure slapstick! And of course, Paul is the one who specifically advised his readers to be 'fools for Christ' (1 Corinthians 4:10), something that both he and his opponents agreed was exemplified by his own crazy behaviour (2 Corinthians 11:21–8).

There is even some evidence of the use of clown skills in connection with Jewish religious celebrations, as in the story of how the rabbi Simeon ben Gamaliel juggled with no less than eight flaming torches (*Sukkah* 53a). But it was not until the twelfth century that they again came into prominence in the Church, with the development of the Feast of Fools in France. This was a period when, in general, the

Church was dominated by thinkers such as Thomas Aquinas (1225–74) and the Scholastics, though even Thomas valued 'folly' in the Pauline sense as an essential part of theology, and in the same period Francis of Assisi (1182–1226) exemplified most clearly of all what it meant to be a fool for Christ, talking to animals, kissing lepers, and generally turning conventional behaviour and wisdom on its head. Indeed, the early Franciscans called themselves 'fools of Christ', preferring what they called 'heart knowledge' over 'head knowledge' (though it was the latter that eventually won the day).

In the medieval Feast of Fools, which started as a New Year celebration, the figure of the clown was used for two purposes, first as an interrupter to highlight or draw attention to something of particular significance in the liturgy, and then also as a means of poking fun at the pomposity of church life. In this connection, minor clergy would dress up and parody their superiors, imitating the pomp and ceremony by wearing funny clothes, burning old shoes to create 'incense', and even on occasion taking donkeys to church and having them 'say' ('hee-haw') the responses.[15] At this period, of course, ordinary worshippers had few ways of connecting with formal worship, which was in Latin, a language none of them knew, and for them the holy fools could be empowering and inspirational, and provided something they could easily relate to. Inevitably, the work of these fools came to be connected with power struggles in the Church, and when their activities were outlawed towards the end of the fifteenth century it was as part of a broader process of the marginalization of the laity and opposition to their desire for faith to be more celebratory and less penitential. In a sense, therefore, the banishment of the holy fools was indirectly one of the factors that led to the Reformation – an irony, if ever there was one, in the light of the fervent opposition to the arts that emerged especially among the Calvinist reformers. But the classic holy fools had three distinguishing marks, all of them continuing the prophetic and radical strands of biblical faith personified by the prophets before them. They had a passionate commitment to Christ, living as he did and gladly accepting ridicule; they had a strong sense of eschatological purpose, as they continually drew attention to the conflict between the world's values and God's values; and they had a clear commitment to social justice, demonstrated in the way they were prepared to challenge the dominance of the rich and powerful.

Foolishness and the Character of God

Apart from the obvious relevance of all this to the situation in which Christians now find themselves vis-à-vis post-modernity, there is also a significant christological dimension which we should consider, for the image of Jesus himself as a clown is one that seems to have particular power to address the needs of today's people.[16] In one sense, of course, the significance of Jesus never changes. But his meaning has been articulated and presented over the centuries in many diverse ways. For example, to the earliest generations of Christians, suffering continual and often organized persecution, the image of Jesus that spoke to them most powerfully was as a good shepherd who would lead them to safety. To medieval Christians in Europe, facing the incredible suffering inflicted by the black death and plague, he became a tortured figure on a cross who would share their pain – while Christians inspired by the Enlightenment vision often found it more helpful to imagine him primarily as a great teacher or rabbi. In a world as diverse as ours, there is unlikely to be any one way of depicting Jesus that can speak with the same universal appeal as some of these earlier images appear to have done in their own more restricted contexts. But the presentation of Jesus as a clown seems to me to have a particular relevance at this time, especially to people in the Western world, who need to take themselves less seriously and learn to listen to others – though what I have seen of the way Christian clowning is received in the non-Western world suggests it may not be altogether irrelevant there as well, for when properly understood it presents a radical revolutionary challenge to the political and economic status quo, which is exactly what oppressed people and minorities all around the world wrestle with, as they struggle to be heard and to be taken seriously. The figure of the clown embodies central Christian beliefs about Jesus, and expresses them in ways that words (which are having a hard time today anyway) can never adequately do. The clown is a symbol of joy, who embodies simplicity and points to the pleasures to be found in the everyday things of life. The clown is a symbol of hope, a character who never gives up believing that the impossible will someday become possible: everyone knows that the clown is going to fall off the slackrope, or the unicycle, or get a custard pie in the face, but will always get up and start over again. In addition, the clown is a nonconformist who humbles the exalted and exalts the humble, a vulnerable lover who continually expects goodness from others, but who often receives abuse and rejection instead. It is the clown who most poignantly demonstrates the foolishness and weakness of the gospel:

> Like the jester, Christ defies customs and scorns crowned heads. Like a wandering troubadour he has no place to lay his head. Like the clown in the circus parade, he satirizes existing authority with regal pageantry when he has no earthly power. Like a minstrel he is costumed by his enemies in a mocking caricature of royal paraphernalia. He is crucified amidst sniggers and taunts with a sign over his head that lampoons his laughable claim.[17]

The more we explore the theological implications of mime and clowning as prophetic ministries, the more obvious it becomes not only how closely this all integrates with traditional aspects of Christian theology, but also how specifically relevant it is to the kind of concerns we meet among post-modern people, especially those groups that I have described as the desperate poor, the hedonists and the spiritual searchers. The word 'clown' itself is related to the old Anglo-Saxon term 'clod' which refers to a simple sort of person who would be allocated to menial tasks. This is the lowest form of servant, a person who seems to have no significant power at all. If you think of clowns in the circus, they are not traditionally the centre of attraction or the star performers. On the contrary, they serve to draw attention away from themselves and toward those others who are the key players. This is how the New Testament describes Christians, as God's servants whose calling is to draw attention to Christ (John the Baptist being perhaps a key example here, Mark 1:7–8). More than that, traditional clown make-up in itself reflects the core of the gospel, with its symbolism of death (white face) and resurrection (the colours of life). Even before anything has been said or done, a clown's face speaks about the journey from death to life, from crucifixion to resurrection, Good Friday to Easter Day – and beyond. Over and above this, clowns in whiteface are ageless and sexless, transcending time, race, and culture. This is why they can so readily cross cultural boundaries, for as clowns they do things that they would be unable to do as regular people (such as overturning the cultural rules that say men should not cry, or women should not be angry). Clowns accept people as they are; they are the original rainbow people of God, expressing what it means to be fully human and in the process giving voice to the theology found in New Testament passages such as Galatians 3:28. In this context, Christian clowns (as distinct sometimes from circus clowns) affirm other people, allowing them their own space for reflecting on and engaging with the gospel.[18]

In the light of this, it is not surprising that clowns encourage inter-action – another central gospel value that also speaks powerfully to today's people. Clowns never just give a performance, but create a two-way communication. Nor do they stay in a circumscribed place, but (and this is a contrast with what usually happens in church) they move outside the lines and mix with people in such a way that every-one becomes involved (for which, see New Testament passages such as 1 Corinthians 12:4–26, 14:26–33). At the same time, clowning is not directive or prescriptive. It is not as if there is only one way for faith to be understood or expressed, but, like Jesus, the clown gives each person the opportunity to think and reflect upon where they are, and where they wish to be. Jesus never forced his way uninvited into any-one's life, and the clown's ambition is to be like that – opening doors of opportunity, and setting up signposts that will provide spiritual direction rather than prescribing a detailed route map.

If this all seems strange behaviour, and contrary to regular norms of human conduct, then it is. But it is also a reflection of the nature of God, who is neither rational nor logical. The ability to create a non-rational (which is not the same as irrational) space for spiritual nur-ture and challenge is a skill we cannot afford to ignore if we are to have any hope of communicating the gospel effectively in a post-modern culture. Clowns naturally open up a non-rational space for God to work by inviting us to laugh at ourselves in a way that enables us to challenge and question our assumptions, because we never endow human values with too much seriousness. But clowns also speak not only to our reason, but predominantly to the emotions, and that in itself means that their message will reach the parts of our being that other forms of communication fail to touch. These are the parts that we frequently like to keep under wraps, but the parts that need to be transformed if we are to fulfil our calling as human beings made in God's image.

Besides all this, classic comedy is an articulation of the core message of the Bible – someone gets brought down, and then through a non-heroic means is lifted up higher and better than they were before. Things are turned upside down, taboos are broken and set aside – and because the clown is like a child, no one is ever threatened. Is there any better example of what it means to 'turn the world upside down' (Acts 17:6)? Clowning is an expression of vulnerability, and therefore of the central feature of the gospel.

Clowns take on our 'sins' (absurdities, hypocrisies, and so on) and transform them. This is the heart of what it means to be 'fools for Christ's sake' – showing our own weakness and vulnerability, coming alongside others, sharing joys, pains and fears, and in the process pointing to Jesus. He is the most outstanding example of a person of great weakness, who was able to challenge and change the whole world – though he was rejected, and suffered in the process. People can reject a clown – and do. But like Jesus, the clown ministers by coming alongside others, not from a position of power but from a place of weakness.

Creative Spirituality

The more I have reflected on all this in relation to the core values of the gospel on the one hand and the needs of our culture on the other, the more certain I am that there is something quite profound in here that we ignore or marginalize at our peril. There will be, as I have repeatedly emphasized, many different ways of articulating the call of Christ for this generation. We will not all need to go off and become clowns, any more than we will all need to become dancers in the light of what I presented in the last chapter. That would be no more profitable than the mistake the Church has already made, of insisting that all its members be exclusively thinkers and speakers. But if we are serious about fulfilling the evangelistic mandate to share the gospel with all kinds of people, we will most certainly have to revisit some of our inherited assumptions about what it means to be church, in order to create space for these more creative and diverse things to happen – which I think will also be space for God to work among us in new ways.

Most of our churches still have a lot of suspicion about the dramatic arts, even though we regularly incorporate drama without realizing it – whether in the theatrically spectacular processions of traditional liturgical worship, or in the eccentric preaching styles of those in the Reformed tradition who think they dislike drama, but whose repeated gestures are mimetic by any definition, and not infrequently are used in exactly the same way as stand-up comics would use exaggerated and repetitive body movements. The same people can often adopt idiosyncratic and affected styles of speech that, in any other social context, could not be intended to be anything other than comedy. We have to accept that there have at times been particular reasons for Christians to tread warily with these arts. In the

Roman era, theatre was often coarse and immoral, which helps to explain why Christians in the Constantinian age were ambivalent about it. Similar considerations led to Pope Innocent III (1250) seeking to exclude dramatists from the Church, even though the Middle Ages generally had witnessed the emergence of a whole range of productions that presented the Christian message most effectively: mystery plays (telling Bible stories), morality plays (highlighting issues of behaviour), and miracle plays (stories of the saints). Today, we need to recognize that, while the dramatic arts of course have the power to corrupt, they also have the power to heal and to challenge. In that respect, they are no different than the spoken word with which the Church feels more at ease. Without spirituality, mime, clowning, and dance are no different from other human endeavours without spirituality: they can become manipulative, cynical, pessimistic, destructive, and self-serving. The prophets of the Old Testament faced off with false prophets from time to time – but that did not divert them from their mission. When Hananiah challenged Jeremiah's mime by smashing his yoke, he did not abandon the use of props – he went off and made new and more durable ones (Jeremiah 28:10–16). When infused with spirituality, the dramatic arts can be provocative, challenging, and renewing.

Given its stated commitment to a high view of Scripture, it is surprising that it should have been the Protestant tradition that has been most suspicious of anything that could be regarded as connecting with people's imagination, which of course is an indispensable vehicle for the kind of art forms we find in the prophets. The Reformation as such did not necessarily require this conclusion, for Luther himself is reported as having once said that, 'If people are not allowed to laugh in heaven, then I don't want to go there' – and his *Table Talk* is full of jokes. But in the Reformed tradition more generally, and especially among the Puritans, the human imagination was regarded as vacuous and lacking in value, if not endemically sinful, and therefore not only the kind of prophetic communications we have explored here, but even aesthetic concerns in worship were completely banished. For a tradition that has often regarded itself as the prophetic cutting-edge of the Church, it is surprising how readily it rejected the very things that had most obviously characterized the prophetic tradition in the Bible, not only in the Old Testament but also in the portraits of Jesus preserved in the four Gospels. Though Oliver Cromwell's political ambitions soon lost popular support in seventeenth-century England, his success in banning all forms of theatre, and his determination that fun and spontaneity would hence-forth be displaced by rational discourse and moral seriousness, created a legacy which the Churches in the West have scarcely be-gun to escape from even now. We should not, of course, be too harsh in our judgement on these people by reading back the conditions of our own day into theirs. This was a period when, for all sorts of reasons intrinsically unconnected to the Christian faith, rational dis-course was culturally dominant, and in that context it was natural for them to emphasize the significance of the spoken and argued word as an important part of Christian worship and witness. The problem was that the 'liturgy of the word' came to be a 'liturgy of human words' in the form of sermons, rather than a ministration of the Word of God which, since God is creator, comes in many different forms – silence, as well as speaking, not to mention dance, mime, clowning, song, the Eucharist, and many other things besides. If that seems too cynical a judgement, then the underlying agenda of much Reformed thinking was laid bare by an extraordinary series of ex-changes between John Whitgift, Bishop of Worcester, and the Puritan Thomas Cartwright, in what came to be known as the Admonition Controversy. Whitgift proposed that if Scripture was indeed the same thing as 'the word of God', then it should be sufficient merely to have it read in church, without any accompanying explanations at all – to which his opponent responded by insisting that only the preaching could turn the Bible into a spiritually edifying experience. 'Reading is not feeding,' he thundered, 'but is as evil as playing upon a stage . . .'[19] Controversies like that related to the cir-cumstances of their own day, and our mistake has been to universalize them and turn them into gospel absolutes in a way that now, in a culture that is not aural, but predominantly visual, is actually obscuring the gospel, not presenting it. Unless we deal effectively and de-cisively with attitudes like this, we will not make much progress with our evangelism, and we might even find that, far from holding out the word of life to those who are starving, we are actually pre-venting them from finding the spiritual nourishment that they so desperately need.

We will return to this theme in the final chapter. But first, we need to complete our survey of biblical resources that might aid us in our quest to uncover ways to eradicate the stultifying effects of theologi-cal and ecclesiastical McDonaldization, by looking more closely at the nature of the Bible as story.

7 TELLING THE STORY

Post-modern culture is full of paradox and contradiction, and nowhere is this more obviously the case than in relation to the search for a story that will give meaning to life. On the one hand, we are repeatedly being told that post-modern people no longer believe in metanarratives (i.e. some central legitimizing myth, or overarching dogma, that claims to explain universal reality) – yet we are telling more stories today than at any time in living memory, whether we look at the huge numbers of movies now being produced, or focus on the more homespun productions that can be found in the many traditional story-telling networks that are flourishing all over the Western world. Canadian novelist Douglas Coupland knows better than most how to capture the mood and feelings of post-modern people, and in his *Generation X* he tells the story of three friends who have retreated from urban life to spend time in the Arizona desert reordering their priorities and understandings of meaning. Early on, he comments that

> ... it's not healthy to live life as a succession of isolated little cool moments. "Either our lives become stories, or there's just no way to get through them." ... We know that this is why the three of us left our lives behind us and came to the desert – to tell stories and to make our own lives worthwhile tales in the process.[1]

Searching for a New Metanarrative

Story is central to the contemporary quest for meaning, in much the same way as abstract analysis was central to the outlook of modernity. Moreover, though philosophers such as Jean-François Lyotard have claimed that post-modernity is 'incredulity toward meta-narratives'[2] the evidence of popular culture does not uniformly support such a notion.[3] This may well be one of those places where post-modernity, as a popular sociological phenomenon characterized by the attempt to find new ways of doing things in the face of cultural change, has not necessarily espoused the tenets of post-modernism as an ideological outlook.[4] For a striking example, we need only look at the way in which the world of governments and international diplomacy has elevated the concept of 'human rights' into a metanarrative in the post-Cold War period, with such confidence in its all-embracing explanatory power that it is now regularly applied by Western politicians as a means of legitimating their own world dominance without even pausing to ask if this is indeed a universal standard that can be assumed to be self-evident to the whole of humanity.[5] The idea that there is one overarching story that can give meaning to everything else is also widespread in popular culture. James Redfield's book *The Celestine Prophecy* was one of the most widely consulted sources of popular spirituality throughout the 1990s, and continues to be influential. The author's introduction to the book makes it plain that he was setting out what is, by any definition, a metanarrative, a collection of beliefs organized into a truth structure which can explain all aspects of the world and human existence, and provide guidance and direction for behaviour:

> We know that life is really about a spiritual unfolding that is personal and enchanting . . . we know that once we do understand what is happening, how to engage this elusive process and maximize its occurrence in our lives, human society will take a quantum leap into a whole new way of life – one that realizes the best of our tradition – and creates a culture that has been the goal of history all along . . . The following story is offered toward this new understanding . . . All that any of us have to do is suspend our doubts and distractions just long enough . . . and miraculously, this reality can be our own.

Later on, one of the characters comments that 'The most important thing is that we see the *truth* of this *way of life*. We're here on this planet not to build personal empires of control, but to evolve.'[6] The same characteristic can be identified throughout much New Age spirituality. Indeed, the very thing that makes New Age so popular is not that it has no metanarrative, but that it offers a different one than that which the West has traditionally embraced, featuring universalism, pluralism, tolerance, individual choice, mystery and ambiguity in preference to the exclusivity, hierarchy and rationality that dominated the metanarrative of modernity. Moreover, and again contrary to one of the central assumptions of post-modern ideologues, actual post-modern people do believe in absolute truth – but it is a truth that is embodied not so much in what might be called truth structures as in particular values such as freedom, individualism, integrity, tolerance, the importance of nature, the value of a spiritual connection, and the belief that people should serve others beside themselves. Far from being an intrinsically coherent world view in itself, post-modernity is most accurately defined in terms of its reaction against modernity.[7] If modernity turned out to be too scientific, too rational and logical, too Western and individualistic, ignoring the mystical and spiritual side of life and imperialistically imposing a view of absolute truth, then post-modern culture espouses the antithesis of such beliefs. It accordingly values a holistic view of humanity and the world, pluralism and tolerance, openness to the numinous as a worthwhile part of life, a recognition of the importance of intuition, emotion and experience, of Eastern as well as Western models of viewing reality and spirituality, and at the same time stressing connections and relationships alongside individualism, and belief in subjective truth. All of this is not only story, but metanarrative.[8]

Coupland again provides a good example of the acceptance of universal standards, this time in his book *Polaroids from the Dead*, where he has one of his characters reminisce, 'I wondered how I would be judged if just today were to be my entire life. Was I being good? Was I being evil?'[9] In one sense, this is an unfocused rhetorical question, but it is nevertheless indicative of the belief held by many people that, somewhere, there are absolute standards of right and wrong even if we are not quite sure exactly what they might be. Throughout Coupland's novels, his characters consistently display surprisingly judgemental attitudes for people who, in theory, are not supposed to believe in absolute standards backed up by some kind of metanarrative. They regularly criticize people who are superficial, frivolous in their spending, uncaring about the environment, or showing off their superior intellectual knowledge. Moreover, this phenomenon is not restricted to imaginary lives, but can be located very specifically in the way we handle actual questions about the kind of absolute standards implied by metanarratives. A recent article on 'Cultural Relativism and Human Rights' had this to say:

> When reasonable persons from different cultural backgrounds
> agree that certain institutions or cultural practices cause harm,

then the moral neutrality of cultural relativism must be sus-
pended . . . We have moved beyond the idea of a value free
social science to the task of developing a moral system at the
level of our shared humanity that must at certain times super-
sede cultural relativism . . . [this] does not diminish the continued value of studying and affirming diversity around the
globe . . . suspending or withholding judgment because of cultural relativism is intellectually and morally irresponsible.[10]

An article in the US magazine *Scholastic Instructor* highlights the
inextricable connection between story and universal values, with its
account of 'The Heartwood Program . . . [which] uses multicultural
children's stories to present seven universal values: courage, loyalty,
justice, respect, hope, honesty, and love.'[11]

In his study of the emerging post-modern culture, Walter Truett
Anderson had highlighted the same connection ten years earlier: 'To
develop tolerance is to develop a story about stories, a perspective on
all our values and beliefs. We need such a story desperately now, as
much as we need sound environmental management and respect for
human rights.'[12] The increasing popularity of story – told through
many different media – should come as no surprise in the midst of all
our cultural uncertainty. For story provides people with a vehicle
through which to express themselves at moments of pain and tur-
moil. As a genre, it facilitates the articulation of deep insights and
emotions far more easily than detached, rational explanation has ever
been able to do. For many people today, music is the story that
provides the underlying narrative of meaning for life. For others it
is through the movies created in Hollywood, while yet others discover it in the endless conversations that take place in American
coffee shops or British pubs. However it comes to us, story can
become a powerful vehicle for far-reaching challenge and lifestyle
change: 'no more radical activity exists'.[13] But the danger is that we
will allow the narratives that inform our lives to be provided by the
phony stories of consumerism, in which the security of true wisdom
will be replaced by sporadic choices and feel-good experiences. We
are seeing the consequences of this all around us, as people are identified primarily by the style of their clothes, or by what they drink, or
the sort of cars they drive. Not only does this kind of story lack the
power to form community, but at its worst it can also encourage
privatism and a destructive form of individualism. If the only
thing available to us is a fragmented and meaningless story, then

we inevitably become meaningless and fragmented persons ourselves.

Christians, of all people, should have something to say in this context, though all too often we seem to have been content to sit on the
sidelines and be mere spectators in the face of a concerted effort by
certain sections of the media in particular to undermine the Christian
metanarrative and replace it by a McDonaldized mythology gen-
erated by and serving the needs of consumerism. I had a striking
example of this while I was in California writing this book. During
the Christmas period 1999, I attended two 'shows' ostensibly on
Christmas themes. One was a visit to Disneyland. I had been on previous occasions, and like most visitors enjoyed the experience, even
though I knew it was escapist, commercialized and – in the most precise sense of the word – McDonaldized.[14] But a Christmas visit was
quite different from a summer visit, and the essentially empty and
contentless presentation of a Disney portrayal of Christmas left a
bigger impression on me than I had anticipated. Though there was a
studied avoidance of calling it Christmas at all (a common phenomenon in the whole of American culture, where because of a civic para-
noia about anything to do with religion the Christmas season has
uniformly become 'the holidays'), at the climax of the famed Main
Street parade Santa asked the crowd, 'Do you believe in the spirit of
Christmas?' Of course, we all yelled our positive affirmations, though
even as I joined in I had already started to wonder what it was that
we were applauding. There was certainly an attempt to weave some
kind of metanarrative that would make us all feel good about something, but it consisted of an odd pastiche formed out of bits and
pieces of the stories of Aladdin, Snow White and the Seven Dwarfs,
The Lion King, Alice in Wonderland, and other traditional stories that
have come to be associated with the Disney movies and theme parks.
At best, this is a fragmented and unsatisfactory effort at creating a
new metanarrative – nor is it limited to the Disney empire, for with
variations from place to place this is the kind of Christmas story that
now seems to be accepted and promoted throughout much of the
Western world. Yet, in spite of the criticisms that can be levelled
against such efforts to redefine a major Christian festival, beneath it
all there is still an intrinsically spiritual question about the nature of
good and evil, and the meaning of all things. Have we as Christians
been too ready to accept the cultural conspiracy of late modernity
that would replace a traditional metanarrative that has both a human
and a cosmic dimension by one that exhibits only vague strivings for

spiritual meaning? By way of contrast, at the same Christmas season I also attended a production of *The Glory of Christmas* at the Crystal Cathedral (part of the Reformed Church of America), a church whose integrity as a creative contextualization of the gospel in its (southern Californian) culture I have come to appreciate more every time I have been there. Located only a few blocks away from Disneyland, this was one of the most impressive statements of the Christian meta-narrative that I have ever seen. Moreover, as I reflected on both the contrasts and connections between the two, I was struck by the way in which the values being espoused by the new emerging 'secular' metanarratives are frequently rooted in the Christian story itself, and I began to wonder if our own inability to live within the critique that the Christian story brings to our lives accounts in some way for our evident reluctance or inability to share the story itself with a new generation. It is not just the unchurched people mentioned in a pre-vious chapter who need to hear the Christian metanarrative afresh, but all of us, including especially those of us in the Church, who often seem too happy to live, worship, and witness in ways that can appear to be denying some of the central themes we claim to believe in. In this context, one of the greatest needs of the hour is for us to tell the story, for our own sakes as well as for the sake of the world.

Orality, Literacy, Rationality and the Bible

The Bible itself is almost unique in the world of religious literature because it consists, not of abstract philosophical and religious ideas, but of stories. The entire book is one big story, and those sections which are not (such as the legal prescriptions of the Old Testament) are there to provide essential background information so that we may more readily appreciate the nature of the stories. Moreover, the Bible is not just a static kind of story, but is itself the end product of stories that were continuously told and retold, whether the traditions of the ancestors repeated over many generations in ancient Israel or the narratives about Jesus orally communicated among the earliest groups of Christians. Even those parts of the story that can seem dull and unappealing when read from the pages of a book may well have been the very passages that brought it all to life when it was origin-ally heard as story, as Douglas Adams has shown in his discussion of biblical narratives as 'grandparent stories'.[15] Since biblical interpreta-tion as it has been handed down to us is the product of an Enlightenment-inspired methodology based on reverence for that slippery concept known as 'pure reason', it should surprise nobody to learn that theological exegesis has generally ignored the story form, and created the impression that the stories are just peripheral, and the 'real thing' is to be found in intellectual abstraction. That is not to say that it was a waste of time for previous generations to translate the stories into categories of what we would now recognize as 'systematic theology'. In a world where detached rationality was highly prized, and where the endeavours of Greek philosophy had created a series of common thought forms and vocabulary through which people of different cultural backgrounds might speak to one another and be understood clearly, extrapolating universal principles out of the stories was a natural and inevitable part of contextualizing the Christian faith.

However, any kind of systematizing of stories into principles will always remain a tentative enterprise, because at any given moment it can only be done in terms of whatever the contemporary modes of thought might be, and these will inevitably be limited and time-conditioned. Moreover, all systematic presentations of ideas are to some extent isolated from other presentations which begin from different assumptions and philosophical starting points. At best, they can only ever be a part of the total picture. The collapse of the Enlightenment consensus has highlighted the reality of that, and we now appreciate (to take the second point first) that historically, the categories of Greek philosophical discourse (which to a great extent were the inspiration behind modernity) have, in world terms, been only one of many possible ways of understanding reality. Anyone who has ever struggled to try and relate traditional Western concepts to, say, the ancient world views of the Indian subcontinent will realize that, without the creation of some third interpretive category, it is an impossible task. Even though the religious teachers of both cultures were addressing the same underlying questions of the meaning of life, they were not speaking anything like the same language when it came to providing answers. That kind of difference can be recognized quite easily, and Christians can – and do – take appropriate steps to re-contextualize their inherited beliefs into the thought worlds of different national cultures. But we seem to find it harder to appreciate that the gulf between traditional formulations of Christian belief and the emerging culture of the West is now at least as great, and requires the same kind of re-contextualizing if our message is to be heard, let alone understood and either rejected or accepted. In the post-modern context, there are fewer and fewer shared categories available within which we might articulate anything at all in philosophical abstractions. Increasingly, in this circumstance, we are reverting to some of the characteristics of an oral culture in order to communicate with one another. In this setting, we do not make sense out of things by means of linear logic, but through stories, shared experiences, and relationships. Inevitably, story once again has become a primary vehicle for meaning.

Theology has paid lip service to all this for some time now, though even those scholars who have recognized the value of the story form have typically not been content just to hear the story, but have instead substituted the analytical concepts of propositional modernity with nostrums drawn from the equally propositional world of post-modern deconstruction and semiological analysis.[16] It seems that stories are an embarrassment to theology, serving at best only as illustrations of propositional ideas. But from the perspective of the Church's mission in post-modern culture, this is getting things the wrong way round, and Clark Pinnock justifiably proposes that 'We should redefine heresy as something that ruins the story and orthodoxy as theology that keeps the story alive and devises new ways of telling it.'[17] The reason why story is important in mission should be obvious, for a story always evokes a response. It takes us up into it, and it is not possible to read or hear a story without it impinging on our own story, or even becoming our story. The Enlightenment-inspired idea that we should stand outside a text in order to comprehend it has not only encouraged several generations of scholars to endow what could never be more than provisional opinions with an unreasonable claim to universal truth, but it has also undermined the Church's confidence in its own traditional stories as vehicles for human transformation. To be effective in post-modern mission, we need to reverse that trend. Today's pluralistic world has very many similarities with the world of the New Testament, some of them quite specific, as for example the popularity of Gnostic-like movements within the New Age. We do well to remember that, in the kind of pluralistic world inhabited by the first Christians, it was stories and community that made the difference.

Christian faith actually began with stories. Indeed, the way the stories that Jesus told, and the stories they told about him, have been preserved in the New Testament Gospels in different forms indicates that they were all repeatedly used in diverse contexts in the life of the early Church, as they were adapted to different evangelistic situations as a means of contextualizing the gospel. One early form critic even argued that story was of such central importance to the mission and worship of the first Christians that he believed there was a special calling of story-teller, whose gifts could be set alongside those of apostles, teachers, healers, and so on.[18] Jesus no doubt found stories to be a natural vehicle for spiritual teaching, because they had long served that purpose in Jewish culture. But as a communication style, telling and listening to stories also embodied aspects of what Jesus wanted to say about God in a way that abstract propositions never could. Because stories can reflect and integrate with the experiences of everyday life, they were particularly suited to relating to a God whose essence was more personal than metaphysical.

In an interesting article on what he calls 'story exegesis', Carl E. Armerding highlights six advantages of hearing the Bible as story (which, I suggest, may not necessarily be the same thing as *reading* the Bible as story).[19] Though he was not, as far as I know, writing with any particular missiological purpose in view, it is striking to observe how relevant these points are to the concerns of post-modern people:

- Using the Bible as story takes account of all scholarly methods, but is not exclusively bound to any of them. To the purists, this is eclecticism, or even opportunism, which modernity would generally dismiss as being too prone to subjectivity. But the concern to identify truthful insights from many different sources, and to mould them into a new synthesis, is very much where today's spiritual searchers in particular find themselves. In his book *Baby Busters: The Disillusioned Generation*, George Barna quotes the testimony of a twenty-year-old called Lisa Baker, who described her spiritual aspirations in the following terms: 'All I want is reality . . . Help me to understand why life is the way it is, and how I can experience it more fully and with greater joy. I don't want the empty promises. I want the real thing. And I'll go wherever I find that truth system.'[20] It is easy to dismiss what can look like a pick-and-mix approach to spirituality, and though there are some who use their freedom of choice in a casual way, to imagine that all spiritual searchers fall into that category is to be far more cynical than the facts allow.
- Coming to the Bible as story does not prejudge its possible meanings, and it honours the integrity of the text as it is, rather than dismantling it. A major criticism levelled against the methodologies of modernity relates to the tendency to take things to pieces in a reductionist manner. This of course was intrinsic to the world view of Newtonian and Cartesian science, and it came to be taken for

granted that the only way to understand anything at all was to reduce it to its component parts. This was a major contributing factor to the unthinking exploitation of the world's natural resources, and it was the middle of the twentieth century before we realized (too late) that the cosmos is more than just the sum of its individual parts. Conventional Western medicine was led up the same blind alley, from which it is only now beginning to recover, with the recognition (obvious to most of the world's people) that human beings are not only living machines, but have feelings, emotions, relationships and personal history that impinge significantly on their well-being. It is out of concern for these mistakes that postmodern people prefer to emphasize the need for holistic solutions to life's challenges. Yet our inherited ways of understanding Scripture depend on the very same reductionist model that is now seen to be so inadequate. 'It is ironic that for many years theologians tried to emulate scientists with their precise methodologies built upon the factual and logical portions of scripture, only to discover that in the height of such scientific emulation, science was turning back toward mystery . . . there is more to God than dissecting scripture and taking sermon notes.'[21] One way of addressing that concern will be to reinstate the value of the Bible as story.

■ Stories leave open questions related to the spiritual and the supernatural. Stories are often full of the unexpected and the unexplained – and this applies not only to ancient fairy stories but (even more markedly) to the stories told in Hollywood movies. Angels, spirits, UFOs, visitors from other planets, and a whole collection of other both specific and vague influences from alternative levels of being are now so common in the stories we tell that no one with any connection to contemporary culture could fail to encounter them in one way or another. The huge interest in psychics, readings from tarot cards, channelling of messages from extraterrestrials and spirit guides – not to mention a good deal of the interest in so-called 'alternative' therapies – all stems from the same concern to locate something or someone from beyond ourselves who may yet bring redemption to our troubled world. The majority of us are probably not wholly convinced of the reality of all these things in the way in which modernity would have defined certainty. But still we find ourselves fascinated by the 'what if' scenarios with which they present us. Those whom I have called the secularists in a previous chapter will generally dismiss all this as naïve wishful thinking, and highlight it as further evidence of the potential disintegration of civilization as we have known it, and therefore another good reason why we need élites like them to continue to lay down public policy in ways that will save us from ourselves. But the renewed interest in hearing and telling stories which include such elements, whatever the medium, may well be connected to a heartfelt longing for some kind of living connection with the spiritual that 'may not be simply a resurgence of gullibility but a genuine re-awakening of hunger for a reality which Enlightenment thinking has quenched but could not eliminate.'[22] It should not escape our attention that in this context, story encompasses all three of the characteristics of prophetic witness which we identified in Hosea 12:10 (word, mystery and drama).

■ Because they focus on the whole spectrum of human experience, stories speak directly to our life concerns as we encounter them existentially moment by moment. In particular, stories do not divide life into categories of the cognitive, the affective, the relational, and so on. William J. Bausch expresses it like this: 'Propositions are statements on a page; stories are events in a life. Doctrine is the material of texts; story is the stuff of life . . . theology is a second hand reflection of . . . an event; story is the unspeakable event's first voice.'[23] The healing of our emotions is one of the most pressing needs today, and story can be a means of addressing those concerns that otherwise might be too painful to deal with. A striking example of that would be the way in which Jewish story-teller Elie Wiesel has dealt with the horrors of the Holocaust, by acknowledging the evil but thereby also confronting and disempowering it.[24] But we all use stories in this way, as a vehicle for dealing with confused emotions, whether in relation to everyday irritations or significant crises such as the deaths of our loved ones or the disintegration of relationships. Anyone who is a parent will recall that a distraught child can often be restored to calm by having a story told to them. Stories affirm who we are, not only in times of confusion but also at moments of ecstasy. They do this by inviting us to use our imagination, something with which many Westerners have a problem, because the modernist paradigm has told us that it is less than real, and may even be downright misleading. No wonder so many of us suffer so much pain, and struggle to find identity, when human maturity has been defined only in terms of those capacities located in the left hemisphere of our brains, and growing up has been identified with the possession of cognitive skills and the loss of imagination. Part of this can be attributed to the historical dominance of male ways of doing things, and the rising interest in story-telling today may be, in part, motivated by a search for feminine values in a culture formed by patriarchal values. Whatever the reasons, we do ourselves psychological damage, and deny significant aspects of the gospel, when we lose sight of the wholeness for which we are created. It is the rediscovery of imagination as a God-given gift that will help to restore us: 'The imagination enables us to live in multi-leveled, multi-colored truth, and to receive the truth which is pervaded by mist and mystery. It is also the human power that opens us to possibility and promise, the not-yet of the future.'[25]

■ It is incredibly easy for stories to cross cultural boundaries. This too is one of the pressing social needs of today, for though we pay lip service to the value of learning from other cultures than our own, we still struggle with it, corporately if not as individuals. Racial integration was a problem even in Jesus' day, and he used stories to address this with great effect (e.g. the Good Samaritan, Luke 10:29–37). Listening to one another's stories is a key to social transformation. That was one of the secrets of Dr Martin Luther King Jr, who not only attacked racism as a philosophical position, but used his speeches as an opportunity for telling the story of what it felt like to be African and American in the 1960s. More than anything else, it was learning – often for the first time – what it was really like for his children and their friends that swayed the hearts and minds of middle-of-the-road white Americans to join his crusade for civic equality. If more of us knew how to use story in this way, we could probably address many of today's more intransigent social debates more effectively than we are doing. For example, if issues about sexual orientation were addressed less as abstract concerns about physiology or human rights, and more through the sharing of personal stories by both gay and heterosexual people, it would be likely to bring a different dimension to bear on the discussion of such matters. I suspect that if churches could learn how to conduct an audit of their life not so much through the application of analytical principles copied from the social sciences or business management, but by listening to the stories of different people both in their own faith community and in the wider local context, they might make more progress in evangelism than most of us are capable of doing right now. The same will be true for those church leaders who struggle with knowing how to challenge their people to change. Unless we listen to all the varied stories of those people, and place them alongside the story of the church itself, we will find that constructive change evades us, for changing the culture of a church is actually an exercise in changing its story, and we need to know what it is – and empathize with its nuances – before we can do that.

■ This takes us to the final point highlighted by Armerding, that stories invite participation. I would want to change that slightly to read 'transformational participation'. This is a fundamental underlying principle of the biblical pattern of the handing-on of traditions, where the story of what is past is not a collection of abstract facts – still less dead historical memories – but something living and lively which can illuminate and reshape the story which is unfolding in the present. In this connection, stories only become truly life-changing when they are shared with others, and here Jesus provides us with a striking example of someone who knew the power of doing that. In one of my previous books, I highlighted the story of Jesus and the woman at the well (John 4:7–42) as a significant paradigm for the evangelistic task,[26] and the underlying dynamic of everything that takes place in that episode is determined by the fact that Jesus, first of all, listened to the woman's story as an indispensable precondition for gaining permission to share his own story – and it was from within the intricate interweaving of the two that he was then able to empower her to initiate change in her lifestyle in a way that was affirming and liberating as well as challenging. We shall return to the significance of this in relation to story and the evangelistic task shortly.

First, however, we need to think through some of the theological implications of all this.

Three Connecting Stories

In effect, there are three stories running alongside one another in the Christian world view. In an earlier book, I identified them respectively as God's story, Bible stories, and personal stories,[27] and I will retain that terminology here, partly to maintain continuity with that previous discussion, but also because I can think of no better way of describing them. By God's story, I mean something like what has traditionally been thought of as 'natural theology', which is not so very much different from what Matthew Fox calls 'creation-centered spirituality', namely the notion that this is God's world, and therefore

God is at work in it, not only on a cosmic scale but also in relation to the lives of individuals and communities. In his extensive study of how people come to faith, John Finney identified a small but significant cohort of people who begin to explore spiritual meaning in life for no other reason than that they have an experience of some kind which comes from beyond and outside themselves, drawing their attention to some other dimension of existence.[28] Even as I have been writing this book (this chapter!) I received a totally unexpected letter from a woman I had never met, in her mid-thirties, who told me that she had started reading some of my books because, as a secularist (in the sense defined in chapter 4) she had received healing for a particular complaint, and the healing (which was contrary to the expectations of medical science) could only have come from a supernatural source outside of herself. Since she did not believe in such things, she obviously had a major problem on her hands, but having tested it all as rigorously as she knew how (she is a university professor in England, so she had no shortage of ideas), she concluded that only one explanation was possible: there must be a God, and that God, for unknown reasons, was benevolently involved in her life. Now, as a further step in her spiritual journey, she was exploring Christian beliefs in an effort to help her make sense out of what had taken place. I am finding that this kind of experience, of God being at work in ways that, though specific, are not related to any particular context of either Christian revelation or Christian teaching, is increasingly spoken of today. I mentioned my encounter with David on a Californian beach in a previous chapter, and I could easily multiply examples of such occurrences. There is no way of knowing whether more of this is going on now than would have been the case twenty years ago, or whether it is just that the prevalence of these themes in so many movies and TV shows is alerting us to the possibility of such experiences – or whether we just speak more easily of such things than we once did. Perhaps a combination of all three is at work here, for Finney's researches showed that the discovery of God at work was linked for many people to events such as childbirth, while the even more extensive (though less focused) research reported by David Hay has provided 'convincing evidence that [religious experience] is widespread and that, in a word, it is normal' – though it will surprise no one who has read this far that he continues with the observation that 'Unfortunately, this religious "empiricism" tends to be damaged, even crushed, by a catastrophic loss of morale because of a widespread taboo concerning religion, arising from

Enlightenment ways of thinking.'[29] In relation to Christian evangelism, this is likely to be an increasingly significant area of concern, not least because it is one topic that transcends some of the boundaries between the various groups of people I identified in chapter 4, and is virtually the only way in which totally secular people ever seem to become interested in matters of faith. Paradoxically, it is the one area where I find Christians regularly begin to feel uneasy. I can only imagine that this is because, for the most part, we too have bought into the Enlightenment paradigm rather uncritically, for there is no shortage of such material either in the Bible or Christian history. What we call all this – whether it is supernatural, spiritual, mystical, numinous, transcendent, or whatever – seems less important than that we recognize its reality. But we need to realize that the one thing we cannot do is control it or produce it to order, which is one reason why I would distinguish the kind of divine activity I have mentioned here from what goes on when churches hold healing services or engage in the exercise of charismatic gifts such as glossolalia. If God is truly at work in our world, then the most effective evangelism will take place when we recognize what God is already doing, and place ourselves alongside that, rather than imagining that God can only work in ways that we might either orchestrate or approve of.

The second kind of story that is integral to the Christian world view consists of the Bible stories. The order in which I am listing these three interweaving stories is not significant: they are all, for me, of equal importance theologically, though missiologically I want to suggest that different ones will emerge as more consequential for different people in different times and places. It would easily be possible to write a complete book on the Bible as story, so what can be said here will of necessity be somewhat constrained. It should be obvious that, though the Bible is story, it is not all one story but rather consists of a multiplicity of diverse stories, some of which reveal far more of the selfishness of humans than they do of the love of God. It is not surprising therefore that, historically, it has been possible for the Bible to be used – and abused – as justification for imperialistic exploits and oppressive governments. The Bible itself contains examples of all that, and more besides. But it is only by using the texts in a fundamentalist kind of way that such interpretations can seem plausible, and I believe that when we look to what may be called the central story-line of the Bible, far from upholding it as a book of terror, it actually challenges many of the understandings that have been imposed upon it, particularly by interpreters during the dominance of the modernist paradigm. The very first page of the book of Genesis insists that all people were made 'in the image of God' (1:26–7), a concept which undermines any sense of racial superiority of one group over another, while another key text explains the promise to Abraham and Sarah as being for the blessing of 'all the families of the earth' (Genesis 12:2–3). Though xenophobia surfaced more than once in the history of ancient Israel and – because the Old Testament is a national archive, is documented in its pages – there were always dissenting voices, whether they be the universalism found in post-exilic writers such as Second Isaiah, Jonah or Ruth, or earlier prophets such as Hosea (who in 1:4 denounced what was applauded in 2 Kings 9:17–37) or Amos (1:3–2:8). While it would be impossible to deny that biblical narratives have sometimes been pressed into service in the formulation of expansionist policies, they have only functioned in that way in a context whose essential characteristics were formed by other influences, namely the increasing secularization of Western culture, not to mention human sinfulness.

In using the Bible stories we need to be aware of all these issues, while recognizing that there is a centre to the narrative, and that is provided by the prophetic critique of human behaviour found in the Hebrew Scriptures, and the teaching and example of Jesus contained in the New Testament Gospels. The right question to ask of the Bible stories is therefore not, 'What am I to do?' (for that could be answered in different ways, depending on which story we choose), but rather, 'Of which story do I wish to be a part?' Placing this in the context of our earlier discussion of metanarratives, the key question is going to be about appreciating what kind of metanarrative the Bible is, and properly understood I believe it actually challenges and questions the oppressive attitudes that previous generations have sought to justify on the basis of its teachings. That is why these stories are always going to be normative. Being a Christian entails placing the story of Jesus at the centre, and living on the basis of it. It is not open to us to rewrite or revise this story. But in sharing the story today, we must never forget that Jesus did not come to announce a speculative philosophy, or to communicate propositional truths about theology. His message consisted in the announcement of the possibilities opened up for humankind by the arrival of God's kingdom (which elsewhere I have characterized as 'God's way of doing things'[30]), and the invitation to follow him and thereby to enter the community of those who would self-consciously seek to do God's will. It is through the Bible stories that we enter into the definitive world of images that show us that better world for which we are all longing, and that is the fulfilment not only of the human dream, but also of the divine intention.

Finally, there are our own personal stories. Though I have chosen to illustrate what I mean by God's story by reference to the ways in which God works unexpectedly and unannounced in the lives of individuals, that is not what I mean by personal stories in this context. The stories of God at work generally burst in unexpectedly, from outside ourselves and certainly from beyond our normal expectations. Personal stories are more intentional reflections about ourselves and our life journeys. They involve the sharing of those things we have discovered to be true, and which might in turn be helpful to others as they struggle with the same issues of identity and meaning. Personal stories in this sense are therefore a shared experience, for they only become stories when other people hear them. They might easily involve our reflections on the meaning of the Bible stories as they relate to our own lives – following a pattern initiated at least as long ago as the first century, when the author of John's Gospel chose to intersperse his stories of Jesus with his own thoughts about their significance. In this sense, dialoguing about our own stories in the broader context of God's story and the Bible stories has always been central to the life of the Church. In the best sense, this is what the tradition of the community has been about, the sharing of our own experiences of life and God, as a way of encouraging one another, creating hope in one another, and in the process learning from and being corrected by one another. Moreover, the sharing of our stories in community can help us more fully to enter into the reality of the Bible stories, for though the experts do not always see the full range of possibilities, a text does not mean just anything we might like it to mean, and sharing with others is a key way of sorting out what is worthwhile and what is unhelpful. In a world where so many people's individual stories seem to be fragmented and meaningless, the open and honest sharing of personal experiences is the one thing above all others that will hold out the possibility of hope and renewal to those whose lives are broken. In that connection, we do well to remember that the God of the Bible is not the immutable God of the philosophers, but a suffering God whose power is shown supremely through a story of weakness and vulnerability. We will encourage one another more effectively when we are honest about our struggles than when we pretend we have it all together. If the personal stories of Christians are going to help others on the spiritual journey, it will not be because our stories are different, but precisely because they are no different. Our lives are just as broken, fragmented and dislocated – but the really good news is that by connecting our personal stories with God's bigger story, and the Bible stories, we can be empowered in the struggle to find direction, meaning and purpose.

Stories and Truth

Some readers will no doubt be wanting to ask which one of these three stories is normative. I want to answer that, in their different ways, all three are. Without any one of them we would not have an adequate understanding of Christian spirituality. In terms of our mission, however, I suspect that different types of story will be more important to some people than to others, and maybe different types of story have been more important at different historical periods. There is no doubt that listening to and sharing stories can play a central part in the renewal of our worship and witness today. Learning about other people's stories will be the first step in inviting them to follow Jesus. One of the problems of Christendom was that we assumed everyone else shared our story, and Christians still easily make the same mistake. That is both a consequence of and a contributing factor to the way our churches are able to attract only one kind of person. People naturally gravitate toward those communities where they can recognize themselves and their own concerns through the shared stories and symbol systems which are determinative of the group's life. Of course, it is impossible for us to hear every single person's story, but we can still learn the shared stories of particular groups within our culture, such as those identified in chapter 4, or indeed other groupings that may be age determined or ethnically or gender related. When people can recognize themselves in the kind of stories that bother us, they will be attracted. Though there will be some who might still be attracted by abstract propositional truth claims, they are now in a clear minority. That is not to say that, in the overall scheme of things, truth claims are unimportant to the Christian, as I hope I have made clear in my comment on the Bible stories. But for most people they will not be an entry point into the life of discipleship. Most people will be drawn to the church because they feel it is a place where they can comfortably belong, because it is a good 'fit' for their concerns. While personal stories might therefore be the door through which they enter the space that is the community of Christ's people, once they begin to explore that space in the company of others, they will however discover that there is more to it than that – not only Bible stories and God's story, but other spiritual riches that refuse to be categorized in this way. It is something like this that Clark Pinnock is getting at when he observes that, because there are so many different ways of telling the greatest story of all, there will also be 'many paths of sound doctrine, not just one path.'[31]

Before we leave this topic, I want briefly to relate it to the cultural change that is taking place in Western society. Though one central feature of post-modernity consists of a move from a word-based to an image-based culture, like most generalizations this one is only a partial reflection of a far more complex reality. One of the biggest revolutions of the twentieth century was also one of the last, the emergence of the Internet and the World Wide Web, and most commentators are agreed that it has only just begun to exert an influence on the way we communicate. The most surprising feature about it is that, though it does indeed have lots of pictures, it is intrinsically text-driven. Search engines look for keywords, not key images, and the most widely used feature of all, e-mail, is entirely word based. Whereas a generation ago people were abandoning the written word as a means of daily communication with friends and colleagues, preferring to use the telephone instead as a more 'immediate' medium, we are now returning in droves to our keyboards for some of the most intimate exchanges of our lives. What seems to be progressive and technologically futuristic is actually taking us back to a way of conversing that belongs to the sort of oral culture that many people thought had disappeared long ago. For though e-mail uses words, it does not produce literature. We do not write letters on e-mail; we have conversations. If a friend sends us a query, we do not craft a response with the precision we might otherwise have invested in a hard copy that would be sent through the mail; we reply in the same terms as we would use if we were in the same room, shouting a reply over our shoulder. In this sense, we are reverting to many of the characteristics of an oral culture. Much of the information circulating on the web takes the form of story, whether it be urban myths, or the sharing by individuals of information about themselves on personal web sites. We can see the same process happening in other contemporary media, with the popularity of rap and country music (both devices for telling stories), not to mention the incredible attraction of

TV soap operas for audiences all over the world. The differences between oral and literary cultures have been well documented by Walter Ong, though he assumed that the connection between the two was to be understood developmentally, in the sense that orality would inevitably be superseded by literacy, and therefore those literate cultures where orality still survived were in some ways anomalous.[32] More recent developments in communication suggest that this is too simplistic a way of looking at it, for though the majority of people in contemporary Western societies are literate, in the sense of being able to read and write, growing numbers of us prefer to live in ways that are functionally illiterate, valuing oral and visual stories and relationships more highly than the written word.

Many of those people whom I characterized as traditionalists in chapter 4 have always been oral people at heart, as also have the desperate poor. Increasingly, however, other groups are adopting that way of dealing with meaning, at least in those parts of their lives over which they have control (their working lives usually still being dominated by literate practices). Those I have described as hedonists express themselves in this way, for what is the culture of a rave, if not an oral culture in this technical sense? The same is true for many of the spiritual searchers, who are probably more convinced than most that our love affair with words and rationality has harmed our potential for personal fulfilment. Taking this seriously will have significant consequences for the Church and its message. For people operating in this kind of context tend not to learn things by studying them (at least, not if study is defined in a logical, analytical, conceptual sort of way), but by doing them – or, more exactly, by being shown how to do them. Mentoring will often be a more effective way of enabling such people to see the point of discipleship, and this can take place in a variety of contexts. For example, most church leaders will have noticed the way that many people are quite happy to be part of what might be considered the 'fringe' life of the church by volunteering to do things, whether it be painting and decorating, coaching a sports team, running a parent and toddler group, or any number of other activities – but these same people will often not come to a service. The difference is that the one is focused around doing, whereas the other is dominated by more abstract rationality. I wonder what church might be like if, instead of starting by teaching people about the faith and then asking them how they might work it out in practice, we operated the other way round. Doing that would create a more realistic context in which to share stories – our own and the Bible stories – for what is more natural when looking after children, or working together on some project, than for us to both listen to and talk with those who are our companions? That is the context in which we can most easily share one another's burdens, and explore how faith might inspire and inform daily life. It is also, interestingly, a context which the sociologist Emile Durkheim identified as the matrix out of which interpersonal bonding is most likely to grow.[33] Telling stories, in whatever way and through whatever medium it is done, opens up new spaces in which people can feel safe (for their stories are as important as everyone else's), and in a Christian context that should be a safe space in which faith can be nurtured, as those who have found new direction through following Jesus introduce others to the hope that is within them (1 Peter 3:15), and meeting with one another becomes a meeting with God. Biblical faith is intrinsically relational, not exclusively propositional, and telling stories will always be a key way of exploring the meaning of that.

Linking all this back to the image of McDonaldization explored in earlier chapters, it is worth noting that it is the power of the story that has ensured not only the survival, but the growing prosperity of the fast-food business. Given all the negative characteristics identified by Ritzer and others who have written on the theme, it is surprising that anybody at all would wish to support such establishments. Not only is the 'iron cage' of efficiency, calculability, predictability and control an unattractive vision of life, but according to some health experts the food itself is neither nutritious nor life-enhancing. But the way in which fast-food restaurants are promoted and advertised generally focuses not so much on the actual food, as on the experience to be gained by patronizing them – for example, by freeing up time for harassed parents to be able to spend quality time with their children, while not needing to prepare meals for them or clearing up afterwards. Discussion of the subject among sociologists routinely highlights the image of eating hamburgers as 'party time . . . nostalgia time . . . community time . . . and friendship time',[34] while one commentator on the phenomenon has gone so far as to claim that 'McDonald's success is due to their creation of a narrative that is not necessarily true but rather provides us with a sense of personal identity, a sense of community life, a basis for conduct, and explanations of that which cannot be known'[35] – an opinion reinforced by the claim of Deena and Michael A. Weinstein, that McDonald's overtly evokes religious themes with 'the Golden Arches as a symbol of consumer heaven where Ronald McDonald reigns as demi-god'.[36] Christians have a narrative which, in its pristine form, claims to be able to deliver all these things – and more – in a uniquely satisfying form. Yet all too often, the narrative that we share with the public is not this great and wondrous story, but a sad litany of personal and community dysfunction that is unlikely ever to be attractive to anyone. Not only have we unthinkingly accepted the negative aspects of McDonaldization, but if it really is true that people are more likely to discover identity, community, morality and mystery in a restaurant than they are in the church, there must be something quite fundamentally flawed in our present expressions of church that is actually preventing people from either perceiving or experiencing some of the key promises of the gospel.

8 DREAMING THE CHURCH OF THE FUTURE

'Is the Church dying or living?' That was the question put to me recently at a seminar on the renewal of spirituality in the Church. I have to admit that, of all the questions I might have anticipated, that was not one of them. In fact, I found myself struggling to know how best to answer it. As I have emphasized several times in this book, it seems to me to be a singularly pointless exercise for us to look for scapegoats among previous generations of Christian leaders. We cannot rewrite the past, and we should be grateful for the contributions of those who have gone before us, taking heart from those things that they got right, but not afraid to learn from their mistakes. It is easy enough to see what some of those mistakes were, not least in relation to the culture of modernity. Though some sections of the Church undoubtedly failed to appreciate the difference between gospel values and secular values, it was not intrinsically misguided for Christians to engage with the rationalist-materialist culture of that era, and to seek to contextualize the gospel within that frame of reference. Most of our present difficulties have been created by the fact that Christians appear to have realized later than almost everyone else that the cultural outlook was changing, and we have therefore not played as full a part as we might have done in helping to shape the emerging culture. However post-modernity is to be defined, everyone can see that the challenges facing the Church today are quite different from what they were even as little as five or ten years ago. The challenge to us – as it has been to every previous generation – will be how to contextualize the Christian faith relevantly in ways that will reflect the values of the gospel.

So is the Church living or dying? There is a theological answer to that, which is far from irrelevant to our concerns here: the Church will only live insofar as it is prepared continually to die in order to experience afresh the resurrection power of the Holy Spirit (John 12:24). Coincidentally, the sociological answer also contains within it the same implied conclusion. For if my application of the

McDonaldization thesis to the Church has any plausibility at all, then it must be obvious that the Church simply cannot expect to continue to survive for long into the twenty-first century in its present form. There will always be those who will experience the Church's current practices and procedures as the 'velvet cage', but for all the reasons identified by Ritzer they are likely to be a diminishing group within Western culture. Merely doing more of the same will not be the way that the gospel will be communicated effectively to those increasing millions who are searching for something that will make life more tolerable and hold out the prospect of personal fulfilment. Notwithstanding its undoubted attractions, at the end of the day we know that consumerism doesn't satisfy. A McDonaldized existence is less than fully human – which may be one reason why a McDonaldized form of Church has managed to produce so many nominal believers. Though pre-packaged consumerist spiritualities (both Christian and others) may appear to work for a time, they will not ultimately quench the spiritual thirst of the human spirit any more than the non-stop consumption of food or household goods can meet the fundamental needs of those who are struggling to make sense of the personal emptiness that can be induced by a commercialized commodity culture.

Even though it will frustrate some of my readers, I have resisted the temptation to provide anything like a blueprint for the Church of the future. I do have a pretty clear idea of what a Church for post-modern people could look like – and it is a Church that I think would be as open and welcoming to the desperate poor as to the spiritual searchers and the other groups I have enumerated. But my picture is prescribed by the circumstances in which I find myself, and I simply invite you, the reader, to reflect on the stories and ideas I have shared here, and ask yourself what the church might now need to look like in the neighbourhood where you have been called to be salt and light (Matthew 5:13–16). I do however want to summarize some of the conclusions of my argument in relation to two key areas of church life: worship and mission. But before that, there are a few general comments that will be worth making in relationship to Christian attitudes in the context of post-modernity. One of the unexpected bonuses of the upheavals now taking place in Western culture is to be found in the fact that increasing numbers of people are constantly searching for 'something else', in the seemingly endless quest to identify that elusive magical ingredient which will give added value to their lives. As was suggested in a previous chapter, different groups are expressing this concern in their own ways. Some are genuinely dissatisfied with life as they experience it, and concerned that there seems to be a vacuum at the centre, with no secure place to seek for guidance about values and meaning. Others are influenced by peer pressure, exploring spirituality for no reason more profound than that the circles in which they move consider it to be 'cool' to do so, and they want to make sure they are not left behind by the culture. Others are curious about the unknown, simply because we now know that it exists, and science has admitted it no longer believes it can supply all the answers. One of the consequences of the McDonaldized culture in which this search is taking place is that, for the most part, people are less likely to be concerned about the discovery of universal spiritual truths than they are about following what can seem to be just the latest spiritual fads. It is not hard to understand why some Christians find themselves cynical about the reality or sincerity of all this, but at this point in time anything that looks like cultural elitism is not going to offer a solution, and might even increase the gap that already exists between church culture and the wider world. The fact that so many people are exploring spirituality does not mean they are satisfied with what they have found, or that they will stop searching. Douglas Coupland puts into words what many feel but are unable to articulate for themselves, especially among the spiritual searchers whom I have identified as the key group to which the Church ought to be able to relate most readily: 'I must remind myself we are living creatures – we have religious impulses – we *must* – and yet into what cracks do these impulses flow in a world without religion? It is something I think about every day. Sometimes I think it is the only thing I should be thinking about.'[1]

Christians can easily read that sort of statement and conclude that they can comfortably continue to do business as usual, because if serious people start to think about religion, sooner or later that will inevitably lead them into meaningful dialogue with the Church. But that conclusion does not necessarily follow, not least because 'thinking' about religion for today's people does not generally imply rational reflection on theological propositions. It is more likely to involve personal wrestling with the kind of question that I raised for myself in the first chapter, that is, 'how can we make sense of the Church?' While truth claims are bound to feature eventually in any effort to address that question, for the vast majority of people such concerns will rarely form their initial entry point into the debate.

Community and Mystery

So what will the entry points be? Back in the mid-1990s, some of his political opponents were mystified that US president Bill Clinton could command such a high level of support among the voters, when he had apparently made so many mistakes in his personal as well as his professional life. His response came to be regarded as a sort of iconic representation of his entire presidency: 'It's the economy, stupid!' Because he had dealt effectively with the big issues that mattered most to people – job security and the expectation of financial growth – other incongruities in his performance could be overlooked and criticized in a benevolent rather than a destructive way. I think the same thing is true of the Church today. People can see that Christians have their problems, they can appreciate how and why otherwise honourable people can sometimes be forced into compromising positions that can look like hypocrisy – and they can accommodate these, because that is what life is like. If we had it all together we would be less than human. But there are two aspects that will be absolutely central if the Church is to regain spiritual credibility among today's people. We can take Clinton's phrase, and replace 'the economy' with 'community and mystery'. Interestingly, these are the very matters that Paul Tillich highlighted more than fifty years ago as the aspects of Protestantism that he believed would become increasingly problematic in the post-war culture that he saw emerging even then.[2]

Though not everyone will necessarily admit to it, or even know how to articulate it, people in all the groups identified in chapter 4 are desperately searching for a place where they can belong and be valued. In a world of dysfunctional relationships, in which people are hurting and constantly being put down, either by other individuals or by the more impersonal operations of the system in general, for the majority the entry point to anything that might be regarded as 'fullness of life' (John 10:10) will begin and end when they find a safe space where they can be themselves and be affirmed and lifted up in the struggle to be human. This should not be difficult for Christians: it is, in effect, the message of the very first page of the Bible, that humankind – in all its diversity – is made in the image of God (Genesis 1:26–7). The mention of God in this connection highlights another key element of the historic Christian faith, namely that people find their true fulfilment not only as they relate to one another, but as they relate to God through one another. Indeed, the ways in which we do so are supposed to be reflective of those relationships which are at the centre of God's own being. Theologically, one might say that the traditional doctrine of the Trinity provides a model for both community and mystery within the Church – though that is not the way that those who are as yet not Christians will express it. They are going to be far more likely to judge the authenticity of the Church by experiencing the community and the mystery first, and then reflecting on what they have experienced. In missiological terms, a key theological question will then be: what do people experience when they engage with the Church? To put it in another way, does the Church have a problem with its semiology, or sign symbols? Has the image evoked by mention of 'Church' – depending, as it does, on the way ordinary people experience it in their regular life-world – somehow become detached from the foundational values-world of Christian faith? Or, in a more homely image, have we failed to practise what we preach? One of the major reasons for the success of McDonald's restaurants has been the corporation's ability to promote a wholesome image of its own purposes: 'The McDonald's Golden Arches have themselves become eloquent cultural icons which not only physically locate the outlet but iconically summarize the McDonald's promise – to provide a sense of security and inclusiveness, and to be included in the McDonald's family.'[3] Christians would not be the only ones to question this somewhat pretentious claim – for can anything as ephemeral as a fast-food restaurant (even one of impeccable quality) possibly provide meaningful 'security and inclusiveness'? But that is not the point. Instead, we need to ask ourselves what kind of images are conjured up by the Church? Can we claim with any plausibility to be a locus for meaningful community and mysterious spirituality – even though both of those are central values of the gospel? In my book *Faith in a Changing Culture*, I included some discussion of two contrasting models of church. The first was what I called the traditional model, which among other things is characterized by a concern for boundaries and controls whose sole purpose is to limit access to only certain kinds of people. The other, which I suggested would be a more appropriate expression of some central values of the Christian faith, was what I called the stakeholder model, in which there could and would be a place for diverse types of people, who might be at different stages in their journey of faith, but who would be bound together by their commitment to one another and to the reality of the spiritual search, rather than by inherited definitions of institutional membership.[4] Those who have found this differentiation helpful – and, judging from the size of my postbag, there have been very many of them – now need to be prepared to do something about it, and actively engage in the creation of stakeholder churches which will be welcoming and open places for all who are serious about exploring the reality that is God – who, we should never forget, is greater than any or all of us, and therefore the idea that we somehow have a monopoly on God, or that God can do nothing in the world without our aid, is certainly inadequate and might also be blasphemous.

We easily describe the church as a 'community of faith', but all too often community is the one thing that people fail to find among us. I have referred to the novels of Douglas Coupland at many points throughout this book, and for Christians who are serious about understanding the nature of the spiritual search among younger people in particular, they are an invaluable resource. The key theme to which he repeatedly and insistently returns is the centrality of the happiness that can be created by the interactions between friends who like one another, and the importance of a safe and open space in which meaningful relationships with others can blossom. After much discussion of the state of the world and the meaning of life, one character affirms: 'All I care about is that we're still together as friends'.[5] In the context of that kind of community, individuals learn how to make decisions in partnership with other people, they discover how to receive and to give support, and in the process of doing so they end up by not only finding their own identity but also exploring the grand meaning of things ('metanarratives'). Alongside this vision, of course, Coupland repeatedly highlights how difficult it is to find such a space or such people in today's fragmented world. In *Shampoo Planet*, someone comments that all too often life amounts to 'too many experiences but no relationships'[6] – yet the desire for meaningful community is so powerful that at the end of the day any kind of relationship is going to be better than nothing: 'People without lives like to hang out with other people who don't have lives. Thus they form lives.'[7]

This concern to find personal identity not in an isolated individualistic existence, but through belonging to groups of like-minded people, can be documented all over the world today. Such communities are increasingly assuming the role once occupied by relational ties within the family, as more and more people find themselves cast adrift through the breakdown of meaningful community in their homes. The ideal modernist vision was for us to be separated autonomous individuals, what Tillich memorably described as 'the atomistic solitude of the individual within the mass'[8] – but everywhere we look today, people are desperate to reverse that trend and insist that we do not need to face the discontinuities of life alone, but can – and should – do it with the support of others. Feminist thinking has served to highlight much of this, though it hardly needed an extensive philosophical undergirding to make the point, for in everyday life women (unlike men) have always sought to be connected with others in networks of friendship and mutual support. In the context of today's Church, all these factors can provide an atmosphere within which the impetus towards active community-building can flourish.[9]

None of this is at all alien to the historic Christian tradition. On the contrary, it is nothing more than a restatement of the central teaching of the Christian Scriptures. But of course the Church is not like that. As a community, many people find us unreceptive to any but our own type, and unduly critical and dismissive of the perceptions and experience of others. Audre Lorde's frequently repeated dictum is relevant to the Church here, as she reminds us that 'The master's tools will never dismantle the master's house'.[10] If church is to become widely perceived as a locus of community and mystery, we will be unlikely to accomplish it merely by moving the things we already have and do into different configurations. We will need to apply ourselves to the creation of different kinds of places to inhabit (both literal and metaphorical), that will be built using different tools, and brought to birth by the intermingling of many different stories of faith and hope. An intrinsic part of this will be a conscious engagement with the perception held by many that – despite our claims to the contrary – it can be hard for them to discern anything that they can easily recognize as the presence of God in what we are doing. One of the consequences of the Enlightenment was the privatization of religious belief, and Weber himself highlighted the fact that an overdependence on rationalized ways of being would inevitably lead to the demystifying of the world.[11] In the light of what we have already noted about the McDonaldized state of the Church, it need not surprise us to discover that a sense of mystery has been one of the casualties of this process. But when the Church actually accepts this outcome, and the spirituality of its members becomes just one preference among many about how best to spend one's leisure time, then it goes without saying that something significant has been lost. For the point of spirituality is the need to feel a part of something greater and more mysterious than ourselves, and the widespread search for these missing elements in today's culture provides yet more evidence for Ritzer's view that significant numbers of people are wanting to break free of the 'iron cage' of McDonaldization. In terms of the historic Christian faith, this experience of dislocation and spiritual search ought to be the one place where Christian values and beliefs can most naturally intersect with and engage today's culture. Instead of worrying about how to 'update' our music, or the clothes worn by clergy, should we not be examining some rather more central matters of the faith? After all, Jesus' charisma derived not from trivialities of that sort, but from the simplicity and clarity of his message. He just told the truth, was not embarrassed to speak about God in simple language that even a child could understand, and welcomed to his side anyone with even the vaguest interest in what he was about.

The mention of Jesus highlights another respect in which the Church's semiology is often confused and uncertain. No doubt one of the criticisms that will be made of my argument in this book is that, for some, I have probably seemed to place an undue emphasis on the arts, and in particular on those arts that could be described as embodied. For generations, Christians have been uneasy about the human body in the context of spirituality. But I have included such an emphasis not out of any desire to be trendy or 'cool', but because it is actually a core theological belief of the Christian faith. The incarnation is absolutely central, and without it none of the rest of Christian belief would make any sense at all. But where are the sign symbols of incarnation in today's Church? One evidence is easy to identify, and undoubtedly constitutes one of the jewels in the otherwise tarnished crown of the contemporary Church – and that is in the magnificent achievements of Christians in seeking to alleviate the burden of human suffering and poverty all around the world. Without the deeply incarnational ministries of organizations such as Christian Aid in Britain, or World Vision in the USA – not to mention multitudes of unknown heroes who have given themselves unreservedly to improve the lot of others – humankind would be immeasurably poorer today. Those whom I have categorized as spiritual searchers generally express great admiration for that aspect of incarnational ministry. But they also remind us that this is not the only way in which Christian faith could or should reflect incarnational values. There are other key aspects of Christian practice that we can profitably revisit with the same question in mind. For example, in what sense could what we do in worship be characterized as incarnational? And what is distinctive about our methods and models of sharing the spiritual journey with others that would qualify them to be described by that same adjective? Tex Sample has correctly identified the importance of the doctrine of incarnation (to which I would also add the doctrine of creation) as a central issue for the Church's relationship to today's culture: 'When so-called "traditional" churches are out of touch with the people who live around them, the problem is not that they are irrelevant, but that they are not Incarnational.'[12]

Words and Images for Worship

I have made no secret of the fact that I think the renewal of worship is likely to be fundamental to any effective engagement with most of these questions. It is what the Church most characteristically does, and (though they rarely use the actual term itself), meaningful worship is what very many people today are looking for. In a previous book, I ventured to offer a definition of worship as 'All that we are, responding to all that God is',[13] and astute readers will instantly recognize that a definition like that is the exact opposite of the McDonaldization process. It implies that, far from there being only one way to worship appropriately, there will be many different styles that can authentically reflect the nature of God, and highlight the core elements of Christian faith. Worship with integrity will assume a multiplicity of forms, and those things which I have highlighted in previous chapters in the course of surveying some of the biblical resources that may help us to explore this multifaceted nature of true worship are quite literally the tip of a very large iceberg. They are certainly nothing like exhaustive, and I have singled them out for particular mention here not because I believe that either individually or together they constitute the whole of what worship is about, but because they point to some aspects that have been forgotten or ignored, and to which we ought now to pay particularly careful attention in the light of the new emerging culture.

Ironically, though, the one area of contemporary church life in which there is more acrimony than almost any other is connected with worship. I have already referred to the so-called 'worship wars' that seem to have broken out all over the Church as the need to examine what we now do (with a view to changing it) has stirred up intense and acrimonious passions. The arguments often look as if they are about music – those who like contemporary styles *versus* those whose preference is for classical composers – but the issue is much broader than that, and really focuses on the shift from the kind of word-based culture typified by modernity to the more obviously image-based culture now emerging under the guise of post-modernity. The change from one to the other is not, in the most absolute sense, quite as stark and undifferentiated as that statement perhaps implies, and one of the ironies of our ostensibly image-oriented culture is that there is more print today than at any previous time in history, and even new technologies such as the World Wide Web are predominantly word-based. But as a general trend, the move from word to image is unmistakable, and it has wide-ranging implications not only for worship, but for the whole of Christian belief and practice. What is now happening in this cultural shift can be compared to what took place with the invention of the printing press, something which, if it did not exactly spark off the Protestant Reformation, certainly became an incredibly powerful tool of mass communication in the hands of the Reformers and their successors. Regrettably, today's Christians have not had anything like the same level of foresight to enable them to grasp hold of the new opportunities now available. Some are simply unaware of the magnitude of the cultural change that is taking place, and are 'clergy and laity committed to literate culture who simply don't see what all the commotion is about . . . and who wonder why the church can't continue to do what it has done all along.'[14] Others can see what is going on, and what it means, and take refuge in the opinions of people like Neil Postman, who imagines that what he regards as the displacement of the rational by the visual will inexorably lead to the pathological disintegration of civilized society.[15] When coupled with a simplistic exegesis of the Bible, which seems to be able to demonstrate that anything to do with art (and therefore anything visual or tactile) is somehow theologically unacceptable, it is not difficult to see the attraction of such a viewpoint to many Christians. But a more subtle approach to these issues will show us the real source of such misgivings. Paradoxically, the development of writing itself created the same sense of dismay, and claims of superficiality were commonplace among those who preferred oral methods of communication. Plato, for example, criticized the rise of literacy in terms that could have been written yesterday: 'This invention will produce forgetfulness in the souls of those who have learned it . . . They will not need to exercise their memories, being able to rely on what is written.'[16] He too was suspicious of art, believing that words were somehow more profound than images, and criticized artists for misleading 'children and fools' by replacing 'truth' or 'real things' with 'the imitation of appearance'.[17] It is easy to complain that people are thinking less today, but that is not an accurate assessment of the situation: what we need to realize is that we are actually now thinking differently. Mitchell Stevens puts his finger on what is going on with his observation that 'The word's distress causes most *educated* people distress.'[18] So far as the Church is concerned, we need to wake up to what this change means. For just as literacy made possible (in some senses, even produced) abstract, cognitive analytical ways of reflection, so the increasing dominance of image is actually creating different ways of regarding reality. The medium really is the message, and the means we use to express our thoughts have the effect of shaping, and even changing, the thoughts themselves. This seems to me to be absolutely central to any talk about mission and worship in today's Church, for while the Church continues to operate in a literary format the majority of people are now operating within a visual format, and those whose brains operate in the one will not necessarily understand those who prefer to work with the other. Connecting them is like trying to load a single computer with two incompatible operating systems: it doesn't work. Even as I have written that last sentence, I realize that some readers will have no idea what I'm talking about because they still manage to live as if computers had never been invented – and that in itself is yet another evidence of how detached some Christians have become from the wider culture, especially as it is experienced and lived by younger people.

Many of the Church's problems over how to contextualize worship in this new situation arise from the way in which we have allowed literate culture to be absolutized as if it was the only way of doing things. This assumption extends not only to words themselves, but also to the sort of words that are regarded as appropriate, and thence to particular styles of music. In a world of cultural ferment and experimentation, the Church often appears to be hopelessly committed to what is in reality a McDonaldized view of what is and is not acceptable in worship, though it does not always appear that way because in this instance the McDonaldization process is not generally centred on simplistic marketable commodities but on an essentially élitist approach which is over-dependent on the kind of literate discourse traditionally embraced by the educated upper middle-classes – and that, by definition, is something that educated people who think about such issues are likely to be either unable or unwilling to notice, because to do so would automatically challenge their own social dominance.[19] In a fascinating discussion of some of the practicalities of this, Marva Dawn eloquently pinpoints the predicament in which many church people find themselves. In her book *A Royal Waste of Time*, she launches into a vigorous attack on a reviewer of one of her previous books, in which she had used the imagery of food to describe worship, making her dislike of what she called 'Burger King worship' abundantly plain. The reviewer had questioned her proposals for the renewal of worship, on the basis that the majority of people would not share her preference for the spiritual equivalent of 'a fancy French restaurant', but would actually want to choose the populist 'Burger King' version instead, because 'in a given week it feeds a lot more people, and the food meets the needs.'[20] In response, she reasonably asks whether worship should always be 'easy to digest' – a sentiment that would certainly resonate with those I have called spiritual searchers, who seem prepared to invest enormous amounts of time and effort into learning a whole new way of being in order to read books such as *The Celestine Prophecy* or *A Course in Miracles*. Moreover, in identifying pre-packaged worship with what I have labelled McDonaldization, she asks a fairly obvious question: 'Will we learn diversity at Burger King?'[21] So far, so good. But the problem is that she fails absolutely to realize that what she recommends as an alternative offers at least as little diversity as what she so vehemently decries. The only difference is that her choice in McDonaldized worship arises not out of popular culture, but from the classic preferences of Western intellectual discourse. In this world, 'culture' is not about how people live their lives on a daily basis, but becomes something to be 'read', as if it was some kind of text whose deepest meaning is to be found not in what people think they are doing, but in what literate élites consider to be meaningful because it is possible to turn it into a collection of rational abstractions, analysed by those who have been trained in the skills of having ideas about ideas. The narrowness of this type of reality is every bit as McDonaldized as the sort of pre-packaged (for which read 'popular') music and liturgies about which Dawn is so angry (and noone who reads her writings can doubt that she truly is an incredibly angry person: 'worship wars' is definitely no exaggeration here!). Readers may think I am choosing an easy target, for Dawn certainly does write in an especially confrontational way and therefore readily invites criticism. But she also typifies a mentality that is widespread in many churches, and her work can therefore be assumed to speak for many others who, though they might not express their antipathy toward popular culture in quite such an extreme fashion, nevertheless share the same underlying opinions.

On this view of the nature of worship, anything connected to popular culture (especially anything visual or tactile) is to be rigorously opposed,[22] and Dawn does indeed come perilously close to saying that those who are unable to cope with literate culture can hardly be regarded as authentically Christian:

> If we always have to have everything presented to us visually, how can we pay attention to texts, or imagine Moses or the disciples, or contemplate the presence of God? . . . The very medium itself emphasizes feeling and amusement rather than linear, rational thought. This is especially destructive for a faith that is based on what we know about the God who transforms us through the renewal of our minds . . .[23]

Of course, things are nothing like as simple as that, and one only needs to ask what that kind of statement might imply about the capacity for faith of, for example, people with learning difficulties, or sufferers from dementia – or indeed, children – to see that the identification of spirituality with rationality raises more questions than it is supposed to solve. In addition, though, it seems to me to be significantly at odds with much of the evidence of the Bible itself, as I have sought to demonstrate in previous chapters. With a world view of that sort, the doctrines of creation and incarnation would not merely be relegated to the margins, but discarded entirely, certainly as any kind of practical models for Christian living or believing. Dawn realizes this implied contradiction, and in other passages struggles then to rehabilitate a more holistic view, insisting (for example) that worship should be 'filled with splendor . . . with symbols and other works of art, with a wide variety of musical sounds, with texts and preaching full of images and thought-provoking challenges, with silences that give inspiration free rein'[24] and that 'Christianity is not simply an intellectual assent to a set of doctrinal propositions . . .'[25] I mention Dawn's works here not so much to engage in a wide-ranging critique of them, but because I think this ambivalence is typical of where many churches find themselves in relation to worship, especially in the mainline denominations. On the one hand, they can see that what they have traditionally done no longer has the attraction it once did, even for those who are in the Church let alone those who are not – but at the same time, they are resistant to the exploration of other styles of worship that seem to be working, especially if they come from the independent or charismatic churches and use contemporary musical styles. These are then castigated by being labelled as McDonaldized in some way, which means that any changes that may be proposed turn out to be allowable only within a very narrow frame of reference, namely the kind of music and the sort of symbols with which those who hold the power in church boards and committees now feel most comfortable. So classically-oriented music and liturgies are regarded as good, sophisticated, faithful to the tradition, and spiritually enhancing, while popular music and home-grown artistic endeavour is dismissed as commercialized, simplistic, lacking in depth, and so on. Dawn is an outstanding example of this very tendency, for notwithstanding her stated dislike of predictable and pre-packaged worship of what she calls 'the Burger King variety', she then insists that '. . . I believe unremittingly that it is *utterly dangerous for churches to offer choices of worship styles . . .'*[26] If that is not a McDonaldized view of worship, then I don't know what is. The only difference is that the uniformity of one kind of culture (the classical, élitist and rational) is acceptable, even praiseworthy (and, by implication, identified with the will of God), whereas the presence of another (the populist, visual, and emotional) is not (and may easily be dismissed as the work of the devil).

Where does all this lead us? Here, I want to make just a few very simple and obvious points. One is that if the Church can only handle its own brand of élitist artistic appreciation, and inclines to adopt the Kantian position that would dismiss a more embodied form of artistic expression as 'barbarism',[27] then it deserves to be struggling to relate Christian faith to the wider culture. Peter Berger has pointed out the way in which today's spiritual search is deeply connected with the search for something that will give ordinary people a voice: 'In country after country . . . religious upsurges have a strongly populist character. Over and beyond the purely religious motives, these are movements of protest and resistance against a secular elite.'[28] Christians will want to protest that we are not a 'secular elite', but that will be unconvincing to the spiritual searchers, for they tend to see the two things as different sides of the same coin. If the Church shares the same élitist outlook, that will only serve to reinforce the prior opinion held by most searchers, that the Church is, in any case, 'unspiritual', an epithet which by definition will then be used to classify it as yet another modernist institution that has no understanding of the post-modern search for meaning and value. But the spiritual searchers are not going to be the only group who will find cultural elitism a barrier to spiritual growth. In his book *White Soul*, Tex Sample has comprehensively demonstrated how this attitude has led to the alienation of working-class people from the churches in North America, and I believe the same thing is largely true in Britain.[29] Though there is not a direct correlation between conventional definitions of 'working class' and what I have called the traditionalists, the traditionalists undoubtedly include a large proportion of blue-collar workers. Moreover, these are not the only two groups who find themselves on the cultural margins of the Church, for the hedonists do as well, and for more or less the same reasons. Nor should we ignore the potential for covert racism that is offered by this mono-cultural attitude to what is acceptable and appropriate in the Church. In the 1950s and 1960s, large numbers of immigrants from former colonies settled in what they thought was their 'Christian' homeland, only to discover that their traditional styles of worship were not welcomed by British Christians. As a result, many of them lost faith altogether, while the Afro-Caribbean community as a whole was forced to retreat into churches that it founded for itself, where worship would not be constrained by the values of white, Western middle-class tastes. I remember myself being taken as a child to visit family friends who worshipped in a church in the London suburb of Herne Hill, where many immigrants had settled, and sitting through a sermon in which the black members of the congregation were berated for everything from their appearance to their lifestyle. Though I was not yet a teenager, I thought at the time that this was an odd way for the followers of Christ to behave, and looking back just on my own narrow exposure to such attitudes, it is hard to reach any other conclusion than that the rejection of such people (whose faith was, in reality, a good deal more vibrant than that of the church leaders who rebuffed them) was one of the most outrageous examples of overt racism (sin) there has ever been in the British Christian community. All that is now a matter of regret for many, of course, and some will be embarrassed that I have even mentioned it here. But I wonder if we have really learned the lesson, for the Church continues to perpetuate exactly the same mistake in relation to other groups within the wider population. When Christians dismiss other people's ways of doing things, not only do they marginalize their tastes in music or whatever it happens to be, but they are also sending out signals to the people who like these other approaches to life, implying that they themselves are simplistic, lacking in depth, inadequate, and so on – and therefore, by implication, if they are in the

Church they will need to be controlled, improved and otherwise worked upon by those who are in charge. But who would want to join that kind of outfit – especially when those with such high opinions are doing the very same things, albeit within their own boundaries of taste? When people who prefer classical music complain about others who sing a one-line charismatic worship song twenty times, how do they justify themselves then singing a one-line Taizé chant twenty times? Speaking personally, I have no problem with either of these worship styles, but such complaints only serve to highlight the fact that the McDonaldization of worship is by no means limited to just one approach. Ironically, one of the criticisms levelled at sociologist George Ritzer is that in the development of his McDonaldization thesis he was himself motivated by regret at the replacement of an élitist high culture with the mass culture of McDonaldization, though I would suggest this is another point at which the Church's experience can help to redefine aspects of the McDonaldization thesis itself, as it demonstrates that the options are not (as Ritzer assumes) between a classical Western culture that offered freedom and the 'iron cage' of consumerism in the guise of McDonaldization, for the underlying attitudes of the Church provide strong evidence of a highly McDonaldized form of classical culture, which has itself become an 'iron cage' for many people.[30]

Worship, of all aspects of church life, ought to create a context in which people can be themselves, which is another way of saying that we need spaces where we may celebrate the way God has made us. By definition, that means there will never be any kind of universalized blueprint for relevant worship, and to try and produce one would just be another form of McDonaldization. The ways in which Christians actually celebrate their faith ought – by theological definition – always to be highly diverse. That means – of course – that there will be a space for those whom I have criticized here for being too élitist. There is nothing wrong with the classical tastes of the educated classes. But to imagine, as many do, that this is the only authentic way of being human and spiritual is to make a huge mistake. Moreover, given the cultural context of today's world, the overall trend will certainly need to be away from such genteel good taste and its accompanying literate discourse, and in favour of worship that will be embodied, and that will place the mutual sharing of stories of faith at the centre of its search for meaningful human community, not to mention its obedient commitment to the gospel.

Mission

Mission is another key area of Christian activity that cries out to be released from the influences of McDonaldization.[31] This is hardly surprising at all, for in one sense mission is the Church's equivalent of marketing, so there is a natural temptation here to turn the gospel into a pre-packaged product, if only because that is the way that many other things are promoted and sold in today's world. It is also of course a methodology whose origins and rationale are to be located in the culture of modernity, something which alerts us yet again to the ambiguous position in which we now find ourselves – for at the same time as we are asking serious questions about the underlying assumptions that have led to an increased rationalization of our lives, human beings have never been as rationalized as we are now, and even if we do not necessarily like it we do tend to accommodate to it. In reflecting on an appropriately Christian style of mission for this time in history, we will inevitably need to remind ourselves again of how we have reached this point, and where we might now go.

Modernity was founded on three significant epistemological assumptions: knowledge is certain, knowledge is objective, and knowledge is inherently good. Not only have these beliefs had a profound impact on culture in general, but they have also deeply influenced much reflection on the nature of Christian evangelism. For knowledge to be certain meant that for anything to be real it must first be scrutinized by reason, through the mind; to be objective implied that the emotions and intuitions were to be set aside – while the goodness of knowledge was generally assumed to be self-evident, especially 'scientific' knowledge, which by definition was supposed to be unadulterated by having been filtered through the affective dimension of human nature. Since such achievements were evidently open to anyone, by virtue of being the traditional Cartesian rational autonomous individual, personal freedom of choice also came to be regarded as a non-negotiable cultural value. Insofar as post-modernity is rooted in the desire to move beyond this world view – albeit within the frame of reference provided by modernity itself – post-modern people and their aspirations can be understood by comparing and contrasting their outlook with that of the generations who immediately preceded them.

Today's people can accurately be described as 'post-rational', in that the emphasis on knowledge being what comes from the mind has been supplemented – and in some cases displaced – by a renewed emphasis on the concept of 'mystery'. Though rational discourse has a place, it is no longer perceived as having a monopoly on understanding. Knowledge, therefore, is no longer 'objective' in the old sense, because feelings and emotions are regarded as valid interpreters of reality – while the idea that knowledge is ultimately good is the least plausible notion of all, in the light of the twentieth century's legacy of devastation and destruction, in the natural world as well as in human lives. In the process of these changes, 'truth' itself has also been redefined, and tends to be understood not in relation to some external authority, but from within the experience of the individual. Christians have often perceived a problem in all this, and express a sense of both frustration and suspicion with a world view that can appear to be dominated by judgements about 'what works for me'. It is certainly easy to question the integrity of this kind of approach to the spiritual search, and even a writer as sensitive as Lesslie Newbigin has done so with his caustic comment that 'The unknown god is a convenient object of belief, since its character is a matter for me to decide. It cannot challenge me or pose radical questions to me.'[32] On a definition of truth based on the premises of modernity, that can sound a plausible conclusion – and, at this point at least, Newbigin was more of an unreformed Enlightenment thinker than I think he wanted to be. But when we understand the post-modern mindset in its own terms, behind all the posturing there is still a search for absolute truth. This is yet another example of the way in which 'human beings are now being restructured in their senses, feeling, knowing, and reasoning'.[33] Though by the standards of conventional literate discourse, a statement regarding 'what works for me' might sound like a denial of the possibility of absolute truth, it is actually a manifestation of the search for truth – not only that, but it contains some inherent absolutes itself. That something *works* is a value judgement, especially when set alongside the conviction that modernity failed to 'work' (which is another value judgement). Spiritual choices that 'work' tend to be seen as those which increase love, provide inner peace and a sense of meaning, and establish a safe space where people can feel they belong. The belief that all this is worth looking for is itself an absolute belief, as also is the idea that we should choose something that will suit us. The post-modern mindset is not, however, merely a form of glorified individualism, still less of selfish choices, for it is 'post-individual'. Increasingly, an individual's personal story is not regarded as something detached and autonomous, but as having meaning only when it is incorporated within a wider community as an integral part of the knowing process in such a way that any one person's narrative becomes a part of the transcending story.

What does all this have to do with effective mission? What underlying principles might inform a style of mission that grows from the bottom upwards – from the personal spiritual search of today's people – rather than being imposed from the top downwards? The top-down style has dominated for so long – for centuries! – that we probably should reflect even on what it means to ask the question in that particular way. I want to suggest that posing it like this brings together several strands both of human experience and of the biblical and Christian tradition in a way that can help us to articulate a strategy for mission that will be thoroughly contextualized in postmodern culture as well as firmly grounded within the history of Christian people. The strands that I want to bring together include the experience of women as they have reflected on the nature of the male-constructed culture we have inherited, the many New Testament images which depict spiritual discovery in terms of birth, growth and nurture, and the mission practices of the early Celtic Church. In turn, this will raise some far-reaching questions about the way in which we might appropriately do theology, indeed what theology might consist of, in today's world – though I do not propose to seek an answer to those questions here: to do that adequately will require another book.

The fact that women operate according to a different paradigm than men has been recognized for a long time. Classic studies by men (!) like Piaget and Freud concluded that women's moral reasoning was underdeveloped and illogical – a position that was challenged especially by Carol Gilligan's 1982 study of how women think, with particular reference to their moral development.[34] She demonstrated that what had previously been regarded as 'low levels' of moral development in women were misleading indicators, not least because they had been based on what were assumed to be absolute standards, derived exclusively from the empirical study of male ways of being. The reality, however, was that women used different values than those commonly taken for granted by men, values that had been either ignored or simply missed because it had not been possible for the female perspective to be heard in a world dominated and defined by patriarchal values. Modernity eventually recognized this, but in that cultural context the best that could be offered was the chance for women to share the same opportunities and privileges as men, but only insofar as they were able or willing to adopt male ways of doing things. One of the significant differences between that and the emerging post-modern culture is that women have now begun to find opportunities to do things in their own natural way, releasing knowledge from within, using gifts and abilities that are intuitive to the human person, and having them affirmed and valued.

Like other aspects of contemporary culture, there are many ambiguities and discontinuities about the picture I have just sketched all too briefly. Patriarchy, in common with other underlying principles of modernity, is not dead, and many women find themselves still struggling to be authentic to themselves in a man's world. I would not in any way wish to diminish or play down the tensions and pain this can create in particular circumstances. But as a general cultural trend, there can be no doubt that all the movement is towards affirming and valuing a different way of doing things. What this different way might be has been neatly summarized in *Women's Ways of Knowing*, a book written by four female writers in which they report the results of their empirical research among a group of women drawn from widely diverse sectors of the educational and social spectrum.[35] The idea of a community of writers producing such a work is itself a statement about a different way of doing things, reflecting one of the convictions to which I have already referred, the idea that truth will emerge not from the autonomous rational individual by him or herself, but in a context of communal sharing and exploration. Having identified four key characteristic ways in which these women gained knowledge ('Received Knowledge', 'Subjective Knowledge', 'Procedural Knowledge' and 'Constructed Knowledge'), they were also able to recognize common threads within all four categories:

> They want to avoid what they perceive to be the shortcoming in many men, the tendency to compartmentalize thought and feeling, home and work, self and other. In women, there is an impetus to try to deal with life, internal and external, in all its complexity. And they want to develop a voice of their own to communicate to others their understanding of life's complexity.[36]

Another conclusion was that women want to see all knowledge as a construction, and truth therefore becomes a matter of context. Theories are not to become truths, but merely models to aid understanding: 'Women tend not to rely as readily or as exclusively on hypothetico-deductive inquiry, which posits an answer (the hypothesis) prior to the data collection, as they do on examining basic assumptions and the conditions in which a problem exists.'[37] Furthermore, for these women it was not enough merely to be told that they had the capacity or the potential to become knowledgeable or wise. They needed to know that they already knew something (though by no means everything) and that their innate knowledge was of value in itself. Knowledge gained through life experiences needed to be as important and real and useful as the abstract cognitive knowledge imparted in the conventional Western educational process. Such knowledge does not need to culminate in the statement of general propositions, because truth itself can be understood as a process of construction in which the knower participates, and a passion for learning is unleashed. One of the interviewees, a woman called Lydia, commented that 'It isn't the finding the truth that's so wonderful. It is in the looking for it, the exploring, the searching. If you were to ever think that you've finally arrived at it, you've blown it. Truth gets more elusive the older I get.' She then went on to recall the poem 'Ithaca' in which Ulysses searches for home, but added that for people today it is not so much the getting home that is important, as the travelling. The journey is a lot more important than the destination.[38] This kind of statement has enormous and significant implications for the Church and its mission, as also does the renewed emphasis on intimacy and the priority of relationships in the context of a quest for personal wholeness. Whereas men have generally inclined to put career consolidation ahead of idealism and intimacy, women more usually consider the effects that their lifestyle choices will have on others, especially those with whom they are in close relationships.[39] The one exception to that may be women who fall into the category of what I have called corporate achievers, who (as I pointed out earlier) are the one group most fiercely committed to modernity – and to be successful in that world it is essential to embrace its values and practices.

The relevance of all this for the Church has been highlighted from a completely different starting point by Stanley Grenz in his article 'Star Trek and the Next Generation: Postmodernism and the Future of Evangelical Theology'.[40] By comparing and contrasting the characters in the original television series of *Star Trek* with those in the series *Star Trek: The Next Generation*, he illustrates the differences between modernity (the original) and post-modernity (the next generation). In particular, Mr Spock (one of the original heroes) played a dominant role as the ultimate Enlightened rational individual (even though he was from another planet): totally detached and objective, with no emotions, all of them qualities that enabled him to solve whatever problems might arise. Insofar as women appeared in the first series, they had either successfully taken on male characteristics such as intelligence and restraint of emotions, or they represented the stereotypical objects of male sexual fantasy. *Star Trek: The Next Generation*, however, presents a very different perspective. Intelligence is no longer defined by reference to Enlightenment-inspired ideals, but is derived from the wisdom of the whole cosmos, represented by the part played by humanoids from all over the universe. There is no exact equivalent to the perfect detached rationality of Mr Spock, because a character who can fix everything is now redundant: the starship *Enterprise* is typically delivered from difficulties only when all the crew members work together. A prominent person in this respect is Counselor Troi, a woman specially gifted in perceiving the hidden feelings of others. In other words, not only is a woman's intellect affirmed, but so is the intuitive method whereby she has gained her knowledge. Grenz highlights other contrasts between the two series: in the post-modern *Next Generation*, time is no longer linear, reality is not always what one sees, and the rational cannot always be trusted. And whereas the original series generally ignored spiritual concerns, *The Next Generation* includes a supernatural character, Q.

What does all this mean in terms of mission? I think it was Martin Luther who observed that 'If you preach the gospel in all aspects with the exception of the issues which deal specifically with your time – you are not preaching the gospel at all.' The Church – especially in its evangelical Protestant wing – set itself to address the questions thrown up by modernity so self-consciously that George Marsden has claimed that 'evangelicalism – with its focus on scientific thinking and empirical approach, and common sense – is a child of early modernity'[41] – a claim affirmed also by Paul Tillich who wrote of Protestantism more generally that

> It has become a "theology of consciousness" in analogy to the Cartesian philosophy of consciousness . . . The personality was cut off from the vital basis of its existence. Religion was reserved for the conscious centre of man [sic]. The subconscious levels remained untouched, empty, or suppressed, while the conscious side was overburdened with the continuous ultimate decisions it had to make. . . *A religion that*

does not appeal to the subconscious basis of all decisions is untenable
in the long run and can never become a religion for the masses.[42]

The way in which the Church engages in mission still generally
reflects that mindset. So – to continue the *Star Trek* imagery – what
might *The Next Generation* in mission look like if it is to have any hope
of engaging with what Tillich called the subconscious levels, and
which today we might more readily identify as the search for a
mysterious, intuitive and deeply personal spirituality?

The book *Women's Ways of Knowing* highlights what it calls the
'midwife-teacher' model as typical of the emerging culture, which I
believe points to new possibilities in apologetic method. The terminology emerged as the researchers struggled to identify a model that
could be used by teachers in order to accommodate students who
learned in different ways. The women on whose experience the
research was based expressed a belief that they already possessed
latent knowledge, and they consequently desired to gain further
knowledge not so much from the traditional 'banker-teacher' who
would merely deposit knowledge in the learners' heads (Tillich's
'theology of consciousness'), but from the 'midwife-teacher', whose
approach would be to draw existing knowledge out of the learner,
and assist students in giving birth to their own ideas, thereby making
their own tacit knowledge explicit and at the same time elaborating
it.[43] It will be worth pursuing this image a little further, and asking
what a 'midwife-evangelist' might look like.

In relation to the role of a midwife, three concerns are significant.
The primary one is the preservation of the vulnerable child, 'to preserve the postmodern's fragile newborn thoughts, to see that they are
born with their truth intact, that they do not turn into acceptable
lies.'[44] In addition, though, is a concern for the midwife to foster the
child's growth, to 'support the evolution of the thinking of the post-
modern individual' – a concept which places the focus on the innate
knowledge of the child rather than on the information supplied by
the midwife-evangelist. In this context, the midwife-evangelist will
gladly and openly contribute whatever she knows when it is appropriate, but will remain clear that the 'baby' is not hers but belongs to
the one whom she helps. The evangelizing cycle then becomes one
of confirmation – evocation – confirmation, and so on. Midwife-
evangelists can help individuals to deliver their own spirituality into
the world, though they will also be available to share their own
knowledge and help to put others into conversation with voices –

past and present – in the culture and the Church.[45] The opportunity to both value and utilize their own innate knowledge and spirituality in everyday life is something that many people complain is lacking in the contemporary Church.

Another issue that can be encapsulated within this model is the post-modern person's need for 'practical information', something which invites the midwife-evangelist to adopt a 'problem-posing' method that will begin from the recognition that knowledge (even – especially – knowledge of God, or Christ) is not the property of the evangelist. Once this kind of evangelist enables people's innate (God-given) knowledge and spirituality to be openly acknowledged and articulated, then a further significant concern of maternal thinking becomes central: 'The mother must shape natural growth in such a way that her child becomes the sort of adult that she can appreciate and others can accept.'[46] This has the effect of promoting an atmosphere in which wholesome development can take place, something that has been described as a 'yogurt' atmosphere (full of vitality and movement from within), as distinct from the traditional 'movie' atmosphere (in which individuals are spectators of other people's growth).[47]

I remember having a conversation just a couple of years before the end of the twentieth century, in the course of which my companion encapsulated the challenge of the new millennium in this question: What are we bringing to birth at this time of the changing of the ages? It was a question deeply rooted in the story of the first changing of the ages – the coming of Christ – which of course focused in a very literal way on the birth of Jesus at Bethlehem. The more I have reflected on it, the more obvious it has become to me that this is exactly the right metaphor for us to explore and use in our evangelism at this point in time. It clearly roots us in the past, for the Bible is full of images of personal transformation and new possibilities, while the image of 'new birth' has for many people been a favourite way of describing conversion to Christ (John 3:1–8).[48] But it also enables us to look to the future, not only in the sense that it is a relevant image for post-modern culture, but also because it opens out possibilities of who we might yet become, rather than dwelling on who we have been. In that sense, it has built into it the eschatological element of Christian hope and expectation, that has sometimes been lost in past methodologies of mission, with their over-emphasis on past failures and consequent minimizing of future possibilities. For a mother, the image of birth is a natural one to apply to Christian growth and development, and it also relates to the increasingly popular trend among women who also belong to the group I have called spiritual searchers, of rediscovering the spiritual power of physical cycles, and using what is natural as an entry point for what is spiritual – or, rather, insisting that there is no distinction to be drawn between the physical and the spiritual. Men, on the other hand, have historically been more comfortable with using images of death as the starting point for an understanding of spirituality, something that inevitably places all the emphasis on final conclusions, and therefore concerns itself with who is guilty for what, and in what measure.[49] This has often engendered the kind of judgemental attitudes that people today find so unappealing. Starting from birth is not only profoundly scriptural (the incarnation!), but also makes available a different set of images for effective evangelism. This spirituality does not ignore guilt and mess and judgement (because of its freedom to acknowledge the embodiment of human life, it can actually more easily name sins that have often been ignored), but the darkness of death is displaced from the centre, and the key focus is the excitement of moving forward hand in hand with God as little children ourselves on the journey, knowing that before us lies growth, discovery, exploration, and renewal of life. Starting from birth, we can encourage one another, support one another, and hold out that generous spirit of acceptance and affirmation that is not just one of the most desperate needs of today's people, but is also one of the central values of God's kingdom. I have always been impressed with the missionary style of Jesus precisely for these reasons: that he was consistently honest about the mess that is sin (in the broadest sense, not just defined in terms of human actions), and yet he never instilled a sense of guilt and failure in the people he met, but always held out the possibility of new start, further stages on the journey, personal renewal, and fresh empowerment to be the best people they could possibly be, because we are all made in God's image.[50]

The more I reflect on it, the more certain do I become that this shift of imagery will not only be an appropriate contextualization of the gospel in the post-modern world, but it also connects with other significant aspects of Christian history whose importance have sometimes been missed in the past. In his book *Recovering the Past*, John Finney compares and contrasts what he identifies as the Roman and the Celtic styles of mission, with the one roughly approximating to the inherited male-inspired model and the other to what I have called here the 'midwife-evangelist' model, beginning not from images of death but from the possibilities of new life.[51] Though sharing some of the misgivings of those who worry that 'Celtic Christianity' might too easily become a figment of the post-modern imagination, rather than a reflection of history 'as it actually was', he is still able to identify some key characteristics that distinguished the way the Romans did things from the way the ancient Celts both celebrated and shared faith. I have to say that I do not personally share the opinion of those historical purists who deplore the use of the Celtic saints as inspirational models for the emerging culture of post-modernity. If there is exaggeration or misunderstanding of some of their ideas, then that is perhaps inevitable given the distance in time that now stands between us and them, and the scanty sources of our information about them. But the Judeo-Christian tradition has never been reticent about using images from the past to inform and inspire its future vision. The process can be traced as far back as the Hebrew Bible itself, whose writers were continuously rewriting and reinterpreting the history of the Israelite nation in order to map out the shape of a plausible future for themselves. If they occasionally put a romantic spin on the stories they recorded, they never did it for the purpose of falsifying history (a notion that itself would only make sense in a modernist context), but in order to perceive more clearly the purposes of God.

In his analysis of the early Celtic mission (which, incidentally, he does believe can be verified historically), Finney identifies three trends which he also traces in what he calls 'the new evangelism' that he believes is emerging within British churches today. He characterizes these as: 'From the Damascus road to the road to Emmaus', 'From Doctrine to Spirituality', and 'From missions to mission' – all of them 'moving from a Roman to a Celtic model. The best modern evangelism goes where people are and listens, binds together prayer and truth, celebrates the goodness and complexity of life as well as judging the sinfulness of evil, and sees truth as something to be done and experienced as well as to be intellectually believed. It walks in humility.'[52] If the Roman model was (and is) the McDonaldized version of Christian faith, then the Celtic model is undoubtedly going to be good news for those whose lives have been blighted by the 'iron cage' of an inflexible spirituality which pays too little attention to the fundamental biblical doctrines of creation and incarnation. It is also striking that these three characteristics listed by Finney are all significantly different from a Cartesian style of mission, and bear remarkable similarities to what we are now hearing when women are given the space to speak with their own voice, rather than within the categories of patriarchal culture.

It is no doubt a cliché to say that the Church today stands at a crossroads. However it may be expressed, we certainly face some clear choices. We can either continue with the modernist approach that views authority as rooted in some kind of universal systematic methodology, and which will enable us to speak with certainty even though others may not be in a position to hear – or we can construct a different sort of authority, based on personal, individual experience and freely acknowledging the kind of ambiguities and uncertainties that will always be implicit in any approach which places a value on such things. The exploration of an embodied spirituality through the arts will be intrinsic to this second approach, which I believe offers a new prospect of enabling us to create the kind of personal spaces which will allow people to entertain the thought of participation in the Christian story precisely because its starting point is the possibility of a meaningful spirituality that begins from within the context of human experience rather than being offered as a pre-packaged, McDonaldized religious product. That is not to say that its main rooting will be within human experience, for on any kind of Christian understanding human life only finds its truest meaning by reference to the life of God, shown to us and shared with us through Jesus Christ. But the divine will be nurtured in a community context, where people who are friends can help one another towards personal maturity, and where no one need apologize for uncertainty, knowing that whatever new insights might emerge will always be somewhat tentative in nature, for none of us can ever hope to fathom the being of God. For some Christians, this approach will certainly be far too risky, though for those prepared to take the risk, it will hold out new possibilities of personal healing and wholeness in a fragmented world, as well as the prospect of a Church renewed in its own soul. Actually, its weakness will be the real secret of its power, and in that respect it will be incarnational in every sense of the word, for this is how Jesus himself came bearing the good news. And even St Paul – often unfairly castigated as a revisionist commentator on the message of Jesus – reminded his readers in Corinth (who, of all people, were tempted to think that they could best do God's work in their own way and by their own power) that 'God chose what is foolish in the world to shame the wise; God chose what is weak in the world to shame the strong; God chose what is low and despised in the world, things that are not, to reduce to nothing things that are . . .'

(1 Corinthians 1:27–8). For those struggling to find new ways of being church in the context of rapid cultural change, that is perhaps the best news of all, and the most truly empowering message for the post-modern age.

NOTES

Chapter 1: Cultural Change in Personal Perspective

1. The earlier ones were: *Faith in a Changing Culture* (London: HarperCollins, 1997); *What is the New Age Still Saying to the Church?* (London: HarperCollins, 1999); *Cultural Change and Biblical Faith* (Carlisle: Paternoster Press, 2000).

2. See *Cultural Change and Biblical Faith*, 94–5.

3. For an overview, see Hilary Lawson and Lisa Appignanesi, *Dismantling Truth: Reality in the Post-Modern World* (New York: St Martin's Press, 1989); and for specific examples, cf. Jacques Derrida, *Writing and Difference* (Chicago: University of Chicago Press, 1978); Richard Rorty, *The Consequences of Pragmatism* (Minneapolis: University of Minnesota Press, 1982), *Objectivity, Relativism and Truth* (Cambridge: Cambridge University Press, 1991); Michel Foucault, *The Order of Things* (New York: Random House, 1970).

4. Peter Brierley (ed.), *UK Christian Handbook Religious Trends No. 2: 2000/2001* (London: Christian Research, 1999); Peter Kaldor *et al.* (eds.), *Taking Stock: a Profile of Australian Church Attenders* (Adelaide: Openbook, 1999); National Council of Churches, *Yearbook of American and Canadian Churches* (Nashville: Abingdon Press, annual); George Barna, *The Index of Leading Spiritual Indicators* (Dallas: Word, 1996); Barna Research Group, *Never on a Sunday: the challenge of the unchurched* (Glendale: Barna, 1990); Roger C. Thompson, *Religion in Australia: a History* (Melbourne: Oxford University Press, 1994); Muriel Porter, *Land of the Spirit? The Australian Religious Experience* (Geneva: WCC, 1990); Grace Davie, *Religion in Britain since 1945* (Oxford: Blackwell, 1994); Steve Bruce, *Religion in Modern Britain* (Oxford: Oxford University Press, 1995); Wade Clark Roof, *Spiritual Marketplace: Baby Boomers and the Remaking of American Religion* (Princeton NJ: Princeton University Press, 1999).

5. Cf. Francis Fukuyama, *The Great Disruption* (London: Profile Books, 1999), 52–60. For more on this distinctive phenomenon of American (especially Protestant) Christianity, see Conrad Cherry and Rowland A. Sherrill, *Religion, the Independent Sector, and American Culture* (Atlanta GA: Scholars Press, 1992); Andrew Greeley, *The Denominational Society* (Glenview IL: Scott, Foresman & Co., 1972).

6. Fukuyama, *Great Disruption*, 238–9.

7. This need for relevance to family or personal needs can even transcend

traditional religious boundaries, such as that between Protestants and Catholics. See the experience reported by Leith Anderson of people from traditionally Catholic families joining his (Protestant) church because of its programmes for children, but announcing in advance their intention to return to their roots once their children are grown up (Leith Anderson, *A Church for the 21st Century*, Minneapolis: Bethany House, 1992, 32).

8. See Grace Davie, 'Europe: the exception that proves the rule?' in Peter Berger (ed.), *The Desecularization of the World* (Grand Rapids: Eerdmans, 1999), 65–83.

9. William D. Hendricks, *Exit Interviews: revealing stories of why people are leaving the church* (Chicago: Moody Press, 1993), 224–5. Similar statements can as readily be found among those leaving church in Britain: cf. Michael J. Fanstone, *The Sheep that Got Away* (London: MARC, 1993); Philip Richter and Leslie J. Francis, *Gone but not Forgotten: Church Leaving and Returning* (London: Darton, Longman & Todd, 1998).

10. He writes of 'a correlation between people coming alive to their emotions and their exit from the church' and goes on to observe that as his interviewees struggled to reconcile their own self-discovery with their experience of church life they regularly described themselves as 'moving closer to God but further away from the church' (*Exit Interviews*, 267–8).

11. See my *Changing Culture and Biblical Faith*, 78–103.

12. Don Browning, *A Fundamental Practical Theology* (Minneapolis: Fortress Press, 1991).

13. George Ritzer, *The McDonaldization of Society* (Thousand Oaks CA: Pine Forge Press, 1993, rev. edn 1996); *The McDonaldization Thesis: Explorations and Extensions* (Thousand Oaks CA: Sage Publications, 1998).

14. *Fundamental Practical Theology*, 35.

15. ibid., 8.

16. Cf. Gustavo Gutiérrez, *A Theology of Liberation* (Maryknoll NY: Orbis, 1988). For some further comments on applying this more broadly, see also my *Faith in a Changing Culture* (London: HarperCollins, 1997), 177–85.

17. Browning, *Fundamental Practical Theology*, 22–3.

18. ibid., 1.

19. *Mission and Evangelism – an Ecumenical Affirmation* (Geneva: WCC, 1982), section 13.

20. *Stigmata* (1999), directed by Rupert Wainwright; written by Tom Lazarus and Rick Ramag; produced by Frank Mancuso Jr, and starring Gabriel Byrne, Patricia Arquette and Jonathan Pryce. Distributed by MGM/UA.

21. For more on formative influences in my own spiritual journey, see my book *Tune in to the Bible* (London: Scripture Union, 1989), 11–20; and the article 'To see the world as God sees it: through the Cross', in Ruth Harvey (ed.), *Wrestling and Resting: Exploring Stories of Spirituality from Britain and Ireland* (London: CTBI, 1999), 10–12.

22. Encapsulated most clearly in W. Lillie, *Studies in New Testament Ethics* (Edinburgh: Oliver & Boyd, 1961) and *The Law of Christ* (Edinburgh: Saint Andrew Press, 1966, 2nd edn).

23. J.M. Robinson (ed.), *The Nag Hammadi Library in English* (New York: Harper & Row, 1977; rev. edn San Francisco: HarperCollins, 1988).

24. Ziauddin Sardar, *Postmodernism and the Other* (New York: Pluto Press, 1998), 43.

25. ibid., 13.

26. R. Descartes, 'Discourse on the Method', part 4, section 32, in J. Cottingham, R. Stoothoff, D. Murdoch (eds.), *Philosophical Writings of Descartes* (Cambridge: Cambridge University Press, 1985), vol. 1, 127.

27. Linda Woodhead, 'Christianity according to its Interpreters' in *Reviews in Religion and Theology* 1997/4, 11–12.

28. *Faith in a Changing Culture*, 63–4.

29. Cf. Janet Litherland, *Everything New and Who's Who in Clown Ministry* (Colorado Springs: Meriwether Press, 1993), 57–9, 81–2, 132–3, 258–9.

30. *Fundamental Practical Theology*, 30.

31. ibid., 250.

32. ibid., 171. For more on the notion that mainline denominations have their theology to blame for their demise, see J. Edward Carothers, *The Paralysis of Mainstream Protestant Leadership* (Nashville: Abingdon Press, 1990).

Chapter 2: Rational Systems and Human Values

1. See, for example, Hans Bertens, *The Idea of the Postmodern* (New York: Routledge, 1995); David Harvey, *The Condition of Postmodernity* (Oxford: Blackwell, 1989); David Lyon, *Postmodernity* (Buckingham: Open University Press, 1994).

2. For studies of the ways in which this affected lifestyles, cf. Hugh Cunningham, *Leisure in the Industrial Revolution* (London: Croom Helm, 1980); Philip A.M. Taylor (ed.), *The Industrial Revolution in Britain: Triumph or Disaster?* (Lexington MA: Heath, 1970); Stella Davies, *Living through the Industrial Revolution* (London: Routledge, 1966); E.R. Pike, *Human Documents of the Industrial Revolution in Britain* (London: Allen & Unwin, 1966).

3. Aram Vartanian (ed.), *La Mettrie's L'Homme Machine* (Princeton NJ: Princeton University Press, 1960), 197. Cf. René Descartes, *A Discourse on Method* V, translated by John Veitch (London: J.M. Dent, 1912), 43–5.

4. For a discussion of the implications of management systems in relation to human and, especially, spiritual values, see Russell Ackoff, *Creating the Corporate Future* (New York: John Wiley & Sons, 1981). For a distinctively theological perspective on this, see M. Fox, *The Reinvention of Work* (HarperSanFrancisco, 1994).

5. For examples of this – if proof were needed – see the novels by Douglas Coupland: *Generation X* (New York: St Martin's Press, 1991), *Shampoo Planet* (New York: Pocket Books, 1992), *Life after God* (New York: Simon & Schuster, 1994), *Microserfs* (New York: HarperCollins, 1995), *Polaroids from the Dead* (New York: HarperCollins, 1996).

6. Francis Fukuyama, *The Great Disruption* (London: Profile Books, 1999).

7. *The Truman Show* (1998), directed by Peter Weir, written by Andrew

Niccol, starring Jim Carrey, Laura Linney, Ed Harris, Noah Emmerlich. Distributed by Paramount Pictures. *The Matrix* (1999), directed and written by Andy and Larry Wachowski, starring Keanu Reeves, Laurence Fishburne, Carrie-Anne Moss. Distributed by Warner Brothers. *American Beauty* (1999), directed by Sam Mendes, written by Alan Ball, produced by Bruce Cohen and Dan Jinks, starring Kevin Spacey, Wes Bentley, Annette Bening, Thora Birch, Mena Suvari. Distributed by Dreamworks. On the spiritual search reflected in *The Truman Show*, see my *Cultural Change and Biblical Faith*, 154–73.

8. For a succinct and accessible account of the emergence of diverse working lifestyles, see Charles Handy, *The Hungry Spirit* (London: Hutchinson, 1997).

9. The Columbine massacre has been better documented than any others, through the publication of the story of Cassie Bernall: see Misty Bernall, *She Said Yes: the Unlikely Martyrdom of Cassie Bernall* (Farmington PA: Plough Publishing House, 1999).

10. See John Drane and Olive M. Fleming Drane, *Happy Families?* (London: HarperCollins, 1995), 52–70.

11. On extreme thrill-seeking sport, see Rebecca Piirto Heath, 'You can buy a thrill: chasing the ultimate rush', in *American Demographics* 19/6 (1997), 47–51. On sport more generally as a vehicle for spirituality, see S.J. Hoffman (ed.), *Sport and Religion* (Champaign IL: Human Kinetics Books, 1992).

12. For the relationship of this phenomenon to worship, see Tex Sample, *The Spectacle of Worship in a Wired World* (Nashville: Abingdon, 1998), 76–86.

13. George Ritzer, *The McDonaldization of Society* (Thousand Oaks CA: Pine Forge Press, 1993). There was a revised and somewhat expanded edition published in 1996. Page references here are to the original 1993 edition. The idea was first expounded by Ritzer in 'The McDonaldization of Society', in *Journal of American Culture* 6/1 (1983), 100–7.

14. George Ritzer, *The McDonaldization Thesis: Explorations and Extensions* (Thousand Oaks CA: Sage Publications, 1998).

15. Ritzer, *McDonaldization of Society*, 1.

16. Significantly, Weber's original work made a direct connection between the rationalized society and Christianity: Max Weber, *The Protestant Ethic and the Spirit of Capitalism* (New York: Scribner's, 1958 – originally 1904/5). The notion of McDonaldization is not, however, limited to a Weberian understanding of the social process, and in *The McDonaldization Thesis*, 16–34, Ritzer also expounds his ideas by reference to Karl Mannheim's theory on the nature of rationalization.

17. Ritzer, *McDonaldization of Society* (1996 edition), 22–4, who in turn based his argument substantially on Z. Bauman, *Modernity and the Holocaust* (Oxford: Polity Press, 1989). For further discussion of this topic, see Peter Beilharz, 'McFascism?', in Barry Smart (ed.), *Resisting McDonaldization* (Thousand Oaks CA: Sage Publications,1999), 222–33.

18. Cf. Alan Bryman, 'Theme Parks and McDonaldization', in Smart (ed.), *Resisting McDonaldization*, 101–15; Ritzer, *The McDonaldization Thesis*, 134–50.
19. Ritzer, *McDonaldization of Society*, 8.
20. ibid., 26.
21. Richard Münch, 'McDonaldized Culture', in Smart (ed.), *Resisting McDonaldization*, 139.

Chapter 3: The Church and the Iron Cage

1. *Brazil* (1985), directed by Terry Gilliam; written by Terry Gilliam and Charles McKeown; starring Jonathan Pryce, Kim Greist and Robert De Niro. Distributed by Universal Films.
2. Ritzer uses the metaphor of three cages to describe varying responses to the phenomenon of McDonaldization: 'the velvet cage' (those people who like it), 'the rubber cage' (others who appreciate some aspects of a McDonaldized lifestyle, while not wishing to be always constricted by it), and 'the iron cage' (those who find themselves oppressed by it – whom Ritzer clearly believes to be the majority). The terminology of the 'iron cage' was borrowed by Ritzer from Weber, who however originally used it with a different nuance in a totally different socio-historical context. Other scholars have questioned its usefulness as an image, while not doubting the realities which Ritzer highlights. Derek Sayer, for example, helpfully proposes that a better model might be 'the shell . . . on a snail's back: a burden perhaps, but something impossible to live without, in either sense of the word' – explaining that, while 'A cage remains an external restraint . . . [rationalization] . . . is a prison altogether stronger, the armour of modern subjectivity itself. Dependency on "mechanical petrification" has become an integral part of who we are' (*Capitalism and Modernity*, London: Routledge, 1991, 144).
3. George Ritzer, *The McDonaldization of Society* (Thousand Oaks CA: Pine Forge Press, 1993), 135.
4. Cf. J. McClancey, *Consuming Culture* (London: Chapman, 1992), 212.
5. For typical expositions of this view, see Donald A. McGavran, *Understanding Church Growth* (Grand Rapids: Eerdmans, 1980, 2nd edn); Wayne Weld and Donald A. McGavran, *Principles of Church Growth* (Pasadena CA: William Carey Library, 1974); Charles L. Chaney and Ron S. Lewis, *Design for Church Growth* (Nashville: Broadman Press, 1977); M. Wendell Belew, *Churches and How They Grow* (Nashville: Broadman Press, 1971); C. Peter Wagner (ed.), *Church Growth: State of the Art* (Wheaton IL: Tyndale House Publishers, 1986); William M. Easum, *The Church Growth Handbook* (Nashville: Abingdon Press, 1990). Though this school of thinking was much criticized at the time, it did nevertheless serve to highlight the declining condition of churches in Western culture, and was a significant factor in reorienting the thinking of church leaders to realize that the so-called 'Christian' nations of the West are actually one of the most significant mission fields today. For one of the most balanced critiques of

the Church Growth Movement, see Lesslie Newbigin, *The Open Secret: Sketches for a Missionary Theology* (Grand Rapids: Eerdmans, 1978); and for scholars who have built on its insights while seeking to avoid its McDonaldizing tendencies, see Kennon Callahan, *Effective Church Leadership* (San Francisco: Harper & Row, 1990), *Twelve Keys to an Effective Church* (San Francisco: Harper & Row, 1983); Tex Sample, *US Lifestyles and Mainline Churches* (Louisville KY: Westminster John Knox Press, 1990).

6. Ritzer, *McDonaldization of Society*, 182.

7. ibid., 83, 85.

8. For a well-researched corrective to this, see John Finney, *Finding Faith Today* (Swindon: Bible Society, 1992); and for a theological understanding of the diversity of conversion experiences, see Dick Peace, *Conversion in the New Testament* (Grand Rapids: Eerdmans, 1999), who argues that the idea that conversion to Christ is invariably an instantaneous Damascus-road type of experience can only be sustained by an over-emphasis on the experience of Paul and an ignoring of the experience of those who were Jesus' original disciples.

9. The classic account of stages in faith development is James Fowler, *Stages of Faith* (San Francisco: Harper & Row, 1981). Originally based on insights from developmental psychologists such as Piaget and Kohlberg, later formulations of stages of faith development have been adjusted to take account of the criticisms of Carol Gilligan, *In a different voice: psychological theory and women's development* (Cambridge MA: Harvard University Press, 1982), who highlighted the extent to which this was a male model. Though theorists are more likely now to talk of Fowler's six stages as a cyclical rather than a linear model, it has proved difficult to break away entirely from the idea that this is in some way a normative and prescriptive pathway to personal maturity that should therefore be universally applicable to any individual. For more recent applications of the concept, see V. Bailey Gillespie, *The Experience of Faith* (Birmingham AL: Religious Education Press, 1988); Jeff Astley and Leslie J. Francis (eds.), *Christian Perspectives on Faith Development: a Reader* (Leominster: Gracewing, 1992); Mary Jo Meadow, *Through a Glass Darkly: a spiritual psychology of faith* (New York: Crossroad, 1996); A. Eugene Dyess, *Faithing: a reconstructive method* (Lanham MD: University Press of America, 1994).

10. The Orthodox tradition appears to be the only traditional mainline denomination that is actually growing in overall numbers in the UK: cf. Peter Brierley (ed.), *UK Christian Handbook Religious Trends 2000/2001* (London: Christian Research,1999), 2.14, 8.11–8.13.

11. For an instructive discussion of the theme park culture, see Alan Bryman, 'Theme Parks and McDonaldization', in Barry Smart (ed.), *Resisting McDonaldization* (Thousand Oaks CA: Sage 1999), 101–15.

12. For a theologically competent and practical discussion of the difference between 'home groups' and 'home churches', see Robert and Julie Banks, *The Church Comes Home* (Peabody MA: Hendrickson, 1998).

13. Richard Münch, 'McDonaldized Culture', in Smart (ed.), *Resisting*

McDonaldization, 139; Ziauddin Sardar, *Postmodernism and the Other* (London: Pluto Press, 1998), 139. For the same phenomenon in regard to vegetarianism, see Keith Tester, 'The Moral Malaise of McDonaldization', in *Resisting McDonaldization*, 217–19.

14. Sardar, *Postmodernism and the Other*, 259–60.

15. For a corrective, see Christiane Bender and Gianfranco Poggi, 'Golden Arches and Iron Cages', in Smart (ed.), *Resisting McDonaldization*, 22–40. In the second edition (1996) of *The McDonaldization of Society*, 11–13, Ritzer did include a list of positive features of McDonaldization, though his general approach to the phenomenon is still overwhelmingly negative.

16. Cf. Douglas Kellner's comment that 'taking the infamous fast-food company McDonald's as the paradigm of McDonaldization skews [Ritzer's] analysis negatively, missing the dialectics of McDonaldization, its positive and negative features', in 'Theorizing/Resisting McDonaldization: a Multiperspectivist Approach', in Smart (ed.), *Resisting McDonaldization*, 187.

17. Cf. Steven Miles, 'McDonaldization and the Global Sports Store: Constructing Consumer Meanings in a Rationalized Society', in Mark Alfino, John S. Caputo and Robin Wynyard, *McDonaldization Revisited* (Westport CT: Praeger, 1998), 53–66.

18. Ritzer himself made a few peripheral remarks on TV evangelists and the Vatican (*McDonaldization of Society*, 58).

19. For a succinct statement of the issues in terms of the challenges facing the Church today, see John Finney, *Recovering the Past: Celtic and Roman Mission* (London: Darton, Longman & Todd, 1996).

20. This, in brief, is the gist of the criticisms made in Alfino *et al.*, *McDonaldization Revisited*; and Smart (ed.), *Resisting McDonaldization*.

21. Peter Bilharz, 'McFascism?', in Smart (ed.), *Resisting McDonaldization*, 222.

22. George Ritzer, 'Assessing the Resistance', in Smart (ed.), *Resisting McDonaldization*, 238.

23. Ritzer himself has, of course, addressed many of these criticisms in *The McDonaldization Thesis: Explorations and Extensions* (Thousand Oaks CA: Sage Publications, 1998).

24. A. Gouldner, *The Dialectic of Ideology and Technology* (London: Macmillan, 1976), 114.

25. Don Browning, *A Fundamental Practical Theology* (Minneapolis: Fortress Press, 1991), 9.

26. ibid., 135.

27. James A. Beckford, 'Religione e società nel Regno Unito', in *La religione degli Europei* (Torino: Edizione della Fondazione Giovanni Agnelli,1992). The quotation cited here is taken from an unpublished English version of the paper, supplied to me by Beckford.

28. Cf. William Storrar, 'From *Braveheart* to Faint-Heart: worship and culture in postmodern Scotland', in Bryan Spinks and Iain Torrance, *To Glorify God* (Edinburgh: T & T Clark, 1999), 69–84.

29. Ron D. Dempsey, *Faith Outside the Walls* (Macon GA: Smyth & Helwys, 1997), 9.
30. Cf. C.P. Kottak, 'Rituals at McDonald's', in *Natural History* 87/1 (1978), 75–82.

Chapter 4: Whom Are We Trying to Reach?

1. See Arthur Marwick, *The Sixties* (Oxford: Oxford University Press, 1998).
2. On the key role this has played in the Church's evident inability to communicate with this and later generations, see Tex Sample, *The Spectacle of Worship in a Wired World* (Nashville: Abingdon Press, 1998), especially 34–44.
3. That is precisely the spin placed on it in Peter Brierley (ed.), *UK Christian Handbook Religious Trends No. 2: 2000/2001* (London: Christian Research, 1999), 0.3–0.4.
4. For an exploration of this angle with specific reference to the baby boomer generation, see Dean R. Hoge, Benton Johnson and Donald A. Luidens, *Vanishing Boundaries: the religion of mainline Protestant Baby Boomers* (Louisville KY: Westminster John Knox Press, 1994).
5. My definition of these groups is located within my understanding of British culture, though I believe a good case can also be made out for classifying North American culture along similar lines. Readers who are familiar with the three groups identified by Tex Sample as Cultural Left, Cultural Middle and Cultural Right will recognize some rough correspondences between these and the people I have called spiritual searchers, corporate achievers and traditionalists, though I am certain that the cultural mix in both the USA and Britain is infinitely more complex than Sample suggests (see Tex Sample, *US Lifestyles and Mainline Churches* (Louisville: Westminster John Knox Press, 1990)).
6. See, for example, the comments on the Apostolic Church of God in Don S. Browning, *A Fundamental Practical Theology* (Minneapolis: Fortress Press, 1991), 26–33, 243–77.
7. Douglas Coupland, *Life after God* (New York: Simon & Schuster, 1994), 279.
8. Cf. Christine Evans *et al.*, 'I don't like Mondays' in *British Medical Journal* 320/7229 (22 January 2000), 218–19, and ensuing discussion and additional references at <http//www.bmj.org/cgi/content/full/320/7229/218>.
9. *Reel Spirituality*, held on 6 November 1999 at CBS studios, Burbank, California as part of the sixth annual City of the Angels Film Festival.
10. John Street, *Rebel Rock* (Oxford: Blackwell, 1986), 226.
11. Douglas Coupland, *Generation X* (New York: St Martin's Press, 1991), 8. For further discussion of the importance of stories as a way of exploring and expressing spirituality, see chapter 7, 133–54.
12. Walter Ong, *Orality and Literacy* (London: Methuen, 1982), 48.
13. J.B. Trend, *The Civilization of Spain* (London: Oxford University Press, 1944), 88.

14. *A Course in Miracles* (New York: Foundation for Inner Peace, 1975).

15. James Redfield, *The Celestine Prophecy* (New York: Warner, 1993).

16. See my *The Bible Phenomenon* (Oxford: Lion, 1999), 7–10; and, for evidence that I am not the only one to meet such people, cf. Paul Vallely, 'Evangelism in a Post-Religious Society', in *Setting the Agenda* (London: Church House Publishing, 1999), 30–43 (Church of England Board of Mission Occasional Paper No. 10).

17. On all this, see my *What is the New Age Still Saying to the Church?* (London: HarperCollins, 1999).

18. Gregor T. Goethals, *The TV Ritual: Worship at the Video Altar* (Boston: Beacon Press, 1981), 6.

19. For an especially perceptive account of the concerns of such people, see Paul Vallely, 'Evangelism in a Post-Religious Society' in Church of England Board of Mission, *Setting the Agenda: the Report of the 1999 Church of England Conference on Evangelism* (London: Church House Publishing, 1999), 30–43.

20. Leith Anderson, *A Church for the Twenty-First Century* (Minneapolis: Bethany House, 1992), 21.

21. For a succinct critical analysis of this trend, see J.A. Matta, *The Born Again Jesus of the Word-Faith Teaching* (Bellevue WA: Spirit of Truth, 1987).

22. Sample, *US Lifestyles and Mainline Churches*, 145.

23. Peter L. Berger (ed.), *The Desecularization of the World* (Grand Rapids: Eerdmans, 1999), 10.

24. For more on the background to this, cf. Tony Campolo, *Can Mainline Denominations make a Comeback?* (Valley Forge PA: Judson Press, 1995); Robert Wuthnow, *The Crisis in the Churches* (New York: Oxford University Press, 1997).

25. Ziauddin Sardar, *Postmodernism and the Other* (London: Pluto Press,1998), 195.

26. James Redfield, *The Celestine Prophecy* (New York: Warner, 1993), 27.

27. Douglas Coupland, *Microserfs* (London: HarperCollins, 1995), 41.

28. For extensive discussion of this phenomenon, see Eddie Gibbs, *In Name Only: Tackling the Problem of Nominal Christianity* (Wheaton IL: Bridgepoint,1994).

29. Cf. my *Changing Culture and Biblical Faith*, 78–103.

Chapter 5: Celebrating the Faith

1. On the issues surrounding theological education and the nature of ministry, see my *Cultural Change and Biblical Faith* (Carlisle: Paternoster Press, 2000), 104–53.

2. Matthew Fox, *The Reinvention of Work* (San Francisco: HarperSanFrancisco, 1994), 256–60.

3. ibid., 258.

4. ibid., 258.

5. On the consequences of all that for the Church's mission, see Robert

Banks, *Reenvisioning Theological Education: Exploring a Missional Alternative to Current Models* (Grand Rapids: Eerdmans, 1999).

6. Fox, *Reinvention of Work*, 258–9.
7. ibid., 259.
8. ibid., 259.
9. I need to point out here that I am by no means uncritical of his work myself. See my article 'Matthew Fox', in Trevor Hart (ed.), *Dictionary of Historical Theology* (Carlisle: Paternoster Press, 2000).
10. For typical works of this period, cf. Donald Bruggink and Carl Droppers, *Christ and Architecture* (Grand Rapids: Eerdmans, 1965); Gilbert Cope, *Making the Building Serve the Liturgy* (London: Mowbrays, 1962); Peter Hammond, *Liturgy and Architecture* (New York: Columbia University Press, 1961); William Lockett (ed.), *The Modern Architectural Setting of the Liturgy* (London: SPCK, 1964). For broad overviews of the relationship between space and theology, see also Harold W. Turner, *From Temple to Meeting House* (Hawthorn NY: Mouton de Gruyter, 1979); James F. White, *Protestant Worship and Church Architecture: Theological and Historical Considerations* (New York: Oxford University Press, 1964). For what might be regarded as more specifically 'post-modern' contributions, cf. James F. White and Susan J. White, *Church Architecture: Building and Renovating for Christian Worship* (Nashville: Abingdon Press, 1988); E.A. Sovik, *Architecture for Worship* (Minneapolis: Augsburg, 1973); Kennon L. Callahan, *Building for Effective Mission* (San Francisco: Jossey-Bass Publications, 1997); Richard Giles, *Re-Pitching the Tent: re-ordering the church building for worship and mission in the new millennium* (Norwich: Canterbury Press, 1999).
11. See, for example, Leonardo Boff, *Church, Charism and Power* (New York: Crossroad, 1985); Rosemary Radford Ruether, *Women-Church* (San Francisco: Harper & Row, 1985); John Macquarrie, *Theology, Church and Ministry* (New York: Crossroad, 1986); Peter C. Hodgson, *Revisioning the church: ecclesial freedom in the new paradigm* (Philadelphia: Fortress, 1988); Rémi Parent, *A Church of the Baptized* (New York: Paulist Press, 1989); Hans Kung, *Reforming the Church Today* (New York: Crossroad, 1990); Letty M. Russell, *Church in the Round* (Louisville KY: Westminster John Knox Press, 1993); R. Paul Stevens, *The Equipping Pastor* (Washington DC: Alban Institute, 1993).
12. For a succinct account of this, see Gordon Donaldson, *The Faith of the Scots* (London: Batsford, 1990), 65.
13. James F. White notes the same phenomenon in relation to the way Reformed Protestants typically regard their communion tables with great reverence: 'Strangely enough, in many denominations with little eucharistic piety, this is the one spot in the church never approached by the people. It remains more aloft and aloof than in those denominations where people gather round it weekly' (*Introduction to Christian Worship* (Nashville: Abingdon Press, 1980), 82).
14. ibid., 81–2.

15. Aidan Kavanagh, *Elements of Rite: a Handbook of Liturgical Style* (New York: Pueblo Publishing Company, 1982), 21.

16. Individual communion cups were first introduced in the USA in 1894, and then made their first British appearance in 1898 at Thorne Congregational Church, near Doncaster. Their use was justified at the time only by reference to matters of hygiene, rather than theology: cf. D.W. Bebbington, 'Evangelicalism in Modern Britain and America', in G.A. Rawlyk and M.A. Noll (eds.), *Amazing Grace* (Grand Rapids: Baker, 1993), 187. I am surprised that Bebbington seems to imply that individual cups were a specifically evangelical invention, but if indeed they were that would only serve to emphasize my contention here, for of all sections of the Church none has bought into the rationalized Enlightenment vision more enthusiastically than the evangelicals: cf. George Marsden's comment that 'evangelicalism – with its focus on scientific thinking and empirical approach, and common sense – is a child of early modernity' (in *Evangelicalism and Modern America* (Grand Rapids: Eerdmans, 1984), 98). I have been unable to trace either the origins or rationale of the use of processed wafers for bread.

17. Max Weber, *The Protestant Ethic and the Spirit of Capitalism* (New York: Scribners, 1958), 182.

18. National Conference of Catholic Bishops of the USA, *The Liturgy Documents: a Parish Resource* (Chicago: Liturgy Training Publications, 1991, 3rd edn), 321. The entire document is pages 313–39 in this book, and consists of 107 numbered paragraphs. The quotation is from paragraph 14; the italics are mine.

19. James F. White, 'How the Architectural Setting for Worship forms our Faith', in Robert E. Webber (ed.), *Music and the Arts in Christian Worship, Book 2* (Nashville: Star Song, 1994), 548 (= volume 4 of *The Complete Library of Christian Worship*).

20. *The Liturgy Documents*, 332 (paragraph 76 of *Environment and Art in Catholic Worship*).

21. ibid., 321 (paragraph 16 of *Environment and Art in Catholic Worship*).

22. Paul Tillich, *The Protestant Era* (Chicago: University of Chicago Press, 1957, abridged edition), 227.

23. *The Liturgy Documents*, 325 (paragraph 35 of *Environment and Art in Catholic Worship*).

24. Donaldson, *The Faith of the Scots*, 72.

25. *Faith in a Changing Culture* (London: HarperCollins, 1997), 120.

26. Webber (ed.), *Music and the Arts*, 487.

27. Tex Sample, *The Spectacle of Worship in a Wired World* (Nashville: Abingdon Press, 1998), 74.

28. For the story of this, see *Faith in a Changing Culture*, 63–4.

29. For a Christian exploration of this theme, see Martin Blogg, *Healing in the Dance* (Eastbourne: Kingsway, 1988).

30. J.G. Davies, *New Perspectives on Worship Today* (London: SCM Press, 1978), quotations from pp. 20, 34.

31. *De Saltatione* 7.
32. Cf. Mayer I. Gruber, 'Ten Dance-Derived Expressions in the Hebrew Bible', in Doug Adams and Diane Apostolos-Cappadona, *Dance as Religious Studies* (New York: Crossroad, 1990), 48–59.
33. Hebrew *gil/gul* – as found, for example, in Psalm 118:24.
34. For examples, see Exodus 15:20; 1 Samuel 29:5; 2 Samuel 6:14; Psalms 30:11, 149:3, 150:4; Ecclesiastes 3:4; Judith 15:12–13.
35. In addition to Adams and Apostolos-Cappadona, *Dance as Religious Studies*, see the following resources for a combination of historical and biblical studies and practical instructions for introducing movement into worship: Constance Fisher, *Dancing with Early Christians* (Austin: Sharing Company, 1983); Ronald Gagne, Thomas Kane and Robert VerEecke, *Introducing Dance in Christian Worship* (Washington DC: Pastoral Press, 1984); Mary Jones, *God's People on the Move* (Sydney: Christian Dance Fellowship of Australia, 1988).
36. See for example Lamentations 5:15, and compare and contrast with Jeremiah 31:4, 13. The same theme appears in Ecclesiastes 3:4; Psalm 30:11.
37. Examples may be found in Judges 11:34–40, Mark 6:17–28.
38. Mishna *Sukka* IV.9.
39. In the opening paragraph of his classic history of the synagogue, Isaac Levy characterizes it as 'a house of prayer [and] a representative communal institution . . . utilized to intensify the cultural life of the congregations it has served . . . an essential medium for the preservation of the distinctive Jewish identity' (Isaac Levy, *The Synagogue: its History and Function* (London: Vallentine, Mitchell & Co. Ltd, 1963), 5). Cf. also Azriel Eisenberg, *The Synagogue through the Ages* (New York: Bloch Publishing Company, 1974), 62–71.
40. Paul F. Bradshaw, *The Search for the Origins of Christian Worship* (New York: Oxford University Press, 1992), 55.
41. See my *Faith in a Changing Culture*, 128–35; and for a more exhaustive study of preaching, David C. Norrington, *To Preach or Not to Preach?* (Carlisle: Paternoster Press, 1996).
42. Cf. R. P. Martin, *Worship in the Early Church* (London: Marshall, Morgan & Scott, 1964), 24–7, who, on this basis, characterized the worship life of the early church as consisting of 'praise . . . prayers . . . instruction'. A similar, classic treatment of the topic from the same generation is C.F.D. Moule, *Worship in the New Testament* (London: SCM Press, 1961).
43. E.g. Matthew 5:12, where the Greek word *agalliasthe* = Aramaic *dusu*. Cf. Matthew Black, *An Aramaic Approach to the Gospels and Acts* (Oxford: Clarendon Press, 1967, 3rd edn), 158.
44. Davies, *New Perspectives on Worship Today*, 40.
45. Cf. for example, G. Delling, *Worship in the New Testament* (London: Darton Longman & Todd, 1962); Oscar Cullmann, *Early Christian Worship* (London: SCM Press, 1953) – both of which give detailed accounts of worship 'services' with a confidence that is not justified by the evidence.

46. *Oration against Julian* 11, 171.
47. See *On Repentance* II.vi.42–3. 'The Lord bids us dance, not merely with the circling movements of the body, but with pious faith in him . . .'
48. Cf. *Shepherd of Hermas* S 9.xi; Clement of Alexandria, *Address to the Heathens*, xii.119f; Gregory the Wonder Worker, *Four Sermons* i.

Chapter 6: Prophetic Gifts

1. Cf. G.W. Ashby, *Sacrifice: its nature and purpose* (London: SCM Press, 1988); R. Girard, *Violence and the Sacred* (Baltimore: Johns Hopkins University Press, 1977); R.K. Yerkes, *Sacrifice in Greek and Roman religions and early Judaism* (New York: Scribner, 1952); H. Hubert and M. Mauss, *Sacrifice: its nature and function* (Chicago: University of Chicago Press, 1964); J.F.A. Sawyer and M. Douglas, *Reading Leviticus: a conversation with Mary Douglas* (Sheffield: Sheffield Academic Press, 1996).
2. This is the fellowship offering of the Old Testament (Leviticus 3:1–17; cf. Exodus 24:1–8; Joshua 8:30–5; 2 Samuel 6:17; 1 Kings 8:63–4). Other major types of sacrifice were gift offerings (Leviticus 1:1–17, 2:1–16, 23:1–25), sin offerings (Leviticus 4:1–5:13) and guilt offerings (Leviticus 5:14–6:7; Numbers 5:5–8). The ritual of the annual Day of Atonement was a specialized form of this (Leviticus 16:1–34; 23:26–32; Numbers 29:7–11). Though they differed in details they all served the same underlying purposes.
3. *Readers Digest Universal Dictionary* (London: Reader's Digest Association, 1987), 981.
4. Claude Kipnis, *The Mime Book* (Colorado Springs: Meriwether, 1974), 1–4.
5. Cf. Albert Mehrabian, *Nonverbal Communication* (Chicago: Aldine Atherton, 1972); *Silent Messages* (Belmont CA: Wadsworth Publishing Company, 1981, 2nd edn).
6. Quoted in David Freedberg, *The Power of Images* (Chicago: University of Chicago Press, 1989), 162.
7. For the accounts of this, see Bollandus, *Acta Sanctorum* (Paris & Rome, 1856), March vii. 751–4. See also Allardyce Nicoll, *Masks Mimes and Miracles: Studies in the Popular Theatre* (New York: Harcourt, Brace & Co., 1931), 17–18.
8. On Genesius, see Herbert W. Workman, *The Martyrs of the Early Church* (London: Charles H. Kelly, 1913), 125–6.
9. For more on all these early mime artists, and references to them in early Christian and secular literature, see Nicoll, *Masks Mimes and Miracles*, 120–8.
10. J.G. Davies, *New Perspectives on Worship Today* (London: SCM Press, 1978), 106.
11. Cf. Mikhail Bakhtin, *Rabelais and his World* (Bloomington: Indiana University Press, 1984), 196–277; for the social realities behind this form of prophetic activity, see Michel de Certeau, *The Practice of Everyday Life* (Berkeley CA: University of California Press, 1984), 37–40.

12. A recent study of this theme is Douglas Adams, *The Prostitute in the Family Tree* (Louisville: Westminster John Knox Press, 1997); but see also Conrad Hyers, *And God Created Laughter* (Atlanta: John Knox Press 1987); Mark Liebenow, *Is there Fun after Paul?* (San Jose CA: Resource Publications, 1987); Yehuda T. Radday and Athalya Brenner, *On Humour and the Comic in the Hebrew Bible* (Sheffield: Almond Press, 1990); Thomas Jemielty, *Satire and the Hebrew Prophets* (Louisville: Westminster John Knox Press, 1992); J. William Whedbee, *The Bible and the Comic Vision* (Cambridge: Cambridge University Press, 1998); and for a study that explores the topic in the wider context of world religions more generally, Ingvild S. Gilhus, *Laughing Gods, Weeping Virgins* (London: Routledge, 1997).

13. Liebenow, *Is there Fun after Paul?* 24.

14. ibid., 31.

15. Cf. Barbara Swain, *Fools and Folly during the Middle Ages and the Renaissance* (New York: Columbia University Press, 1932).

16. For examples, see Michael Frost, *Jesus the Fool* (Sydney: Albatross, 1994); Elizabeth-Anne Stewart, *Jesus the Holy Fool* (Franklin WI: Sheed & Ward, 1999).

17. Harvey Cox, *Feast of Fools* (New York: Harper & Row, 1969), 140.

18. On clowning and Christian values, see Janet Litherland, *The Clown Ministry Handbook* (Colorado Springs: Meriwether, 1990, 4th edn).

19. For more on this, cf. D.J. McGinn, *The Admonition Controversy* (New Brunswick NJ: Rutgers University Press, 1949), 189–91.

Chapter 7: Telling the Story

1. Douglas Coupland, *Generation X* (New York: St Martin's Press, 1991), 8. Coupland is not alone in this conviction, of course: cf. the claim of communications specialist W.R. Fisher that 'All forms of human communication need to be seen fundamentally as stories', in *Human Communication as narration: toward a philosophy of reason, value, and action* (Columbia SC: University of South Carolina Press, 1987), 2.

2. *The Postmodern Condition* (Minneapolis: University of Minnesota Press, 1993), xxiv.

3. For much of the following section, I am indebted to research carried out by Kimberly Thacker, a member of a doctoral seminar I taught at Fuller Theological Seminary, Pasadena, California, during the fall quarter of 1999.

4. For discussion of the differences, see my *Cultural Change and Biblical Faith* (Carlisle: Paternoster Press, 2000), 94–5.

5. For a critique of this assumption, see Ziauddin Sardar, *Postmodernism and the Other* (New York: Pluto Press, 1998), 44–84.

6. James Redfield, *The Celestine Prophecy* (New York: Warner, 1993), 226–7.

7. Stanley J. Grenz captures the paradox quite neatly with his observation that 'Whatever else it may be . . . postmodernism is the quest to move beyond modernism. Specifically, it is a rejection of the modern mind-set, but under the conditions of modernity. Therefore, to understand post-

modern thinking we must view it in the context of the modern world which gave it birth and against which it is reacting', in David S. Dockery (ed.), *The Challenge of Postmodernism: an evangelical engagement* (Grand Rapids: Baker, 1995), 90.

8. For examples of how the dominance of abstract theorizing is being challenged by those who wish to make story central to our renewed understanding of the world, see N.K. Denzin, 'The sociological imagination revisited', in *The Sociological Quarterly* 31 (1990), 1–22; S. Seidman, 'The end of sociological theory: the postmodern hope', in *Sociological Theory* 9/2 (1991), 131–46.

9. Douglas Coupland, *Polaroids from the Dead* (London: HarperCollins, 1996), 108.

10. Fluehr-Lobban, 'Cultural Relativism and Human Rights', in *AnthroNotes* 20/2 (Winter 1998), 16–17.

11. 'Character makes a comeback', in *Scholastic Instructor* (October 1999), 25.

12. Walter Truett Anderson, *Reality isn't what it used to be* (San Francisco: HarperSanFrancisco, 1990), 267.

13. Tex Sample, *Ministry in an Oral Culture* (Louisville: Westminster John Knox Press, 1994), 62.

14. For a similar perception, highlighting exactly the same sense of personal ambiguity, cf. Alan Bryman, 'Theme Parks and McDonaldization', in Barry Smart (ed.), *Resisting McDonaldization* (Thousand Oaks CA: Sage 1999), 101–15.

15. Cf. Douglas Adams, *The Prostitute in the Family Tree* (Louisville: Westminster John Knox Press, 1997), 1–11.

16. While it is slightly invidious to single out particular examples of this trend, the kind of thing I am talking about is well illustrated in the following: Walter Vogels, *Reading and Preaching the Bible: a New Semiotic Approach* (Wilmington DE: Michael Glazier, 1986); Mark L. Wallace, *The Second Naiveté: Barth, Ricoeur, and the New Yale Theology* (Macon GA: Mercer University Press, 1990); James W. Voelz, *What does this Mean? Principles of Biblical Interpretation in the Post-Modern World* (Saint Louis: Concordia Publishing House, 1995).

17. Clark Pinnock, *Tracking the Maze* (San Francisco: Harper & Row, 1990), 183.

18. Martin Dibelius, *From Tradition to Gospel* (New York: Scribner, 1931), 70 (originally in German 1919).

19. Carl E. Armerding, 'Faith and Story in Old Testament Study: Story Exegesis', in Philip E. Satterthwaite and David F. Wright, *A Pathway into the Holy Scripture* (Grand Rapids: Eerdmans, 1994), 31–49.

20. George Barna, *Baby Busters: The Disillusioned Generation* (Chicago: Northfield, 1994), 93.

21. C. Jeff Woods, *Congregational Megatrends* (Bethesda MD: Alban Institute, 1996), 91.

22. Armerding, 'Faith and Story in Old Testament Study', 47.

23. William J. Bausch, *Storytelling, Imagination and Faith* (Mystic CT: Twenty-Third Publications, 1984), 28.

24. See Wiesel's own reflections on 'The Holocaust as Literary Inspiration' in Elie Wiesel *et al.*, *Dimensions of the Holocaust* (Evanston IL: Northwestern University, 1977), 5–19. Books which he identifies as inspired by that topic include *Legends of our Time* (New York: Rinehart & Winston, 1968), *The Jews of Silence* (London: Vallentine Mitchell, 1973), *The Town Beyond the Wall* (London: Robson Books, 1975), *The Gates of the Forest* (New York: Schocen, 1982) – and others. For a more recent example of the same phenomenon of stories as a way of dealing with pain, see my *Cultural Change and Biblical Faith*, 87–8.

25. Kathleen R. Fischer, *The Inner Rainbow* (New York: Paulist Press, 1983), 7.

26. See *Faith in a Changing Culture* (London: HarperCollins, 1997), 203–17.

27. ibid., 60–8.

28. John Finney, *Finding Faith Today* (Swindon: Bible Society, 1992). For the statistical evidence on which this is based, see Pam Hanley, *Finding Faith Today: the Technical Report* (London: Churches Together in England, 1992).

29. David Hay, *Religious Experience Today: Studying the Facts* (London: Mowbray, 1990), quotations taken from the Preface.

30. Cf. my *Introducing the New Testament* (Oxford: Lion, 1999, 2nd edn), 111–15.

31. Pinnock, *Tracking the Maze*, 213.

32. Walter J. Ong, *The Presence of the Word* (New Haven: Yale University Press, 1967); *Orality and Literacy: the Technologizing of the Word* (London: Methuen, 1982); cf. also Jack Goody, *Literacy in Traditional Societies* (Cambridge: Cambridge University Press, 1968); *The Interface between the written and the oral* (Cambridge: Cambridge University Press, 1987); *The Logic of Writing and the Organization of Society* (Cambridge: Cambridge University Press, 1986).

33. Emile Durkheim, *The Elementary Forms of the Religious Life* (London: Allen & Unwin, 1964), 209–15.

34. A. Kroker, M. Kroker and D. Cook (eds.), *Panic Encyclopedia: The Definitive Guide to the Postmodern Scene* (London: Macmillan, 1989), 119.

35. John S. Caputo, 'The rhetoric of McDonaldization: a social semiotic perspective', in Mark Alfino, John S. Caputo and Robin Wynyard, *McDonaldization Revisited* (Westport CT: Praeger, 1998), 50.

36. Deena Weinstein and Michael A. Weinstein, 'McDonaldization Enframed', in Smart (ed.), *Resisting McDonaldization*, 63. In his essay on 'Theorizing/resisting McDonaldization', Douglas Kellner makes a similar point with his observation that 'McDonald's is selling not just fast-food, but a family adventure of eating out together, intergenerational bonding and a communal experience' (*Resisting McDonaldization*, 188).

Chapter 8: Dreaming the Church of the Future

1. Douglas Coupland, *Life after God* (New York: Simon & Schuster, 1994), 273–4.

2. Paul Tillich, *The Protestant Era* (London: Nisbet, 1951), 256–7.

3. Joanne Finkelstein, 'Rich Food', in Barry Smart (ed.), *Resisting McDonaldization* (Thousand Oaks CA: Sage, 1999), 76.

4. *Faith in a Changing Culture* (London: HarperCollins, 1997), 145–73.

5. Douglas Coupland, *Microserfs* (New York: HarperCollins, 1995), 358.

6. Douglas Coupland, *Shampoo Planet* (New York: Pocket Books, 1992), 107.

7. Coupland, *Microserfs*, 313.

8. *The Protestant Era*, 256.

9. On the broader issues implied here, see A. Bookman and S. Morgan (eds.), *Women and the Politics of Empowerment* (Philadelphia: Temple University Press, 1988).

10. Audre Lorde, *Sister Outsider* (Freedom CA: Crossing Press, 1984), 123.

11. H.H. Gerth and C.W. Mills, *From Max Weber: Essays in Sociology* (London: Routledge & Kegan Paul, 1970), 139.

12. Tex Sample, *The Spectacle of Worship in a Wired World* (Nashville: Abingdon, 1998), 105.

13. *Faith in a Changing Culture*, 108–44.

14. Sample, *The Spectacle of Worship in a Wired World*, 20.

15. Neil Postman, *Amusing ourselves to Death* (New York: Penguin, 1985).

16. Plato, *Phaedrus*, 67–71.

17. Plato, *The Great Dialogues*, Book X, 463–4.

18. Mitchell Stevens, *The Rise of the Image the Fall of the Word* (New York: Oxford University Press, 1998), 28; my emphasis.

19. Cf. the comment by Gary Alan Fine, 'Art Centres' in Smart (ed.), *Resisting McDonaldization*, 148, that academics (and, I would add, Christians) 'are predisposed to treat the provision of culture to mass audiences as being *in itself* something of which to be wary'.

20. Marva J. Dawn, *A Royal Waste of Time* (Grand Rapids: Eerdmans, 1999), 60. The food imagery had been used in her previous book *Reaching Out without Dumbing Down* (Grand Rapids: Eerdmans, 1995), 183–8. Cf. also Kenneth A. Myers, *All God's Children and Blue Suede Shows: Christians and Popular Culture* (Westchester IL: Crossway, 1989).

21. Dawn, *A Royal Waste of Time*, 61–2.

22. She makes a virtue out of the fact that 'I don't even own a television . . .' (*A Royal Waste of Time*, 76).

23. ibid., 77–8.

24. ibid., 77.

25. ibid., 181.

26. ibid., 98.

27. Kant's own position was somewhat ambiguous, if not contradictory, but for this cf. his *Critique of Judgment*, translated by J.C. Meredith (London: Oxford University Press, 1952).

28. Peter Berger, *The Desecularization of the World* (Grand Rapids: Eerdmans, 1999), 11.

29. Tex Sample, *White Soul: Country Music, the Church and Working Americans* (Nashville: Abingdon Press, 1996).

30. On Ritzer, cf. Martin Parker, 'Nostalgia and Mass Culture:

McDonaldization and Cultural Elitism', 1–18; Robin Wynyard. 'The Bunless Burger', in Mark Alfino, John S. Caputo and Robin Wynyard, *McDonaldization Revisited* (Westport CT: Praeger, 1998), 159–74.

31. I am significantly indebted to Marilee Harris, who was a member of a doctoral seminar that I taught at Fuller Seminary, California during the fall quarter 1999, for many of the insights in this section.

32. Lesslie Newbigin, *The Gospel in a Pluralist Society* (Grand Rapids: Eerdmans, 1989), 21.

33. Sample, *The Spectacle of Worship in a Wired World*, 103–4.

34. Carol Gilligan, *In a Different Voice: psychological theory and women's development* (Cambridge MA: Harvard University Press, 1982).

35. Mary Field Belenky, Blythe McVicker Clinchy, Nancy Rule Goldberger, Jill Mattuck Tarule, *Women's Ways of Knowing: The Development of Self, Voice, and Mind* (New York: Basic Books, 1986).

36. ibid., 137.

37. ibid., 139.

38. ibid., 140.

39. ibid., 150.

40. In David S. Dockery (ed.), *The Challenge of Postmodernism: an Evangelical Engagement* (Wheaton IL: Bridgepoint, 1995), 89–103.

41. George M. Marsden, 'Evangelical, History and Modernity', in *Evangelicalism and Modern America*, ed. George M. Marsden (Grand Rapids: Eerdmans, 1984), p. 98.

42. Tillich, *The Protestant Era*, 256; emphasis added.

43. Belenky *et al.*, *Women's Ways of Knowing*, 218.

44. ibid., 218.

45. ibid., 219.

46. ibid., 220.

47. ibid., 221.

48. For a stimulating account of the biblical background to such imagery, see especially Margaret L. Hammer, *Giving Birth: Reclaiming Biblical Metaphor for Pastoral Practice* (Louisville: Westminster John Knox Press, 1994).

49. For more on this predilection in Western spirituality, see Grace Jantzen, 'Necrophilia and Natality: what does it mean to be religious?' in *Scottish Journal of Religious Studies* 19/1 (1998), 101–21.

50. For more explanation of what I mean by the style of Jesus, consult my *Introducing the New Testament* (Oxford: Lion, 1999), 156–8; *Faith in a Changing Culture* (London: HarperCollins, 1997), 203–17; 'Patterns of Evangelization in Paul and Jesus: a way forward in the Jesus-Paul debate?' in J.B. Green and M.M.B. Turner (eds.), *Jesus of Nazareth: Lord and Christ* (Grand Rapids: Eerdmans, 1994), 281–96.

51. John Finney, *Recovering the Past: Celtic and Roman Mission* (London: Darton, Longman & Todd, 1996).

52. ibid., 47.

INDEX